Illuminate
Publishing

GW01271831

# AQA

# GCSE
# Statistics

## Jayne Roper

### Consultant Editor: Shaun Procter-Green

Published in 2020 by Illuminate Publishing Ltd, P.O. Box 1160, Cheltenham, Gloucestershire GL50 9RW

**Orders:** please visit www.illuminatepublishing.com or email sales@illuminatepublishing.com

(c) Jayne Roper

The moral rights of the author have been asserted.

All rights reserved. No part of this book may be reprinted, reproduced or utilised in any form or by any electronic, mechanical, or other means, now known or hereafter invented, included photocopying and recording, or in any information storage and retrieval system, without permission in writing from the publishers.

British Library Cataloguing in Publication Data
A catalogue record for this book is available from the British Library.

ISBN 978 1 912820 02 3

**Printed by:** Standartu Spaustuve, Lithuania 01.20

The publisher's policy is to use papers that are natural, renewable and recyclable products made from wood grown in sustainable forests. The logging and manufacturing processes are expected to conform to the environmental regulations of the country of origin.

**Editorial, Art, Design, and Production Services provided by:** Westchester K-12 Publishing Services of Dayton, Ohio — A U.S. Employee-Owned Company.

**Photo:** Shutterstock ©: p6 Sergey Nivens; p7 sarsmis; p10 Krawczyk-A-Foto; p17 Justin Black; p21 Zephyr_p; p28 totojang1977; p29 aopsan; p30 rawf8; p31 Jacob Lund; p34 Jagodka; p37 Richard Cavalleri; p38 welcomia; p39 Juha Saastamoinen; p40 Nattika; p41 aaabbbccc; pg61 Ljupco Smokovski; p86 Khakimullin Aleksandr; p95 Eric Gevaert; p112 Sergey Nivens; p127 Realstock; p144 Racheal Grazias; p147 StockStudio; p150 Gayvoronskaya_Yana; p152 yoshi0511; p152 Liudmila Fadzeyeza; p198 Brian A Jackson; p199 Roger Uttling; p204 Africa Studio; p205 Oleksandr_Delyk; p211 Steve Cukrov; p214 Keith Gentry; p220 Paolo Sartorio; p222 Awirut Somsanguan; p223 Boule; p230 Oleksiy Mark; p233 Rocksweeper; p244 asharkyu; p250 sirastock; p280 Africa Studio; p285 Erik Lam; p287 Aler-ego; p288 SpeedKingz; p291 TuiPhotoEngineer; p296 AmenStyle; p297 Jose Luis Carrascosa; p298 Picsfive; p299 Vitalinka; p302 Feng Yu; p306 kan_chana

Adobe Stock ©: p66 catto32; p69 Balint Radu; p70 Rawf8.

**Cover Design:** EMC Design

**Acknowledgements:** The author and publishers would like to thank Claire Shewbridge for her help in proofreading this book, and Claire Irons for her help with Exam Practice Questions in the book.

Checked answers to the questions throughout this book are available as a free download online. Please go to: www.illuminatepublishing.com and search within the Statistics book product page.

Where there is a Solution provided for an Example within the textbook, this might not necessarily be the only possible solution and it has not been provided by nor approved by AQA.

AQA material is reproduced by permission of AQA.

# CONTENTS

# Introduction to Statistics and the Statistical Enquiry Cycle (SEC)

This book has been written to support the AQA specification for GCSE Statistics. As there is limited space within any textbook, I've chosen to cover in the most depth those areas of greatest importance to a statistician.

Statistics is more than just "extra maths" - it is in all our lives every day and as such it needs to be interpreted and understood. You'll find that it is used in many subjects you study at school, so having a greater understanding of it will help with more than just your maths and statistics GCSEs!

Doing a course in statistics will put you that little bit ahead of the game. Understanding how things are presented, and why they might have been presented or interpreted in a certain way, is key to knowing how much you can trust what you read or hear. In a time of fake news, we need people who can decode this world of big data and present it in a fair and unbiased way for everyone to understand.

That's why we need statisticians.  This is what this book is about.

**MORE YOUNG PEOPLE NOW BUYING OWN HOMES**

*US stocks suffer worse week for a decade*

More money than ever going into schools, but less than ever per pupil

**FOOD LABELLING HIDES**
true healthiness of many products

*CHILD POVERTY AT RECORD LEVELS*

85% OF PEOPLE PAYING MORE THAN THEY COULD FOR INSURANCE

This book presents the chapters in a logical teaching and learning sequence, finishing with the Statistical Enquiry Cycle. This SEC is another way of describing how all statistical investigations have a common theme and a commonly accepted route from start to finish. The skills you'll develop in the book are all used together when carrying out a statistical enquiry, and so my final chapter - Chapter 13 The SEC - shows a fully worked example alongside the theory of what needs to be done at each stage.

The textbook layout includes several student-friendly features such as "Advice" panels that highlight details that you might otherwise miss, along with tips to make your work easier. The start of each chapter also lists the topics covered, which are then repeated at the end - I encourage you to reflect on these and maybe use in your revision to check you know the key topics in each chapter. There's also a handy list of the new vocabulary that appears in each topic, with a full definition in the glossary at the back of the book.

# 1 | Data and Tables

## In this chapter you will learn to:

- Identify different types of data
- Sort and order data
- Create frequency tables
- Create tally charts
- Create and use two-way tables
- Identify primary and secondary data
- Identify explanatory and response variables
- Design and describe a valid experiment
- Design and describe a reliable experiment
- HIGHER TIER Identify and describe a control group

## New Vocabulary

- Variable
- Qualitative
- Quantitative
- Discrete
- Continuous
- Categorical
- Ordinal
- Bivariate
- Multivariate
- Raw data
- Frequency distribution table
- Class interval
- Two-way table
- Primary data
- Simulation
- Questionnaire
- Observation
- Secondary data
- National Census
- Experimental data
- Explanatory (independent) variable
- Response (dependent) variable
- Extraneous variable
- Control group
- Valid
- Reliable
- Bias

# Types of data

There are many different types of data, and you need to know what kind of data you are dealing with before you can begin to sort and process it.

In different situations, you have different things that will vary. A question may ask about the favourite ice-cream flavour of a group of people. The answer will vary as you ask different people, so the ice-cream flavour is the **variable**. Often we give each variable a letter so that we can refer back to it more easily.

### EXAMPLE

Identify the variable in each situation and choose a letter to represent it.

     **a.** Jess records the amount of water she drinks in a day.

     **b.** Tess counts the number of steps she takes in a day.

     **c.** Bess asks her friends their favourite fruit.

### SOLUTION

You may have chosen different letters for the variables. That's not a problem, as long as you identify what each letter represents.

     **a.** Amount of water,      $w$

     **b.** Number of steps,      $n$

     **c.** Type of fruit,      $f$

**Qualitative** data describes the quality of a variable. It may be the colour of a car, the texture of a rug, the scent of a flower, an emotion, an opinion...a variable that isn't number based.

**Quantitative** data is data that is number based. It may be a length or a volume or something else measurable, or may be just a numerical value. Quantitative data comes in two forms:

- **Discrete** data is often described as "stepped" data where there are no values between the allowed values. The easiest example of this to understand is shoe sizes. Each shoe size is a number, so it is most definitely quantitative data; you may be a size 5 or a size 5$\frac{1}{2}$, but there is no such size as 5$\frac{2}{3}$!

- **Continuous** data is the opposite of discrete data. It's still a numerical value but there are infinitely many values between the ones we write down. It's usually a value of something we measure, like length. We looked at shoe sizes for discrete data, so let us now consider the length of your foot. This is continuous data because no matter how carefully we measure it, if we had more accurate measuring tools, we would be able to take a more accurate measurement.

**Categorical** data is the name we use for data that has already been put into a category or classified in some way. A simple example of this is egg sizes where we see eggs classified as small, medium, large or extra large.

Categorical data has a special subset of data, known as **ordinal** data, where the categories have a natural order. Ordinal data is often found in surveys when people are asked to judge, for example, if they are *very unhappy, unhappy, neutral, happy,* or *very happy.* We know that *neutral* is higher up the scale than *unhappy,* but we have no idea about how much higher it is – this judgement is personal to each person answering the question. We know the *order* of the *ord*inal data but we might now know the distance between each option.

**Bivariate** data is what we call data that has two values attached to it. It's often related data, such as the mass and height of a person or the heights of a father and his son. Mostly, bivariate data will be quantitative.

## HIGHER TIER

Taking bivariate data a step further gives us **multivariate** data. A vet will keep records about each animal that gives the last mass, date of birth, type of animal, colour, etc. Each record contains multivariate data about each animal.

## EXERCISE 1

1. Niles is sorting through the lost property at school. He is sorting the clothes by size (10, 12, 14, etc...) and colour. Are these variables quantitative, qualitative, discrete, or continuous?

2. Quinlan has to sort out the sports activities for a holiday club. He sorts each person by gender, age, and preferred sport, to put them into groups. Fully describe each variable he is using.

3. Liz keeps records about the dogs in her training class. The card for the owner to complete is:

| Owner name: | | Telephone number: | |
| Dog name: | | | |
| Gender: | | Class attended: | |
| Breed: | | | |
| Mass: | | | |

Describe each variable as fully as possible.

   **a.** Gender

   **b.** Breed

   **c.** Mass

4. Jeff is growing sunflowers using different fertilisers. He is recording the progress of each plant. He notes their height, diameter of flower, fertiliser used, and time taken to germinate. Identify and describe each variable he records.

4.  Carter sells jewellery. He keeps a record of each piece he makes and sells. Give examples of quantitative, qualitative, discrete, continuous, or categorical data he may record about each piece of jewellery.

5.  Bruna runs a holiday letting company. She keeps a record for each property she rents out. Identify quantitative, qualitative, discrete, continuous, and categorical data for each of these variables:

    • Post code

    • Town

    • Number of bedrooms

    • Parking for how many cars

    • Washing machine – yes/no

    • Tumble dryer – yes/no

    • Fire – electric/gas/wood

    • Price per week

    • Distance from railway station (miles)

6.  Asha loans classic cars to film-makers. She keeps a record of each car's details that she can email to interested people before they hire them. Design a record card to keep this multivariate data.

## Grouping data

When we are working with statistics, there are often large amounts of data to deal with. These can be difficult to manipulate when they are in raw data form. **Raw data** is the data that you first obtain – usually unorganised and unprocessed.

This data shows the maximum temperature (in °C) for each day throughout April 2018 in Olivia's garden.

| DATE | MAXIMUM TEMPERATURE (°C) | DATE | MAXIMUM TEMPERATURE (°C) | DATE | MAXIMUM TEMPERATURE (°C) |
|---|---|---|---|---|---|
| 01/04/2018 | 10.7 | 11/04/2018 | 14.2 | 21/04/2018 | 30.6 |
| 02/04/2018 | 9.2 | 12/04/2018 | 12.3 | 22/04/2018 | 27.7 |
| 03/04/2018 | 14.4 | 13/04/2018 | 10.6 | 23/04/2018 | 25.1 |
| 04/04/2018 | 15.3 | 14/04/2018 | 13.6 | 24/04/2018 | 16.6 |
| 05/04/2018 | 14.5 | 15/04/2018 | 21.9 | 25/04/2018 | 19.1 |
| 06/04/2018 | 18.4 | 16/04/2018 | 17.5 | 26/04/2018 | 17.0 |
| 07/04/2018 | 17.9 | 17/04/2018 | 16.4 | 27/04/2018 | 16.3 |
| 08/04/2018 | 19.4 | 18/04/2018 | 20.9 | 28/04/2018 | 13.9 |
| 09/04/2018 | 14.7 | 19/04/2018 | 26.7 | 29/04/2018 | 9.7 |
| 10/04/2018 | 9.5 | 20/04/2018 | 32.9 | 30/04/2018 | 7.5 |

From the raw data, you can tell exactly what the maximum temperature was for the whole of April. You just look for the highest temperature value in the table: 32.9°C on 20th April.

We now need to sort the data into some kind of order. The order you choose will depend upon your data, but this data would look good in ascending, numerical order.

- Temperature (°C): 7.5, 9.2, 9.5, 9.7, 10.6, 10.7, 12.3, 13.6, 13.9, 14.2, 14.4, 14.5, 14.7, 15.3, 16.3, 16.4, 16.6, 17.0, 17.5, 17.9, 18.4, 19.1, 19.4, 20.9, 21.9, 25.1, 26.7, 27.7, 30.6, 32.9

We can easily see that the highest maximum temperature is 32.9°C, but in simply writing the list of temperatures in order of size, we have lost which day that happened on. This is typical; when we begin to process data sets, we begin to lose the details.

We could now turn the ordered data into a **frequency distribution table**, but as there is only one instance of each temperature, it doesn't really help in any way. For other data, creating a frequency distribution table can be useful for spotting natural groupings; not so for our data.

Our data would be easier to handle if we grouped it. We can decide the class intervals and having different **class intervals** can alter how the data looks.

Here is one grouping:

| TEMPERATURE, $t$ (°C) | FREQUENCY |
|---|---|
| $0 \leq t \leq 10$ | 4 |
| $10 < t \leq 20$ | 19 |
| $20 < t \leq 30$ | 5 |
| $30 < t \leq 40$ | 2 |

advice

Note the careful use of inequality signs. Any value of exactly 10°C must only lie in one row; it is included in the first row but the second row does not include 10°C (if it could appear in either row, how would we know which row to put it in?)

The class intervals do not need to be of equal width, so we could choose to group the data differently, in order to break down the large group of 19 values in the $10 < t \leq 20$ class.

Another grouping could be:

| TEMPERATURE, $t$ (°C) | FREQUENCY |
|---|---|
| $0 \leq t \leq 10$ | 4 |
| $10 < t \leq 14$ | 5 |
| $14 < t \leq 18$ | 11 |
| $18 < t \leq 22$ | 5 |
| $22 < t \leq 30$ | 3 |
| $30 < t \leq 35$ | 2 |

**advice**

*You may like to try different groupings on your own data to emphasise or disguise details.*

Although we have still lost a lot of the detail from the original, raw data, we can now see that the highest number of temperatures lie in the $14 < t \leq 18$ class, rather than in the much wider $10 < t \leq 20$ class from the previous grouping.

You can use a tally chart before creating a frequency table. These can be very useful in field work when raw data is happening in real time instead of all data being presented on paper.

## EXAMPLE

Meredith has been asked to investigate possible price rises for a toll bridge. She records the types of vehicle that pass along the bridge. The first 50 vehicles to pass her are:

| | | | | | | | | | |
|---|---|---|---|---|---|---|---|---|---|
| Car | Lorry | Bus | Bicycle | Car | Car | Car | Car | Car | Car |
| Van | Car | Car | Van | Van | Van | Car | Car | Car | Car |
| Bicycle | Car | Car | Car | Bus | Car | Car | Bus | Car | Bus |
| Car | Lorry | Car | Car | Motorbike | Car | Car | Car | Car | Car |
| Van | Van | Car | Van | Van | Car | Car | Car | Car | Car |

Put this information into a frequency table.

## SOLUTION

| TYPE OF VEHICLE | TALLY | FREQUENCY |
|---|---|---|
| Bus | IIII | 4 |
| Car | ⵤ ⵤ ⵤ ⵤ ⵤ ⵤ III | 33 |
| Van | ⵤ III | 8 |
| Motorbike | I | 1 |
| Lorry | II | 2 |
| Bicycle | II | 2 |

Each vertical line represents one vehicle. Once there are five items in a group, the four vertical lines are crossed through by the fifth line to create a "gate". These are known as "five bar gates".

Tally charts are often seen with a frequency column on the right, which saves the reader having to count up for themselves:

**advice**

*It's worth doing a quick addition to make sure you haven't missed any or counted one twice:*
*4 + 33 + 8 + 1 + 2 + 2 = 50*
*We have the correct total number of vehicles.*

## EXERCISE 2

1. Madelaine runs a milkshake bar. The table shows the milkshakes she sold on Wednesday afternoon.

| | | | | | | |
|---|---|---|---|---|---|---|
| Chocolate | Strawberry | Vanilla | Banana | Peanut Butter | Chocolate | Strawberry |
| Chocolate | Raspberry | Raspberry | Chocolate | Chocolate | Vanilla | Strawberry |
| Chocolate | Vanilla | Chocolate | Chocolate | Strawberry | Strawberry | Chocolate |
| Strawberry | Chocolate | Vanilla | Chocolate | Vanilla | Chocolate | Banana |
| Vanilla | Vanilla | Strawberry | Caramel | Banana | Strawberry | Blueberry |
| Banana | Lime | Chocolate | Peanut Butter | Vanilla | Raspberry | Vanilla |

Create a tally chart and frequency table to show the data.

2. The pets being seen in a vets one morning are shown in the table.

| | | | | | |
|---|---|---|---|---|---|
| Guinea pig | Cat | Dog | Rabbit | Tortoise | Dog |
| Cat | Hamster | Rabbit | Dog | Cat | Dog |
| Cat | Rabbit | Cat | Cat | Dog | Guinea pig |
| Dog | Dog | Cat | Chinchilla | Guinea pig | Rabbit |
| Rabbit | Cat | Parrot | Dog | Dog | Cat |

Create a tally chart and frequency table to show the data.

**advice**

*You may like to start off with a tally chart.*

**3.** Polly sets up an ice-cream stand at a village festival. Design and create a frequency table to show the flavours of ice-cream she sells.

| Toffee Ripple | Chocolate | Salted Caramel | Mint Choc Chip | Banana | Chocolate | Toffee Ripple | Cherry-Almond |
|---|---|---|---|---|---|---|---|
| Chocolate | Cherry-Almond | Chocolate | Rum and Raisin | Toffee Ripple | Cherry-Almond | Salted Caramel | Chocolate |
| Cherry-Almond | Chocolate | Pineapple | Pistachio | Chocolate | Coconut | Mint Choc Chip | Toffee Ripple |
| Chocolate | Toffee Ripple | Toffee Ripple | Rhubarb-Custard | Rhubarb-Custard | Chocolate | Cherry-Almond | Coconut |
| Salted Caramel | Banana | Rhubarb-Custard | Mint Choc Chip | Coconut | Chocolate | Rhubarb-Custard | Mint Choc Chip |
| Mint Choc Chip | Coconut | Cherry-Almond | Salted Caramel | Toffee Ripple | Pistachio | Raspberry | Forest Fruit |
| Cherry-Almond | Chocolate | Forest Fruit | Toffee Ripple | Cherry-Almond | Salted Caramel | Chocolate | Rhubarb-Custard |
| Toffee Ripple | Coconut | Chocolate | Cherry-Almond | Salted Caramel | Banana | Mint Choc Chip | Chocolate |

**4.** Over the summer months, Polly covers 20 festivals with her ice-cream stand. The table shows how much she takes at each one (to the nearest £).

| | | | |
|---|---|---|---|
| 245 | 203 | 490 | 354 |
| 686 | 367 | 344 | 274 |
| 488 | 309 | 443 | 256 |
| 350 | 297 | 334 | 573 |
| 419 | 243 | 317 | 642 |

**a.** Copy and complete the frequency table.

| AMOUNT (A, £) | TALLY | FREQUENCY |
|---|---|---|
| $0 \leq A \leq 200$ | | |
| $200 \leq A \leq 299$ | | |
| $300 \leq A \leq 399$ | | |
| $400 \leq A \leq 499$ | | |
| $500 \leq A \leq 599$ | | |
| $600 \leq A \leq 699$ | | |
| $700 \leq A \leq 799$ | | |

**advice**

*Aim to have between 4 and 6 class intervals so that you have a good chance of seeing any data patterns. You can have up to 10 class intervals, but it doesn't mean that 10 will work for all situations.*

**b.** Change the class intervals so that they are unequal and recreate the frequency table. Comment upon how the representation of the data has been affected.

5. Use the Internet to gather data on the maximum temperature reached in at least 40 UK locations yesterday. Present your findings in a frequency table and write a few comments to summarise the data.

# Two-way tables

The frequency tables that we were producing in the previous section each had only one variable: flavour of ice-cream, temperature, type of vehicle, type of pet, etc. In order to summarise data which has more than one variable, we need to use a **two-way table**. You are sure to have used them many times without realising it!

Consider this information:

180 children went on an activity holiday. 63 girls went from Mayfield School. 57 boys went from Riverdale School. All of the remaining children came from Long Valley School and one quarter of those children were boys.

For us to answer the questions "How many boys went on the activity holiday?" we need to put this information into a table. We will need to create a two-way table because we have two variables: gender and school.

We can fill in the information we have been given:

| | | GENDER | |
| --- | --- | --- | --- |
| | | Girls | Boys |
| SCHOOL | Mayfield | 63 | |
| | Riverdale | | 57 |
| | Long Valley | | |

The number of "remaining" children will be 180 − 63 − 57 = 60

One quarter of 60:   60 ÷ 4 = 15, so there are 15 boys from Long Valley School.

60 − 15 = 45, so there are 45 girls from Long Valley School.

| | | GENDER | | |
| --- | --- | --- | --- | --- |
| | | Girls | Boys | TOTAL |
| SCHOOL | Mayfield | 63 | 0 | 63 |
| | Riverdale | 0 | 57 | 57 |
| | Long Valley | 45 | 15 | 60 |
| | TOTAL | 108 | 72 | 180 |

**15**

Quick check on total: 63 + 57 + 45 + 15 = 180

Now that the information is clearly presented in a table, we can use it to work out how many boys went on the camp in total: 0 + 57 + 15 = 72 boys went on the activity holiday.

You can choose whether or not to include a row and a column for totals—in the table above, we have.

When you add up the 63 + 57 + 60 from the total column, it should come to the same figure as when you add up the 108 + 72 from the row total. Both of these figures should be 180, the total number of children on the activity holiday.

## EXERCISE 3

1. Use the two-way table to answer the questions.

|  | Boys | Girls |
|---|---|---|
| Year 7 | 284 | 299 |
| Year 8 | 238 | 252 |
| Year 9 | 244 | 209 |
| Year 10 | 196 | 201 |
| Year 11 | 230 | 215 |

   a. How many boys are there in total?

   b. How many girls are in Year 9?

   c. Which year has the fewest girls?

   d. How many pupils are in Year 11?

   e. Which year has the fewest number of pupils?

2. Cally has organised a trip to London for 200 people. Each person chooses one day trip and one evening show to attend. Use the information to complete the two-way table and to answer the questions.

100 people have chosen to see *Wicked*. 90 people have chosen to go to London Zoo and 10 of these will also be seeing *The Lion King*. 25 people will be going to the Tower of London and 10 of these will watch *Matilda*. 20% of those going to the Imperial War Museum will see *Wicked*. 5 of the 80 people watching *The Lion King* will go to the Tower of London.

| | | DAY TRIP | | |
|---|---|---|---|---|
| | | Tower of London | Imperial War Museum | London Zoo |
| **EVENING SHOW** | Wicked | | | |
| | The Lion King | | | |
| | Matilda | | | |

a. How many people go to the Imperial War Museum?

b. How many people have chosen to see *Matilda*?

c. How many people are going to London Zoo and watching *Matilda*?

d. Is it true or false that there are exactly half the number of people watching *The Lion King* as *Wicked* from those going to the Imperial War Museum? Justify your decision.

3. Sue makes blankets. She offers three sizes: cot, wheelchair, and bed. She has four colour schemes: rainbow, white, blue, or pink. Design a two-way table that Sue could complete to show how many of each size and colour she sold last year.

4. The school production is showing on Wednesday afternoon, Thursday evening, and Friday evening. Teddy has sold child, adult, and senior citizen tickets. 60% of the 800 tickets sold were adult tickets. One fifth of the sales were for Wednesday afternoon and half of these were to senior citizens. The 150 child tickets were split equally across the three showings. Thursday and Friday had equal numbers of adult ticket sales. The Thursday showing had 40 senior citizens attending.

How many senior citizens attended on Friday evening?

5. Use the Internet to gather data about the maximum and minimum temperatures yesterday in eight cities in the world. Present your data in a two-way table.

6. Here is a partially completed table about the A-level choices of some students.

|  | Biology | Chemistry | Physics | TOTAL |
|---|---|---|---|---|
| Male | 36 |  |  | 95 |
| Female |  |  | 41 |  |
| TOTAL |  | 42 | 69 | 175 |

Which of these statements are true? You should give a reason for each answer.

a. There are more male students studying chemistry than biology.

b. There are more female students studying physics than chemistry and biology combined.

c. There are more male than female students.

d. There are more male students than female students studying physics.

# Data sources

Where data comes from can have a massive impact on the reliability of any results we find once we have processed the data. A dog food company wanting to sell a new product may well conduct trials that show favourable results. These results may well be fair and true but they would be more believable if they can be conducted by an independent source.

**Primary data** is collected by the person carrying out the analysis of the data. It may be you, when you ask your friends their favourite breakfast cereal or it may be a medicine manufacturer testing their latest treatment. The data will be raw and may take a lot of work to get into a usable format, but should be accurate and reliable because the statistician had control over what data was collected and how it was collected. This will also be the most up-to-date data available.

Examples of methods to gather primary data:

| TYPE OF PRIMARY DATA | EXAMPLE OF COLLECTION | ADVANTAGE | DISADVANTAGE |
|---|---|---|---|
| Experiment | Actually carry out an experiment! This may be in a laboratory testing a new medicine or timing 50 runners doing 100m sprints. | Laboratory experiments are likely to be easy to replicate with exactly the same conditions as the first time (e.g. temperature, light levels, humidity, etc.) as you can control what else is happening. | If the laboratory experiment is made too clinical, it can be said that the results will no longer mimic those from the real world. Participants may not behave naturally in artificial conditions. |
| Simulation | Design and run a computer program that can mimic the conditions necessary. | A **simulation** should not be too costly or too time consuming. A computer program can be left to run overnight without the need for a person to sit there. | Other factors that appear in the real world may not be able to be considered as part of the simulation, leaving the results a little less realistic than is desirable. |
| Questionnaire | Probably the most familiar collection method of primary data. You design the **questionnaire** to ask questions in order to get the necessary data for the research, e.g. asking what time teenagers like to watch TV before scheduling a new series aimed at the 14-17 market. You can have either closed questions which offer limited response options or open questions where the response is unconstrained. | You can directly ask the questions you need answered. If you are working through the questionnaire face-to-face, it's easy to explain when someone doesn't quite understand the question. Questionnaires returned by post/online are more likely to have honest answers to sensitive questions. | These can be very expensive and time consuming. When working through the questionnaire face-to-face, some people may refuse to answer sensitive questions (age, smoking habits, etc.) or lie about them. |
| Observation | This can be thought of as field work. You may actually be outdoors, counting how many people use a particular footpath or sitting in front of a CCTV camera and recording the colour of vehicles driving by. **Observation** is really a form of natural experiment where the observer has little control over the variables. | As long as the observer does not interact with those being watched, outcomes should be natural and data should be valid and reliable. | The observer must be very careful not to influence the data collected. Car colour may appear orange to one person but yellow to another. This kind of bias can be avoided by training the observer before they go out to perform the work. The group being observed may behave differently than normal because they have a "visitor" in with them, e.g. road users may slow down if they notice someone recording car speeds. This may mean results are unreliable. Also, because this is the natural environment, unexpected variables called extraneous variables can affect outcomes (see next section in this chapter). |
| Sampling | Instead of asking the whole statistical population (census), just a "sample" is asked. A few are selected from the whole to represent the population. You can learn more about this in Chapter 2. | This is a much cheaper option than asking the whole population so will save on time and money. | Sometimes the sample used might not represent the population very well. |

**Secondary data** is data that has been collected by someone other than the person doing the analysis. It is often in a more useful format than raw data, for example in a table. In processing the data to this "cleaner" format, details of the original data may well have been lost. Secondary data can be very useful to a statistician, as someone else has had to pay for the research, so not only is it much easier to access, it will cost less in both time and money.

| TYPE OF SECONDARY DATA | EXAMPLE OF COLLECTION |
|---|---|
| Reference | There are many forms of reference material to access. These could be from historical documents, published journals (very useful for the medical profession), books, maps, newspapers, magazines, Internet surveys, etc. The UK Data Archive at the University of Essex holds a wealth of data on many areas.  http://www.data-archive.ac.uk |
| National Census | The **National Census** is a huge survey, conducted by the UK government every 10 years. Every household in the country is required to complete the survey. They ask how many people are living in each house, the total income of each household, whether the property is owned or rented, ethnic group, religion...the list goes on. It really is a very big survey! The National Census will then play an important role in producing national statistics to compare to previous years and to other countries. Tables of different statistics are generated and published by region, so that parts of the UK can be compared to other parts. http://census.ac.uk |

If you use a secondary data source in your statistics, you should always acknowledge the data source as part of your work. If someone finds a problem with your results, they may be able to track the issue back to the original data.

## EXERCISE 4

**1.** The care workers in Sheffield are being observed this week to record how long they spend with each client and which duties they perform.

   **a.** Give one advantage of collecting the data using this method.

   **b.** Give one disadvantage of collecting the data using this method.

**2.** Give one advantage and one disadvantage of using a census instead of a sample.

**3.** Mair wants to find out the most popular make of tablet computer in the UK. Explain how she can go about this using:

   **a.** primary data                    **b.** secondary data

**4.** Marco is researching reading habits of teenagers. He visits 10 schools to observe the use of the library.

    **a.** What sort of data collection method is he using?

    **b.** Identify one problem with him collecting data in this way.

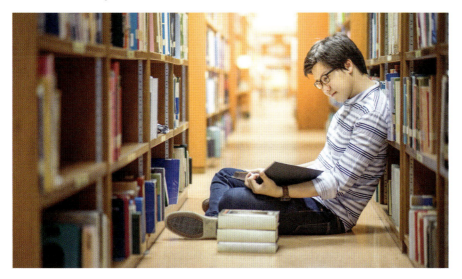

HIGHER TIER

**5.** Amandeep is in charge of the wildlife at a new holiday home site. She needs to work out how many pairs of each kind of animal to introduce in order to establish a good ecosystem on the site. Describe how she can do this and list advantages and disadvantages of your chosen method.

**6.** Describe one advantage and one disadvantage of completing face-to-face questionnaires.

**7.** Ann and Ben are investigating chocolate eaten in a week. Ann suggests looking online, but Ben wants to do a questionnaire.

    **a.** Give one advantage of each method.

    **b.** Give one disadvantage of each method.

    **c.** Suggest two questions, one open and one closed, that Ben could use in his questionnaire.

**8.** Describe one advantage and one disadvantage of completing online questionnaires.

**9.** Matteo has produced a statistical report on the age and masses of soldiers in World War I. Will he have used primary or secondary data? Explain how you know.

# Experimental data and bias

When using an experiment to gather primary data, there may be more variables involved than just the one being investigated. The variable being investigated is called the **explanatory variable** (sometimes also called the **independent variable**). The outcome that you then measure is known as the **response variable** (sometimes also called the **dependent variable**). **Extraneous variables** can also creep (unwanted) into **experimental data** and need to be watched for. These are variables possibly outside of our control that may still affect the outcome of the experiment.

## EXAMPLE

Armaan grows roses to sell. He wants to find out which fertiliser gives the bigger flowers. In his greenhouse, he sets up 10 pots using RosyPosy fertiliser and 10 pots using BigBloom fertiliser.

Describe the explanatory variable and the response variable. Describe any extraneous variables that may affect the outcome of the experiment and how Armaan may possibly overcome them.

## SOLUTION

The two fertilisers are the explanatory variable.

The size of the flowers will be the response variable.

Extraneous variables may be the amount of sunlight each plant receives or whether a plant near to the greenhouse door may get more chilled than a plant near to the back. If the plants are on shelves, those higher up may receive more light. Armaan can try to avoid these situations by having all the plants on the same level. To avoid the "chill" factor, he could alternate the pots RosyPosy, BigBloom, RosyPosy, BigBloom, etc. throughout the greenhouse. This would also help with the potential sunlight issue.

### HIGHER TIER

It's good practice, where possible, to have a **control group** as part of the research, that stay in the same conditions as the rest of the experiment, but are untreated. The control group in the example above would be the 10 pots with no fertiliser as they are in the same greenhouse but receive no fertiliser.

When designing an experiment to gather data, the data must be both **valid** and **reliable** and we must be careful to avoid any **bias**. A valid test is one that does actually test what it's supposed to be testing and a reliable test will give consistent results, no matter who performs the test. As we saw in the previous section, observers without training can also introduce bias but there can be bias from other sources.

| POTENTIAL SOURCE OF BIAS | POTENTIAL FIX |
| --- | --- |
| Researchers themselves may be looking to confirm their hypothesis and so choose to ignore any quirks in the data that could distract from the confirmation they are seeking. | Process the complete data set and see how far away from confirmation this takes things. Review the experimentation process to see if anything needs altering. Re-evaluate whether these quirks can safely be left out of the findings before doing so. It is also sometimes possible to perform experiments 'blind' – meaning participants do not know if they are in the treated group or control group – or even 'double blind' where the researcher may not know either to avoid unintentional (or intentional!) bias. |
| Leading questions in an interview, such as, "Do you agree that people who don't recycle should be fined?" | Test the questions on people before running the interviews in live situations. Review the answers to see if there could be any bias in the wording of the questions or in the manner in which the questions are asked. |
| Social status bias – questions such as, "Do you smoke?", "How much alcohol do you consume each week?", "How much money did you earn last month?" can all be very sensitive to answer. | Try to keep all such questions confidential to get as honest a set of answers as possible. If respondents feel as though they "ought" to answer in a certain way, the collected data will be meaningless. |

## EXERCISE 5

1. Vikki is carrying out an experiment to see which method will boil one litre of water the quickest. She can use the kettle, the microwave, or the stove. Identify the explanatory variable and the response variable in her experiment.

2. Oshra keeps tropical fish in a tank. She thinks that at higher temperatures, more algae grows. She decides to run the tank for one week at each of four different temperatures and measure the amount of algae each week (cleaning away all of the algae each time).

   a. Match up the explanatory and response variable.

   | Explanatory variable | | Amount of algae |
   |---|---|---|
   | Response variable | | Temperature of water |

   b. Can you think of any extraneous variables that may impact the amount of algae seen at the end of the week?

   c. Give one way you could possibly control the extraneous variables you identified in part b.

3. A scientist is interested to find out whether different coloured lights will attract more or fewer moths.

   a. Describe an experiment he could use to find out.

   b. Identify the explanatory and response variables in your experiment.

   c. Could any extraneous variable have an effect on the outcome of the experiment? List any you can think of.

4. Lucille has developed a new drug to slow down the growth of calcium deposits in patients suffering from a disease called scleroderma. She has three groups of patients taking part in a trial to see if the drug works:

   Group A have a 50 mg dose of the drug each day.

   Group B have a 25 mg dose of the drug each day.

   Group C have a tablet that looks like the drug each day but simply contains a vitamin.

   The groups are tested each month, for three months, to see how much additional calcium is in their bodies.

   a. Is Lucille's trial a valid trial? Explain your answer.

   b. Is Lucille's trial a reliable trial? Explain your answer.

   c. Identify the explanatory and response variables in the trials.

   HIGHER TIER  d. Explain the purpose of Group C.

5. Faith has been working on a non-medication treatment to improve memory. Design a statistical experiment she could use to test the effectiveness of her treatment. You should make a note of any extraneous variables that may affect the outcome.

HIGHER TIER

6. Igor has developed a protein shake that can enhance an athlete's performance. He is ready to carry out a statistical experiment to gather statistics. He will use these statistics to help sell the protein shake.

   a. Explain what is meant by a double-blind trial.

   b. Design a double-blind experiment for Igor to test the protein shake.

   c. Describe how your experiment is both valid and reliable.

## You should now be able to:

Identify different types of data

Sort and order data

Create frequency tables

Create tally charts

Create and use two-way tables

Identify primary and secondary data

Identify explanatory and response variables

Design and describe a valid experiment

Design and describe a reliable experiment

HIGHER TIER **Identify and describe a control group**

# Exam Practice Questions

**1.** Rodney wants to open a market stall in his town.

He will sell fruit and vegetables.

Which of these four variables is **discrete**?

    **A.** which fruit and vegetables they like best

    **B.** the number of days in a week they usually buy fruit and vegetables

    **C.** where they usually buy fruit and vegetables

    **D.** how far they live from the market

© AQA 2016

**2.** John collects stamps from all over the world.

Decide whether each of the following variables is discrete, continuous, or qualitative.

**(a)** the length of a stamp

**(b)** the number of stamps in his collection

**(c)** the country the stamp is from

© AQA 2014

**3.** A school has a house system based on kings and queens of England. The following data shows the house that each pupil in a tutor group belongs to.

| | | | | | |
|---|---|---|---|---|---|
| George | Elizabeth | George | William | George | Victoria |
| George | Victoria | Elizabeth | George | George | William |
| William | George | George | Victoria | George | Victoria |
| Elizabeth | Victoria | William | George | Victoria | Victoria |

Complete the tally column and the frequency column for the data.

| HOUSE | TALLY | FREQUENCY |
|---|---|---|
| Elizabeth | | |
| George | | |
| Victoria | | |
| William | | |

© AQA 2016

**4.** Eight dancers take part in a competition.

Each dancer performs a dance which is marked by two judges.

The table shows the scores (out of 10) the judges gave to each dancer.

| | Alex | Nina | Tanya | Rachel | Sam | Cruz | Jess | Mira |
|---|---|---|---|---|---|---|---|---|
| Judge A | 6 | 5 | 10 | 3 | 9 | 3 | 7 | 7 |
| Judge B | 7 | 7 | 9 | 5 | 7 | 6 | 7 | 6 |

**(a)** Which judge gave higher marks on average?

You must show your working.

**(b)** How do you know there was some observer bias?

© AQA 2015

**5.** A food manufacturer advertises that eating their new brand of healthy biscuit "Memo" will increase short-term memory in teenagers.

An experiment is to be set up to test this claim.

Here is a list of the variables that may be connected to the experiment.

**A.** How often the teenager eats "Memo" biscuits.

**B.** The number of words the teenager can remember during the experiment.

**C.** How much sleep the teenager has.

**D.** The number of pets the teenager owns.

**E.** Eating the biscuit "Memo".

**(a)** For this experiment write down which of these variables is:

**(i)** The explanatory variable

**(ii)** The response variable

**(iii)** A possible extraneous variable

**(iv)** A second possible extraneous variable.

**(b)** Is variable D an example of discrete, continuous or categorical data?

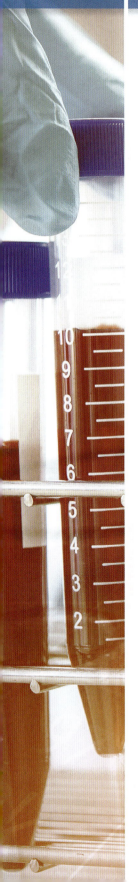

# 2 | Sampling

## In this chapter you will learn:

The difference between a population, a sample, and a sample frame

That "population" can change with each situation

The types of and reasons for using different sampling techniques to avoid bias in your sample

The key features of a simple random sample

The different types of sampling

## New Vocabulary

Sample

Population

Sample frame

Sample size

Random sampling

Stratified

Systematic sampling

Quota sampling

Convenience sampling/ Opportunity sampling

Judgement sampling

# Sampling from a population

**Samples** are used in everyday life; you may have a blood sample taken at the hospital, an interior designer may take fabric samples to show to a client, or you may choose to listen to a sample of a music track before you download it to see if you like it. A sample is just a small piece of something that gives you the overall idea of it.

We use samples in statistics because it is often not sensible to try and look at the entire population or ask the entire population their opinion on something. Try to imagine how much time it would take just to ask everyone in your school if they would like to try a new product in the canteen. You would encounter all sorts of problems, such as keeping an accurate record of who you have spoken to, catching up with people who were absent when you visited their class, and processing the enormous amount of data you will have collected by the end of it.

Now imagine multiplying that for the entire population of a village, town, city, or the country. In real world situations, there are costs associated with large data collection, too, so it's simply not workable. For this reason, we take a sample of the population and collect data from those people.

The **population** consists of everything or everyone being considered (just like the population of a country means everyone in that country). In some instances, we need to survey the entire population, and when we do this, it is called a census. In the UK, we hold a national survey every 10 years.

A statistical population will be different in each situation. For example, it may be all the books in the school library or all of the passengers on a flight.

If a hypothesis states "Girls in 9C can run faster than boys in 9C," then the population is the whole of form 9C (not the whole school).

Compare that with a hypothesis that states, girls can run faster than boys – then the population is all boys and girls! Sometimes, the whole population may not be accessible, and so the people available to appear in the sample become what is known as the **sample frame**, and it's from these people that we would take our sample. If some students from 9C were absent from school on testing day, the sample frame would consist only of those students present.

It is important that when you collect your data, you have not collected biased data. A sample can be biased if the population are not well represented within the sample. For example, if you were collecting data about the method of transport people use to get to work, you are unlikely to have a good spread of answers if you stand outside a railway station and ask your questions. You need to find a way to ensure that bias does not creep in to your sample when sampling as well as when setting the questions.

Before you select your sample, you need to consider **sample size**. The bigger the sample, the more likely you will be to have reliable results, but that also has to be balanced against cost and time constraints. Consideration also should be given to items that are 'destroyed' once used in the sample, such as light bulbs or food samples. Here, there is an argument for smaller sample sizes.

### EXAMPLE

A factory produces 500000 batteries in one shift. Each battery should power a high-power torch for 40 hours. The testing team need to check that the batteries are performing correctly.

   **a.** Explain why the testing team will test a sample and not all of the batteries from one shift.

   **b.** What sample size would you recommend for them to use? Explain why you have chosen this figure.

### SOLUTION

   **a.** The batteries will all be used up once tested, and the company will not be able to sell them.

   **b.** The sample size needs to be large enough to allow a genuine impression of the population to be gained giving reliable results. However, every battery sampled is used up and cannot be sold. It would therefore not make financial sense to test too many. Perhaps a sample of 100 would be appropriate.

# Random sampling

In a **random sample**, each member of the population has an equal chance of being in the sample. A random sample can be selected using the random number generator on a calculator or computer, dice, cards, and random number lists.

The statistician will firstly number each member of the population. Members are then selected by any of the methods above to generate the sample.

## EXAMPLE

There are 40 players in a 5-a-side football tournament. Josh wants to take a 10% sample to ask questions about energy drinks.

    **a.** How many players will Josh need in his sample?

    **b.** Use this player list and random number table (reading across from left to right) to determine which players are in the sample.

| | | | | |
|---|---|---|---|---|
| Tal | Lior | Tamara | Rick | Tom |
| Lita | Bren | Jay | Kez | Sonja |
| Mia | James | Jimmy | Oshra | Mike |
| Jiff | Lilia | Raffy | Jashen | Ranvir |
| Tamir | Milo | Issy | Jake | Jack |
| Zinnia | Jeevan | Cris | Dot | Mal |
| Bri | Helen | Elinor | Daniel | Connor |
| Morgan | Lydia | John | Jasmine | Toby |

| | | | | | | | | | |
|---|---|---|---|---|---|---|---|---|---|
| 84 | 37 | 92 | 78 | 56 | 76 | 62 | 34 | 17 | 52 |
| 21 | 51 | 35 | 87 | 02 | 37 | 19 | 07 | 44 | 84 |
| 76 | 36 | 66 | 31 | 25 | 57 | 53 | 04 | 29 | 32 |

**advice**

*Don't forget to number your population before you begin and then match those numbers to members of the population at the end.*

## SOLUTION

**a.** $\frac{10}{100} \times 40 = 4$ players

**b.** Firstly, number the members of the population using two digits each time: (you can go across or down)

| | | | | |
|---|---|---|---|---|
| Tal **01** | Lior **09** | Tamara **17** | Rick **25** | Tom **33** |
| Lita **02** | Bren **10** | Jay **18** | Kez **26** | Sonja **34** |
| Mia **03** | James **11** | Jimmy **19** | Oshra **27** | Mike **35** |
| Jiff **04** | Lilia **12** | Raffy **20** | Jashen **28** | Ranvir **36** |
| Tamir **05** | Milo **13** | Issy **21** | Jake **29** | Jack **37** |
| Zinnia **06** | Jeevan **14** | Cris **22** | Dot **30** | Mal **38** |
| Bri **07** | Helen **15** | Elinor **23** | Daniel **31** | Connor **39** |
| Morgan **08** | Lydia **16** | John **24** | Jasmine **32** | Toby **40** |

Now use the random number table to select the members of the sample. Any numbers in the table which are higher than 40 are discarded as are any duplicates.

| | | | | | | | | | |
|---|---|---|---|---|---|---|---|---|---|
| ~~84~~ | 37 | ~~92~~ | ~~78~~ | 56 | ~~76~~ | ~~62~~ | 34 | 17 | ~~52~~ |
| ~~34~~ | ~~51~~ | 35 | ~~87~~ | 02 | 37 | 19 | 07 | 44 | ~~84~~ |
| ~~76~~ | 36 | ~~66~~ | 31 | 25 | ~~57~~ | ~~53~~ | 04 | 29 | 32 |

Choosing to read across the rows, the numbers generated are therefore: 37, 34, 17, and 35, which means players Jack, Sonja, Tamara, and Mike would be in the sample.

Instead of using the random number table, you can generate your own list by using the random number button on your calculator.

For example, 0.194 is given when I push Ran# =, so I can choose for that to be 19 or 94 (either is acceptable, but you must be consistent).

You can use dice to generate the random numbers, too. Many different kinds of dice are sold, from 3-faced up to 100-faced! If using the example above and 6-faced dice, I would use three dice and number the players in a different manner. 111 would mean 1 on first dice, 1 on second dice, 1 on third dice, or 213 would mean 2 on first dice, 1 on second dice, and 3 on third dice.

| | | | | |
|---|---|---|---|---|
| Tal 111 | Lior 123 | Tamara 135 | Rick 151 | Tom 163 |
| Lita 112 | Bren 124 | Jay 136 | Kez 152 | Sonja 164 |
| Mia 113 | James 125 | Jimmy 141 | Oshra 153 | Mike 165 |
| Jiff 114 | Lilia 126 | Raffy 142 | Jashen 154 | Ranvir 166 |
| Tamir 115 | Milo 131 | Issy 143 | Jake 155 | Jack 211 |
| Zinnia 116 | Jeevan 132 | Cris 144 | Dot 156 | Mal 212 |
| Bri 121 | Helen 133 | Elinor 145 | Daniel 161 | Connor 213 |
| Morgan 122 | Lydia 134 | John 146 | Jasmine 162 | Toby 214 |

The three dice would then be thrown and corresponding players picked as before. Notice that this is quite inefficient as an awful lot of numbers do not correspond to a person.

Another way to generate a random sample is to number the population, write corresponding numbers onto pieces of card, thoroughly mix the cards and then pick out a suitable number of cards. You've probably come across this idea when people "draw names out of a hat". This is not a recommended method though as it is not possible to achieve a genuine random selection this way.

advice

*If you are using this sampling method, your cards need to be all the same size and every name must be written on a piece of card, before any cards are "chosen".*

# Sampling using stratification

One of the problems with taking a random sample is that it is possible for a section of the population to be missed out when the sample is selected. If you were taking a random sample of students from a school, the selection process may not select anyone from Years 7 or 10. This could make the answers from the people in the survey unrepresentative of the population and could lead to biased survey results.

One way to guard against this happening is to use a sample that is **stratified**. In order to take a sample using this method, we have to divide the population up into different groups or *strata* (strata is the plural of *stratum* which is Latin for 'layer'). We then choose members from each stratum, usually at random, so that we have the same proportion as is found in the whole population.

You will sometimes see reference elsewhere to a stratified sample – technically stratification is not a method of sampling, it simply gets you the number in each strata that then needs to be sampled by one of the other methods. The words used should be "a sample stratified by" and then the type of strata, e.g. gender, age or as in the example below, type of animal owned.

## EXAMPLE

Peak Vets treats 1000 animals in one month: 550 dogs, 250 cats, 197 rabbits and 3 other animals. Explain how to obtain a sample of 100 animals stratified by their type to ask their owners' opinions on the service received.

## SOLUTION

To get a sample size of 100, we would need $\frac{100}{1000}$ of each type of animal.

$\frac{100}{1000} \times 550 = 55$ dogs

$\frac{100}{1000} \times 250 = 25$ cats

$\frac{100}{1000} \times 197 = 19.7$ rabbits

$\frac{100}{1000} \times 3 = 0.3$ other animals

The 55 dogs and 25 cats are whole numbers, but the 19.7 rabbits and 0.3 other animals will need rounding.

Here we would have 55 dogs, 25 cats, 20 rabbits, and 0 other animals. (This will mean that the other animals are not represented in the sample, so it may be better to use 19 rabbits and 1 other animal, but statistically it is 20 and 0.)

**advice**

*When you round the values you get, remember to check that the total number equals the number of the size required.*
*55 + 25 + 20 + 0 = 100*

Now we know how many of each type of animal will be in the sample, we can go on to select those animals that will be in the sample. These animals can be chosen via a random sample within each stratum.

In this first example, everything did round nicely to give the correct final total. This might not always be the case as we shall see here.

## EXAMPLE

An NHS trust wish to survey the performance of their A&E department.

They want to take a sample of 80 patients stratified according to their gender and whether they are adults.

For one week the trust compiles who visits A&E giving the following data.

| NUMBER OF PEOPLE | MALE | FEMALE |
|---|---|---|
| Adult (18+) | 407 | 254 |
| Child (Under 18) | 155 | 99 |

Calculate the number of each type of person who should be in a sample of 80 stratified by these factors.

## SOLUTION

The total number of patients is 407 + 254 + 155 + 99 = 915

To get a sample size of 80 we will need to use $\frac{80}{915}$ of each type of person.

Adult males → $\frac{80}{915} \times 407 = 35.585$

Adult females → $\frac{80}{915} \times 254 = 22.208$

Child males → $\frac{80}{915} \times 155 = 13.552$

Child females → $\frac{80}{915} \times 99 = 8.656$

advice

$\frac{80}{915}$ here is known as the sampling fraction.

We now round these values to the nearest whole number to give the total for each type of person.

Adult males rounds to 36        Adult females rounds to 22

Child males rounds to 14        Child females rounds to 9

Check the total sample 36 + 22 + 14 + 9 = 81, which is one too many.

This has happened because we have rounded up three out of the four times.

To preserve the correct final total sample, we must now round down one of the values which we had actually rounded up. The simplest way is to look for the one which was nearest to rounding down in the first place - this is child males which had a decimal of 0.552, lower than the other two which rounded up.

So, the final sample amounts for each type of person is:

| Adult males | Adult females | Child males | Child females |
|---|---|---|---|
| 36 | 22 | 13 | 9 |

We now would use a standard sampling method, such as random or systematic to obtain the actual people from each type.

# Systematic sampling

Where a data set has no particular pattern or subgroups, we can use a **systematic sample** where we "choose" items from the sample frame at regular intervals, say every 10th or 20th item. With there being no difference between members of the population, we have fewer worries about an unrepresentative sample. This type of sampling is great to use on a production line at a factory where all items in the sample frame are identical.

Firstly, we would number the population and decide upon the sample size. Next, we need to calculate the interval size. We then obtain a starting point using a random technique (dice, ran#, random number table, etc.) and count out the members of the sample from there.

### EXAMPLE

In one hour, a machine produces 500 boxes of cereal. The floor manager wants to take a sample to check the masses are within the allowed limits. Describe how he could take a systematic sample of 50 boxes from those produced by the machine in one hour.

### SOLUTION

Firstly, number each box as it comes off the production line.

A sample size of 50 means we take every $500 \div 50 = 10$th box.

Use a random method to find the starting point (this will be a number between 01 and 10, because we are taking every 10th box.) For example, my calculator gave me a random number of 06.

06 is the first box in the sample, then box numbers 16, 26, 36, 46...496.

# Quota sampling

In a **quota sample**, the statistician is given certain constraints to work within. It may be that the survey is about a new fashion collection in a clothes shop, and the owners have asked for a certain proportion of the sample to be men of a certain age and a certain proportion to be women of a certain age. This can lead to quite unreliable and biased results as people may look like they fulfil the criteria, but in actuality, they do not. Also there will be a certain amount of judgement made by the interviewer.

**EXAMPLE**

Carlos is the new manager of a multi-purpose sports stadium.

He wants to find out what new sports might be popular with customers.

He splits people into age groups 0 – 19, 20 – 39, 40 – 59, 60 – 79, and 80+.

He decides that he will request that his team ask a sample of 100 with 20% of the sample in each age group.

    **a.** Explain why this is quota sampling.

    **b.** Give one advantage of using quota sampling in this case compared to random sampling.

    **c.** Suggest an improvement to his quota sampling method.

**SOLUTION**

    **a.** As the population has been divided into subgroups and a specific proportion (20%) has been determined for each group, this is quota sampling.

    **b.** Random sampling would not necessarily give a good spread of ages within the sample.

    **c.** It seems strange to have 20% of his sample for people aged 80+. He could get some data and find the proportions of customers in each age group and reflect this in the percentage of each age group being asked.

# Convenience sampling

**Convenience sampling** (sometimes known as **opportunity sampling**) is the easiest kind of sample to select. This type of sampling will almost invariably bring bias as the sample members are unlikely to be representative of the population. In order to select the members of the sample, you might take the first $n$ from the sample frame, or if there is no sample frame, you are really just picking those people who are easiest to get.

For example, the first 50 boxes of cereal off a machine at the start of a shift.

### EXAMPLE

Jono uses convenience sampling to take a sample of 40 students at school to ask how they travelled to school that day. He decides to ask the first 40 people through the school gate. Explain why Jono's sample is likely to be biased.

### SOLUTION

People have a tendency to travel to school in groups, whether they walk, cycle, or use the bus. If a bus had just arrived as Jono started to collect the members for his sample, he'd get a large number of bus users and not much else. This could lead him to think that the vast majority of students travel by bus, but this may not be the case at all.

**Judgement sampling** is very similar to convenience sampling, but the person doing the sampling has some element of choice in their sample set. This will almost always lead to bias as the statistician's opinions about how people will answer will affect their choice of sample.

### EXAMPLE

Longbarn council wants to build on an area of parkland, and the local conservation group wants to prevent this from happening. They ask an expert to survey the land to see if there are any reasons why the council should not build. The expert takes samples from the parkland to test for rare animals or rare plants. Explain why this judgement sample is likely to lead to biased results.

### SOLUTION

If the expert wishes to stop the council, he will select samples that show evidence of rare animal or plant life in the parkland. However, if the expert has an interest in the building works, he will select samples that show there is nothing extraordinary living in the parkland. If there does happen to be rare wildlife there of some description, it will be totally up to the expert whether to use the evidence or ignore it.

## EXERCISE 1

1. Tara is starting up a small company selling handmade chocolates. She puts up a post on her Facebook page asking for 20 people to try her chocolates and give feedback. Will these 20 people be a fair or biased sample? Give a reason for your answer.

2. Den owns a club in town and wants to expand. The council have asked him to ask 100 townspeople their opinions on the expansion. Den asks every 10th person, of the 1000 in the club, as they leave his club on Friday night to answer the survey.

   a. What kind of sampling is Den using?

   b. Explain whether this sample group will give views representative of the town.

   c. Suggest a better way to obtain this sample.

3. 80 dogs enter a fun dog show at the village fete. The local newspaper wants to take a photograph of a random sample of 12 dogs. Use this table and the random number table to describe how to obtain the random sample for the photograph. Read across the top row of the random number table. You should list the dogs that will be in the photograph.

| Murphy | Barney | Bruno | Bumble | Milo | Stitch | Poppy | Laddie | Missie | Annie |
|--------|--------|-------|--------|------|--------|-------|--------|--------|-------|
| Betsy | Dolly | George | Beauty | Arthur | Gwen | Beanie | Ollie | Rolf | Penny |
| Pepper | Patsy | Dinky | Toby | Benjie | Betty | Digby | Baxter | Rupert | Rufus |
| Clem | Clint | Bella | Scooby | Basil | Roly | Alfie | Misty | Clark | Rosie |
| Renee | Jeremy | Jessie | Wilson | Dotty | Sniffy | Timmy | Ginger | Blackie | Kissie |
| Lizzie | Finn | Doodle | Paddy | Otto | Karl | Sammy | Barker | Pippa | Archie |
| Holly | Bess | Buddy | Harry | Goofy | Pluto | Blue | Fluffy | Fang | Mick |
| Pebbles | Pablo | Bailey | Ozzy | Charlie | Sky | Cushla | JD | Cookie | Coco |

| 94 | 37 | 92 | 78 | 56 | 76 | 62 | 37 | 17 | 52 |
|----|----|----|----|----|----|----|----|----|----|
| 01 | 51 | 52 | 87 | 02 | 37 | 19 | 07 | 44 | 84 |
| 77 | 36 | 65 | 32 | 24 | 87 | 59 | 04 | 29 | 32 |

4. Sian is hosting a fun 5-km race. The table shows the number of runners in each category.

| UNDER 16 YEARS | 17–25 YEARS | 26–50 YEARS | 51+ YEARS |
|---|---|---|---|
| 49 | 321 | 546 | 84 |

Sian wants to take a 10% sample of runners, using a sample stratified by age.

   a. How many runners are there altogether?

   b. How many runners will be in the sample from each category?

   c. What would be the quickest way to obtain the sample?

   d. Sian wants to know how well runners felt the race was organised.

      i. Why is a sample stratified by age a good way of obtaining these views?

      ii. Suggest another possible way of stratifying.

5. Ben needs to survey 100 people at his local doctors' surgery. He takes the list of patients and contacts every 20th patient.

   a. Explain why this is not a random sample of townspeople.

   b. Give a reason why this method might be better than a random sample.

   c. There are 2000 people registered at this surgery. How many people will be in the sample?

6. Katharine has 100 animals in her dog training classes. She will contact 5% of the owners to ask for feedback (you may assume each owner has only one dog). Use the random number function on your calculator to work out a sample of owners to contact.

7. A club has 240 members, 180 of whom are male. How many men and how many women should be selected for a sample of 30 stratified by gender?

8. In a department store there are 600 workers. 340 work in clothing, 160 work in household goods, 80 work in offices and the rest work in the canteen. A sample of 80 workers is required to discuss the Christmas party. Describe how you would use a random sample stratified by where workers work to select those workers to be asked.

9. Mica has to survey 50 girls aged 14–16 and 30 boys aged 15–17 about an energy drink. Describe how she could obtain her sample using quota sampling.

10. Tina has been asked to find out where the Year 11 students would like to go for their end of year day out. She decides to take a sample of 30 from the 150 in the year. She asks 30 of her friends where they would like to go.

    a. What is the population in this situation?

    b. What type of sampling is this?

    c. Comment on her planned method and think of ways she could improve her sample.

11. The visitors to a small museum are to be asked regarding the facilities available.
    The number of visitors over one week are summarised:

| VISITORS | AGED UNDER 30 | AGED 30+ |
|----------|---------------|----------|
| Male | 84 | 237 |
| Female | 104 | 289 |

    a. Use the proportions from the table to obtain how many should be in a sample of 75 stratified by gender and age.

    b. Why might stratification be a good idea here?

    c. Suggest a possible issue with using this table's data.

    d. Suggest an alternative valid sampling method which could be used.

**12.** A sample of 150 caravan owners is to be asked about their favourite sites.

The sample is to be stratified according to how long they have owned a caravan and how many holidays they take.

Here is data about caravan owners registered with some sites.

| CARAVAN OWNERS | AGED UNDER 40 | AGED 40–59 | AGED 60+ |
|---|---|---|---|
| owned for 0 – 2 years | 23 | 38 | 46 |
| owned for 3 – 5 years | 17 | 34 | 48 |
| owned for 6+ years | 5 | 19 | 59 |

**a.** Calculate the number of owners from each of the known age and length of ownership categories that should be in the sample of 150.

**b.** Sam says, "It would be much easier to just do a random sample, and it would still be fair". Comment on Sam's statement.

## You should now know:

The difference between a population, a sample, and a sample frame

The "population" will change with each situation

The reasons for using different sampling techniques

To avoid bias in your sample

The key features of a simple random sample

The different types of sampling

# Exam Practice Questions

1. There are 38 houses on a street numbered 1–38.

   Use these random numbers to obtain a random sample of five houses from 1–38.

   | 25 | 16 | 44 | 87 | 25 | 09 | 40 | 11 | 12 |

   © AQA 2014

2. A coach company takes weekly trips to the seaside.

   The manager wants to interview some of the passengers on a trip. There are 53 passengers.

   (a) Write down one reason why the manager might want to take a sample rather than carry out a census.

   (b) What population does the manager select from?

   (c) Briefly describe how the manager could obtain a random sample of 10 passengers.

   © AQA 2015

3. A school has 600 pupils.

   The headteacher wants to choose 8 pupils to appear on an advertising poster for the school.

   He decides to select 8 pupils using simple random sampling.
   He numbers the pupils from 001 to 600.
   He uses this table of random digits.

   | 068 | 944 | 408 | 875 | 163 | 977 | 574 | 946 |
   | 916 | 745 | 538 | 936 | 053 | 538 | 436 | 988 |
   | 011 | 444 | 733 | 097 | 300 | 643 | 040 | 752 |

   (a) He starts with 068 and reads **across** each row.
       Write down the number corresponding to each of the 8 pupils he selects.

   (b) Give **one** reason why this method may not be a suitable way to choose pupils for the poster.

   © AQA 2017

4. The table gives details about the 800 people who will attend a concert at a theatre.

   | MEN | WOMEN | BOYS | GIRLS |
   |-----|-------|------|-------|
   | 321 | 360   | 72   | 47    |

   The owner of the theatre wants to survey 40 of these people.

   (a) The manager suggests asking the first 40 people who arrive at the theatre.
       Write down the name of the manager's sampling method.

**(b)** The owner of the theatre decides to use stratified sampling.
Work out the number of men that should be surveyed.

© AQA 2016

5. The personnel department at a company wants to find out the views of staff on certain issues. It decides to carry out a survey on a sample of staff.

   **(a)** Give **one** advantage of doing the survey on a sample of staff rather than doing a census.

   **(b)** Write down a possible sample frame that the personnel department could use when picking the sample.

   The table shows information about the staff employed by the company.

| | | Number of male staff | Number of female staff |
|---|---|---|---|
| | Assistant | 236 | 249 |
| JOB TITLE | Manager | 383 | 492 |
| | Senior Partner | 75 | 65 |

   **(c)** The personnel department decides to choose a sample of 160 staff, stratified by job title and gender.
   Work out the number of male managers that it should choose.

© AQA 2015

6. A youth club has 72 members. The leader decides to select six members at random to go on a sailing course. He numbers the members 01 to 72 and uses the random number table below to make his selection.

| | | | |
|---|---|---|---|
| 29 | 44 | 76 | 56 |
| 44 | 51 | 38 | 00 |
| 07 | 21 | 92 | 17 |

   **(a)** Starting with 29 and reading across each row, write down the number of each of the six members that he selects.

   **(b)** The youth club has 48 boys and 24 girls as members. Calculate the number of boys and girls the leader should include in a stratified sample of members.

7. The table shows how many students are in a school.

| | Lower School | Upper School | Sixth Form |
|---|---|---|---|
| Male | 360 | 240 | 208 |
| Female | 385 | 201 | 173 |

**(a)** Chelsey wants to survey 120 students from the school using a stratified sample. Work out how many male students Chelsey should include in her survey from the Lower School.

**(b)** Twenty-five students from the sixth form are to be chosen. Describe a method of choosing a random sample of these sixth form students.

**8.** A council proposes that a new secondary school is built to serve the three villages, Lower Hadstow, Upper Hadstow, and Great Hadstow.

The total number of adults living in the three villages is 8000.
The council wants to survey a sample of adults living in the three villages to find out what they think about the proposal.

**(a)** The headteacher of Great Hadstow Primary School suggests the council should ask a sample of parents of students at her school.

Explain why this sample may not give reliable results.

**(b)** The council's education officer suggests using a systematic sample of 200 from the 8000 adults living in the villages.

Describe how this sample could be obtained.

The table shows information about the population of each village.

| | PARENTAL STATUS | |
| --- | --- | --- |
| | Adults with young children | Adults without young children |
| Lower Hadstow | 1625 | 1875 |
| Upper Hadstow | 1559 | 841 |
| Great Hadstow | 504 | 1596 |

The council's statistician decides to obtain a sample of 200 adults stratified by village and parental status.

**(c)** How many adults **without** young children from **Lower Hadstow** should be chosen?

53% of the 200 adults sampled supported building a new school.

**(d)** The local newspaper reported the results of the survey.
The newspaper stated that the majority of the adults in the three villages support building a new school.

Explain why this conclusion may **not** be correct.

© AQA 2018

# 3 Charts and Diagrams 1

## In this chapter you will learn to:

- Create and interpret a pictogram
- Create and interpret different kinds of bar chart
- Create and interpret a pie chart
- Create and interpret a histogram of equal class widths
- Create and interpret a frequency polygon

We have already seen that there are different kinds of data; qualitative and quantitative, discrete and continuous. There are many different diagrams to represent the different types of data. It is essential to use the appropriate type of diagram according to the type of data you have.

## New Vocabulary

Pictogram

Bar chart

Bar line chart

Dual bar chart

Multiple bar chart

Composite bar chart

Percentage bar chart

Pie chart

Histogram

Frequency polygon

# Pictograms

A **pictogram** is one of the simplest ways that we use pictures to represent quantitative or qualitative data. Each pictogram must have a key that explains the value of each symbol.

When you create a pictogram for yourself, be careful to choose a symbol that will cut into two or four easily (or more if required). This symbol, for example, 🍦 will not split into two halves or smaller fractions as it is not symmetrical.

## EXAMPLE

Saoirse is knitting hats to give to homeless people. The table shows how many she has made each month, from September to March. Illustrate the data with a pictogram. Remember to choose a suitable symbol and give a key.

| | MONTH | | | | | | |
|---|---|---|---|---|---|---|---|
| | Sep | Oct | Nov | Dec | Jan | Feb | Mar |
| Number of hats made | 4 | 7 | 5 | 11 | 9 | 6 | 3 |

## SOLUTION

Key: 🧢 = 2 hats

**advice**

*You should keep all of your symbols the same size and draw them neatly lined up, vertically. It's not good to have the symbols spread out on one row and squashed on another as the pictogram is a visual representation of your data. Think of the symbols as being in columns, like in a table.*

# Bar charts

You are probably familiar with **bar charts**, too. They are also a nice straightforward picture form of representing data. As with the pictograms, bar charts can be used on qualitative and quantitative data.

A bar chart has:

- a title

- a label for each vertical axis and horizontal axis

- bars of equal width with gaps of equal width between the bars

- a key if it is showing more than one set of data

Here are the different types of bar charts:

### Bar line chart

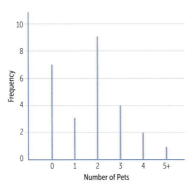

### Bar chart

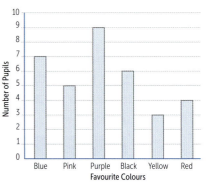

### Dual bar chart

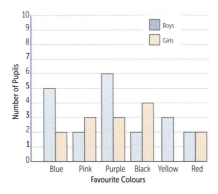

### Multiple bar chart

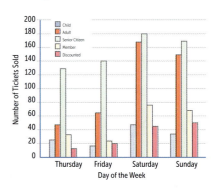

Dual, multiple, percentage, and composite bar charts must always have a key.

### Composite bar chart

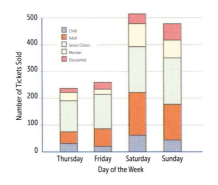

### Percentage bar chart

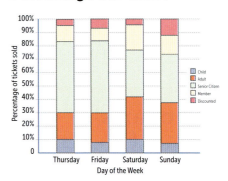

As you can see, we use these types of diagrams to illustrate both qualitative and discrete quantitative data. (Continuous quantitative data requires the use of a histogram – see page 56.)

## EXERCISE 1

**1.**

| | NUMBER OF TRACKS DOWNLOADED |
|---|---|
| Week 1 | ● ● ● ● ● |
| Week 2 | ● ● ● |
| Week 3 | ● ● ● ◖ |
| Week 4 | ● ◖ |
| Week 5 | ● ● ● |
| Week 6 | ● ● ● ● ● ● ● |

Key: ● = 2 Tracks

The pictogram shows the number of tracks Marin has downloaded to her phone during the last six weeks.

**a.** How many tracks did she download in Week 1?

**b.** How many tracks did she download in Week 4?

**c.** How many more tracks did she download in Week 5 than in Week 4?

**d.** During which two weeks did she download the same number of tracks?

**e.** Re-draw the pictogram, using one symbol to represent four downloads.

**2.** Louisa has recorded the number of books borrowed from the school library, by different genre. Illustrate the data with a pictogram.

| GENRE | NUMBER OF BOOKS BORROWED |
|---|---|
| Romance | 22 |
| Sci-fi | 13 |
| Horror | 19 |
| Non-fiction | 12 |
| Crime | 4 |

**advice**

*Remember to include a key.*

**3.** These are the prices (in £) of the last 20 houses sold by TrustMe estate agents.

| | | | | | |
|---|---|---|---|---|---|
| 125500 | 204000 | 120000 | 255000 | 198500 | 210950 |
| 310000 | 155500 | 175750 | 98950 | 166250 | 180000 |
| 115225 | 135000 | 201500 | 178000 | 154500 | 172750 |
| 123000 | 295950 | | | | |

   **a.** Decide upon groups for the data, create a tally chart, and then illustrate the data with a pictogram.

   **b.** Illustrate the data with a bar chart.

**4.** Carro works at a wedding venue. The bar line chart shows the different sizes of table she has available.

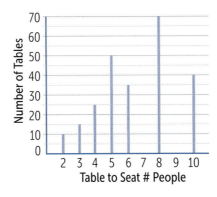

   **a.** How many tables to seat 6 does Carro have?

   **b.** How many tables will seat 5 or more?

   **c.** How many tables does she have in total?

   **d.** How many guests can Carro seat in total?

**5.** Seamus has been on a fishing trip. On Monday he caught 12 lb of fish, on Tuesday he caught 15 lb, on Wednesday he caught 14 lb, on Thursday he caught 21 lb and on Friday he caught 17 lb.

   Draw a bar chart to show the mass of fish he caught each day.

**6.** Freddy went on the fishing trip with Seamus. Freddy's catches were:

| Mon | Tues | Wed | Thurs | Fri |
|---|---|---|---|---|
| 14 lb | 11 lb | 19 lb | 15 lb | 17 lb |

   **a.** Draw a dual bar chart to show Seamus's and Freddy's catches.

   **b.** On which day(s) did Freddy catch a greater mass than Seamus?

   **c.** Freddy says they each had their heaviest total catch on the same day. Is that true? Give a reason for your answer.

   **d.** Did Freddy catch his heaviest single fish on Wednesday? Give a reason for your answer.

**7.** Fraser is studying a group of 500 sheep and their behaviour. He has 5 fields that the sheep can wander between. He keeps a note of how many sheep are in each field, every hour, as shown in the table:

|        | Field 1 | Field 2 | Field 3 | Field 4 | Field 5 |
|--------|---------|---------|---------|---------|---------|
| HOUR 1 | 103     | 90      | 70      | 155     | 82      |
| HOUR 2 | 68      | 141     | 96      | 132     | 63      |
| HOUR 3 | 54      | 168     | 80      | 160     | 38      |

Draw a multiple bar chart to show how many sheep are in each field, each hour.

**8.** The dual bar chart shows how many pupils are wearing braces in each year group.

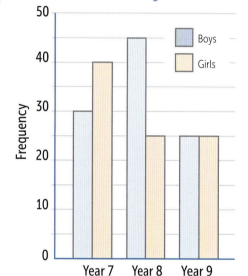

   **a.** How many boys in Year 8 wear braces?

   **b.** How many pupils in Year 9 wear braces?

   **c.** How many girls in Years 7, 8, and 9 wear braces altogether?

   **d.** Illustrate the data using a composite bar chart.

   **e.** Illustrate the data using a percentage bar chart.

**9.** Lou is comparing the numbers of fiction and non-fiction books borrowed at Staplehurst and Wadhurst libraries. She has created this percentage bar chart.

She says that more non-fiction books were borrowed from Staplehurst library than from Wadhurst. Explain why she may not be correct.

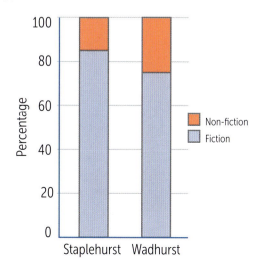

**10.** Maria, Andrea, and Sarah are selling candles. The table shows how many each person has sold.

|  | Strawberry | Raspberry | Lemon | Floral | Cinnamon |
|---|---|---|---|---|---|
| MARIA | 5 | 3 | 1 | 11 | 12 |
| ANDREA | 7 | 1 | 0 | 5 | 14 |
| SARAH | 15 | 7 | 3 | 2 | 6 |

**a.** Draw a composite bar chart to illustrate the data.

**b.** Explain why a dual bar chart cannot be used to illustrate the data.

**c.** Draw a percentage bar chart to illustrate the data, where each bar is made up of three parts, one for each seller.

**11.** This bar chart shows how many cats and dogs Emma saw at the animal health clinic yesterday.

Emma notices that the height of the bar for cats is double the height of the bar for dogs. She tells her boss they saw twice as many cats as dogs.

Explain why she is wrong.

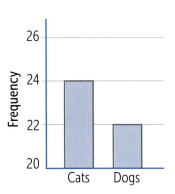

# Pie charts

**Pie charts** are a common way to represent categorical data. You can see at a glance which sector is the largest and smallest and so it's easy to pull some information from them. They do, however, hide their information within and in order to get actual data from them, some work is required.

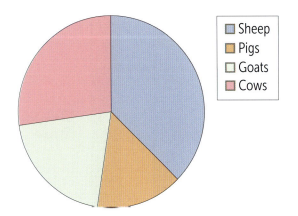

This pie chart shows the animals at a city farm for children.

It's easy to see at a glance that there are more sheep than any other animal because the sector for sheep is the largest. We can also see that the farm has the fewest number of pigs, as the sector for pigs is the smallest.

If we want to calculate the exact number of each animal, we will need to be told how many animals in total the pie chart represents and be able to measure the angle of each sector. It's also vital to have a key so that we know which sector relates to which animal.

## EXAMPLE

There are 40 animals at the city farm. How many of these animals are sheep?

## SOLUTION

Just looking at the pie chart won't help us, there are no numbers there. We will need to use a protractor to measure the angle for sheep.

The angle for the sheep sector is 135°.

We know that there are 360° in a pie chart, so sheep take up $\frac{135}{360}$ of the pie chart. If we multiply this fraction by the number of animals represented in total, we'll have the number of sheep.

$\frac{135}{360} \times 40 = 15$          The farm has 15 sheep.

## EXAMPLE

Mandy is selling pies at a handmade sale. By the end of the sale, she has sold 15 apple, 23 lemon meringue, 11 strawberry, and 11 pumpkin pies. Draw a pie chart to represent the pie sales.

## SOLUTION

First of all, we need to know how many pies were sold in total.

$15 + 23 + 11 + 11 = 60$

We write each type of pie sold as a fraction of the total and multiply by 360°.

For apple then, we calculate:          $\frac{15}{60} \times 360° = 90°$

lemon meringue:          $\frac{23}{60} \times 360° = 138°$

strawberry          $\frac{11}{60} \times 360° = 66°$

pumpkin          $\frac{11}{60} \times 360° = 66°$

advice

*Angles will not always work out to be whole numbers. Once you have calculated each angle, it's worth adding them to make sure you get 360°.*

We now need a circle and a start line coming out from the centre.

From this start line, we carefully draw each angle in. Once each sector is drawn, it should be labelled.

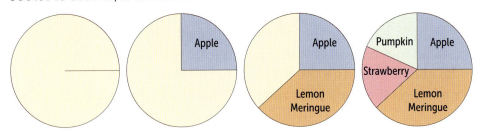

**HIGHER TIER**

Pie charts which represent two sets of data of different total sizes are called proportional pie charts. Higher tier students will need to study this in Chapter 10.

## EXERCISE 2

**1.** Year 11 is holding elections to vote for the Ambassador Student who will greet new students as they join late in the school year. Here are the votes for different candidates:

| Arthur | Sami | Finn | Jo | Elinor |
|--------|------|------|-----|--------|
| 18 | 40 | 25 | 62 | 35 |

Draw a pie chart to represent the votes for each candidate.

**2.** Luther looks at his online orders for the past month. Draw a pie chart to represent his orders.

| Category | Number of orders |
|----------|------------------|
| Books | 32 |
| Music | 10 |
| Films | 15 |
| Clothes | 7 |
| Household | 4 |
| Gifts | 4 |

**advice**

*Remember to label each sector in a pie chart.*

**3.** This pie chart represents 200 vehicles. Calculate how many were lorries.

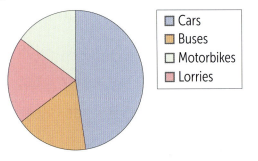

- Cars
- Buses
- Motorbikes
- Lorries

**4.** The bar line chart shows the numbers of animals in some households. Use this information to create a pie chart showing proportions of households with different numbers of animals.

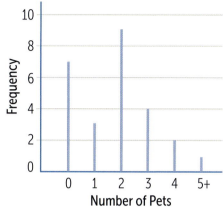

**5.** These pie charts show the items borrowed at two libraries yesterday.

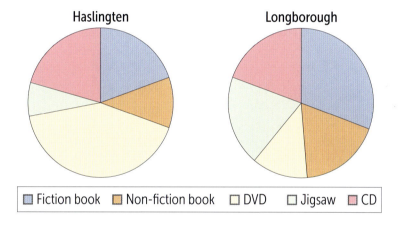

Mabel thinks that more people borrowed fiction books from Longborough library than from Haslingten library. Explain why she may be wrong.

**6.** The pie chart shows the proportion of cats and dogs registered on a health scheme.

There are 130 more cats than dogs. How many dogs are registered on the health scheme?

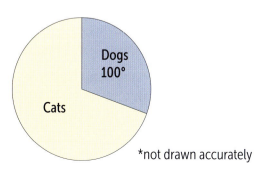

*not drawn accurately

**advice**

*Sometimes you will only be given some of the angles and not an accurate diagram.*

7. 200 students were asked to vote about which snack they would prefer to be able to buy at break time. The pie chart shows the results.

The angle for chocolate is 36° smaller than the angle for fruit. How many students voted for crisps?

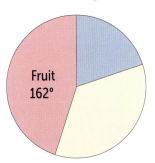

8. The pie chart shows how Aria spends her £150 wage each week.

The percentage bar chart shows how Darla spends her £200 wage each week. Spending on leisure and travel are equal.

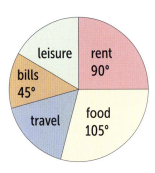
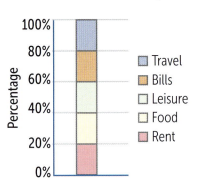

Write three statements comparing Aria's spending with Darla's. Show any calculations you use.

# Continuous data

Until now, the data we have been representing has been discrete. In order to put continuous data into a diagram, it will need to be grouped in some way, and it's only from the grouped frequency distribution that we can draw the diagram. We have a choice of drawing a **histogram** or a frequency polygon.

The easiest histogram to draw is when the groups are all equal width. The histogram will simply look like a bar chart without gaps (remember each type of bar chart has gaps between bars or sets of bars). The scale on the horizontal axis will be a continuous scale on a histogram, unlike that of a bar chart.

The work required if the groups are not all equal is covered in Chapter 10.

## EXAMPLE

The table shows the masses of 80 dogs at dog training club.

Represent the data using a histogram.

| Mass, $m$ kg | Frequency |
| --- | --- |
| $0 \leq m < 10$ | 19 |
| $10 \leq m < 20$ | 30 |
| $20 \leq m < 30$ | 23 |
| $30 \leq m < 40$ | 8 |

## SOLUTION

Each of the classes has the same width, so the histogram will be straightforward. The vertical frequency axis needs to reach as far as 30 and the horizontal mass axis needs to reach as far as 40.

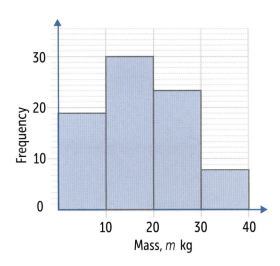

From the idea of a histogram, it's easy to draw a **frequency polygon**. A frequency polygon is drawn by joining where the centres of bars on a histogram would be. This is done by plotting the correct heights at the centre of each class width.

**advice**

*Remember that a histogram does not have gaps between the bars.*

**advice**

*Histograms and frequency polygons are types of frequency diagrams—if you are asked to draw a frequency diagram, you can do either.*

Here is the previous histogram with the frequency polygon drawn over the top. Without first drawing the histogram, the frequency polygon would look like this:

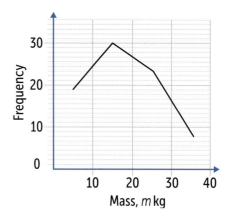

You can see that there is no need to extend the frequency polygon back to the axes (it's not supposed to look like a polygon in maths). If you don't draw the histogram, then you can draw more than one frequency polygon on the same diagram which will make them easier to compare.

## EXERCISE 3

**advice**

*Remember – the scale on the horizontal axis should be continuous.*

1. The table shows information about the speeds ($s$ mph) of 125 vehicles on a motorway.

| Speed, $s$ mph | Frequency |
|---|---|
| $50 \leq s < 55$ | 5 |
| $55 \leq s < 60$ | 9 |
| $60 \leq s < 65$ | 55 |
| $65 \leq s < 70$ | 29 |
| $70 \leq s < 75$ | 24 |
| $75 \leq s < 80$ | 3 |

Draw a histogram to show the information.

2. The table shows information about the heights ($h$ cm) of some women.

| Height, $h$ cm | Frequency |
|---|---|
| $150 \leq h < 155$ | 4 |
| $155 \leq h < 160$ | 13 |
| $160 \leq h < 165$ | 35 |
| $165 \leq h < 170$ | 72 |
| $170 \leq h < 175$ | 54 |
| $175 \leq h < 180$ | 22 |

**a.** Draw a frequency polygon to show the information.

**b.** What percentage of these women are under 165 cm?

**3.** The two tables show how much, in total, 136 shoppers spend (£$t$) on their supermarket shop on Monday morning and on Saturday morning.

| MONDAY MORNING | |
|---|---|
| Total, £$t$ | Frequency |
| $0 \leq t < 50$ | 28 |
| $50 \leq t < 100$ | 19 |
| $100 \leq t < 150$ | 10 |
| $150 \leq t < 170$ | 3 |
| $170 \leq t < 175$ | 54 |
| $175 \leq t < 180$ | 22 |

| SATURDAY MORNING | |
|---|---|
| Total, £$t$ | Frequency |
| $0 \leq t < 50$ | 7 |
| $50 \leq t < 100$ | 5 |
| $100 \leq t < 150$ | 15 |
| $150 \leq t < 170$ | 33 |
| $170 \leq t < 175$ | 54 |
| $175 \leq t < 180$ | 22 |

**advice**

*Technically, money is discrete data, not continuous, but can often—as here—be treated as though it is continuous data.*

**a.** Draw, on the same diagram, a frequency polygon for the information in both tables.

**b.** Use your diagram to comment about the differences in total spend on Monday and Saturday mornings.

**4.** The histogram shows the masses of yarn ($m$, grams) Tanja has left after various knitting projects.

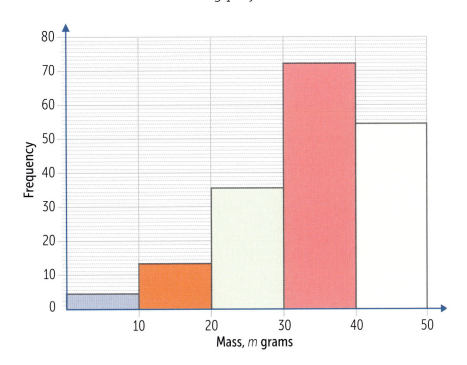

**a.** Complete this table from the histogram.

| Mass, *m* grams | Frequency |
|---|---|
| 0 ≤ *m* < 10 | |
| 10 ≤ *m* < | |
| | |
| | |
| | |

**b.** What percentage of the yarns are at least 30 g?

**5.** Miss Muffet set chemistry homework last week, saying it should take less than 40 minutes to complete. When the class complained that it took them too long to complete the homework, she asks them each how long they spent on the homework and says she will not set the homework today if more than 20% of the class took longer than 40 minutes.

Use the frequency polygon to determine whether the class should get homework today.

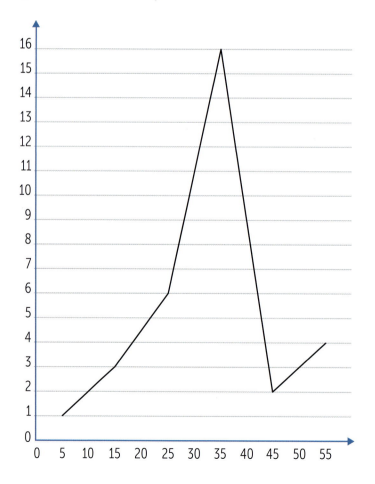

**6.** Here are the lengths (in miles) that some people walked their dog yesterday.

| | | | | | | | | | |
|---|---|---|---|---|---|---|---|---|---|
| 1.2 | 0.6 | 3.4 | 1.5 | 1.4 | 1.1 | 2.6 | 3.1 | 0.9 | 1.1 |
| 3.4 | 2.7 | 1.9 | 1.8 | 2.3 | 4.1 | 2.6 | 1.4 | 1.6 | 1.9 |
| 2.0 | 1.9 | 2.1 | 3.1 | 4.0 | 0.4 | 0.7 | 0.8 | 1.6 | 2.4 |

    **a.** Create a grouped frequency distribution for the data.

    **b.** Draw an appropriate diagram to represent the data.

## You should now be able to:

**Create and interpret a pictogram**

**Create and interpret different kinds of bar chart**

**Create and interpret a pie chart**

**Create and interpret a histogram of equal class widths**

**Create and interpret a frequency polygon**

## Exam Practice Questions

**1.** This table shows the percentages of children of different ages who play instruments.

| | AGE GROUP | |
|---|---|---|
| | 5–7 Years | 8–13 Years |
| Currently play | 65% | 75% |
| No longer play | 5% | 13% |
| Never played | 30% | 12% |

© AQA 2016

Draw a composite bar graph to show this information.

**2.** The table shows the number of cars a garage sold last month.

| Salesperson | Number of Cars Sold |
|---|---|
| Anne | 13 |
| Tim | 12 |
| Ian | 2 |
| Rob | 6 |
| Clare | 11 |
| | Total: 44 |

**(a)** How many more cars did Anne sell than Rob last month?

**(b)** What proportion of the cars sold last month did Clare sell?

Give your answer as a fraction in its simplest form.

**(c)** Draw a bar chart of the sales.

**(d)** The multiple bar chart shows the number of cars that each salesperson sold in 2013 and 2014. Numbers are to the nearest 10.

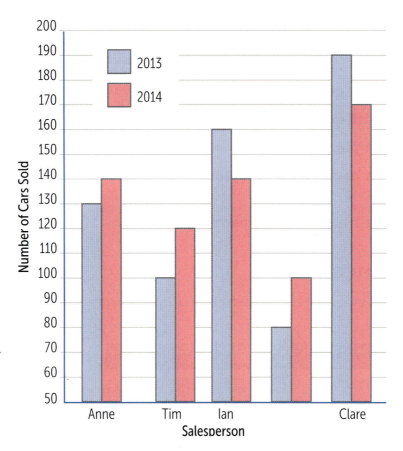

Write down three problems with this multiple bar chart.

© AQA 2015

**3.** A school buys 40 boxes of pens.

The pictogram shows the number of boxes of each colour.

| Colour of Pen | Key: ☐ = 5 boxes |
|---|---|
| Green | ☐ ☐ ☐ |
| Red | ☐ |
| Black | ☐ ☐ ☐ ☐ |

Draw a pie chart to represent this information.

© AQA 2015

**4.** Ahmed has 20 coins as shown.

| | | | | |
|---|---|---|---|---|
| 10p | 10p | 5p | 10p | 10p |
| 10p | 2p | 20p | 10p | 1p |
| 2p | 10p | 10p | 20p | 10p |
| 10p | 5p | 5p | 10p | 10p |

Draw a pictogram for the coins.

© AQA 2013

**5.** There are 120 Year 7 students in a school.
The lunch choices for these students are
shown in the pie chart.

**(a)** Write down the percentage of Year 7 students
who have a school dinner.

**(b)** Work out the number of Year 7 students who
go home for lunch.

**(c)** The number of students who have a packed
lunch is three times the number that go home.

How can you tell this from the pie chart?

**(d)** Here is some information about how the 120
Year 7 students travel to school.
45 walk to school.
10 cycle to school.
One quarter travel by car.
The rest travel by bus.

Draw a bar chart to show this information.

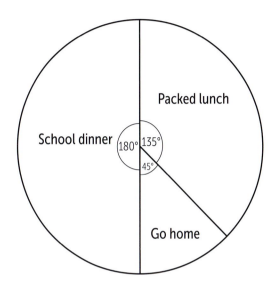

© AQA 2017

**6.** The voltage of 100 12v batteries was tested and the results shown below. Draw a frequency
diagram to represent these data.

| Voltage, $v$ | Frequency |
|---|---|
| $11.0 \leq v < 11.5$ | 6 |
| $11.5 \leq v < 12.0$ | 15 |
| $12.0 \leq v < 12.5$ | 48 |
| $12.5 \leq v < 13.0$ | 23 |
| $13.0 \leq v < 13.5$ | 8 |

**7.** At a village summer fair Claire is running the Buried Treasure Stall. This diagram shows the number of pieces of treasure found after the attempts by 21 scouts at last years' fair.

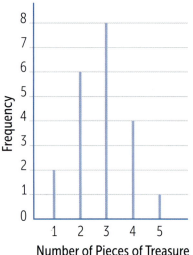

**(a)** How many attempts won 1 piece of treasure?

**(b)** Write down the modal number of pieces of treasure.

**(c)** Work out the range of the number of pieces of treasure won.

**(d)** This year the modal number of pieces of treasure found is 2 and the range is 5 for the 21 Scout's attempts.

    **(i)** Give **two** comparisons of the number of pieces of buried treasure found this year and last year.

    **(ii)** Draw a bar chart to show a possible distribution for the number of pieces of treasure the scouts found this year.

    **(iii)** Name **one** other diagram that could be used to show the data.

**8.** Here is a pie chart

**3-D pie chart showing crops grown in Europe**

■ Wheat
■ Sugar Beats
■ Other
□ Corn

**(a)** Describe why the pie chart is misleading.

**(b)** The table below shows crops grown in North America.

| Type of Crop | Percentage |
|---|---|
| Sugar Beet | 12 |
| Wheat | 26 |
| Corn | 55 |
| Other | 7 |

Draw a pie chart for this information.

**(c)** Write down one **difference** between the crops grown in Europe and North America.

**9.** Years 10 and 11 pupils choose an extra language to study. They can choose either Spanish, German or Mandarin.

**(a)** The chart shows what the Year 10 pupils chose

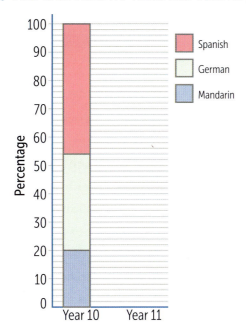

**(i)** What percentage of Year 10s chose Mandarin?

**(ii)** What percentage of Year 10s chose German?

**(b)** 30% of the Year 11 pupils chose Mandarin.
45% chose German.
The rest choose Spanish.
Copy and complete the chart for Year 11s.

# 4 | Probability 1

## In this chapter you will learn to:

Use standard probability words

Use the probability scale

Calculate probabilities

Set up and use probability tree diagrams

Work with mutually exclusive events

Use sample space diagrams

Use formal notation for independent events

Work with basic conditional probability

### New Vocabulary

Chance
Event
Outcome
Likelihood
Probability
Impossible
Certain
Even chance
Unlikely
Likely
Sample space diagram
Mutually exclusive
Independent events
Probability tree diagram
Conditional probability

We often talk about "**chance**":

- the chance it will rain tomorrow
- the chance of Portsmouth Football Club winning the FA Cup
- the chance that the traffic lights will stay on green for us to get through

Probability is a measure of how likely an **event** is to occur with a particular **outcome**. It has its own branch of statistics which is immensely helpful in making weather predictions, estimating the spread of diseases, controlling traffic flow and is used in many other real-world situations. You are most likely to have thought about probability when playing a game; how many times have you played a game, needed a six to start, and waited ages to get that six? I'm sure there will have been discussions about the chances of you having to wait so long! You will see how easy it is to calculate that **likelihood** for yourself.

# The probability scale

When we use words to describe the likelihood of something happening, it's best if we all use the same words on the same scale, then those words will have the same meaning to everyone. In medical trials, everyone needs to use the same scale when describing pain or their conceptions of pain may be vastly different to one another - in which case their responses would be meaningless.

| | | |
|---|---|---|
| **SUBJECTIVE PAIN SCALE** | | |
| | **0** | No pain. Feeling perfectly normal. |
| **Minor** Able to adapt to pain | **1** Very Mild | Very light, barely noticeable pain. |
| | **2** Discomforting | Minor pain, like lightly pinching the fold of skin. |
| | **3** Tolerable | Very noticeable pain, like a doctor giving you an injection. |
| **Moderate** Interferes with many activities | **4** Distressing | Strong, deep pain, like an average toothache. |
| | **5** Very Distressing | Strong, deep, piercing pain, such as sprained ankle. |
| | **6** Intense | Strong, deep, piercing pain like several bee stings. |
| **Severe** Patient is disabled and unable to function independently | **7** Very Intense | Comparable to an average migraine headache. |
| | **8** Utterly Horrible | Comparable to childbirth or a really bad migraine headache. |
| | **9** Excruciating Unbearable | Pain so intense you cannot tolerate it and demand pain killers. |
| | **10** Unimaginable Unspeakable | Pain so intense you will go unconscious shortly. |

*This pain scale was devised by Ferreira-Valente et al., 2011.*

In **probability**, too, we need to all be using the same scale with the same meaning. Here is the probability scale, showing the words and basic likelihoods.

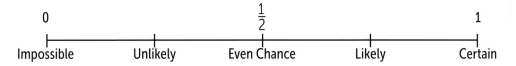

67

*If you ever get a probability that is greater than one, or is negative, you should check your calculations as these values cannot be probabilities.*

- something that has absolutely no chance of happening is labelled "**impossible**" (this is a probability of 0)

- something that is guaranteed to happen is "**certain**" (this is a probability of 1)

- an event that has two equally likely outcomes has "**even chance**" (this is a probability of $\frac{1}{2}$)

All probabilities lie between 0 and 1 inclusive. You can see that "**unlikely**" and "**likely**" appear between 0 and $\frac{1}{2}$, and then $\frac{1}{2}$ and 1 respectively.

## EXAMPLE

Show on the probability scale where the likelihood of each event having the given outcome is.

  **a.** An even number is rolled on a fair, 6-sided dice.

  **b.** The colour of someone's blood is white.

  **c.** You will fall asleep this week.

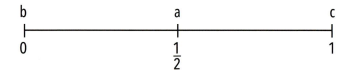

## SOLUTION

  **a.** There are 3 even numbers and 3 odd numbers on a fair, 6-sided dice so this is even chance.

  **b.** It is impossible for blood to be white.

  **c.** Even if you stay up to do a dance marathon or Xbox tournament for a day or two, at some point you are certain to fall asleep this week.

## EXERCISE 1

  **1.** Use the probability words *impossible, unlikely, even chance, likely,* or *certain* to describe each event and outcome.

  **a.** The next puppy to be born in a litter is female.

  **b.** A fair coin will land on tails when flipped.

  **c.** It will rain in Manchester during March next year.

  **d.** A playing card chosen at random will be a heart.

  **e.** I will win the lottery without buying a ticket.

2. Show the likelihood of these outcomes on a probability scale.

   a. The Queen will call at your house for tea today.

   b. A red card is picked when choosing a card at random from a pack of playing cards.

   c. The song "Black Velvet" by Alannah Myles is playing next time you turn the radio on.

   d. Your teacher will give you a test this year.

3. Write down something you know is:

   a. certain      b. impossible

   c. very, very unlikely but not impossible

4. Cally is researching the probability of a person chosen at random in her village being able to drive. Archie says, "They can either drive, or they can't, so it's an even chance." Explain why Archie is wrong.

5. Show the likelihood of each of these events on a probability scale. Discuss your answers with a partner. Were there any differences? For each difference, discuss how the outcome is or isn't affected by your own circumstances.

   a. You will download a new app for your phone this year.

   b. Your brother will buy you a puppy for your birthday.

   c. You will spend an evening next month at the opera.

   d. The answer to a probability question is −10.

# How to work out probabilities

You can now use the probability scale to describe the likelihood of something happening but we usually see probabilities written as fractions, so let's think about that now.

In events such as rolling a fair, 6-sided dice, each result is equally likely to occur. It's not more likely that you'll roll a 2 than a 5; all options 1, 2, 3, 4, 5, 6 are equally likely. Most dice are 6-sided so they are often referred to as a "normal" dice. The word "fair" is telling you that every outcome is equally likely. This is not the case for all sets of events however. For example, in a bag of 3 strawberry and 7 lemon sweets, whilst each individual sweet is equally likely to be picked, there is not an equal chance of picking a strawberry or lemon sweet when choosing at random. In this particular bag of sweets, it is far more likely that a lemon sweet is chosen.

We write the probability of an event as:

$$P(\text{event}) = \frac{\text{number of ways the event can occur}}{\text{total number of possible outcomes}}$$

But you can think of it as:

$$P(\text{event}) = \frac{\text{how many ways you get the thing you want}}{\text{how many things there are altogether}}$$

In the 3 strawberry, 7 lemon sweets example, we get:

$$P(\text{lemon sweet}) = \frac{7 \text{ lemon sweets}}{3 + 7 \text{ sweets altogether}} = \frac{7}{10}$$

$$P(\text{strawberry sweet}) = \frac{3 \text{ strawberry sweets}}{3 + 7 \text{ sweets altogether}} = \frac{3}{10}$$

The probability of something *not* happening is 1 − the probability of it happening because all probabilities add up to 1.

This means that P(lemon sweet) + P(not lemon sweet) = 1, so 1 − P(lemon sweet) = P(not lemon sweet).

You can see this makes sense as the only option other than a lemon sweet is a strawberry sweet and P(lemon sweet) + P(strawberry sweet) $= \frac{7}{10} + \frac{3}{10} = \frac{10}{10} = 1$.

**advice**

*You should only give a probability as a fraction, a decimal, or a percentage. You should NEVER use words such as 1 out of 6, or a ratio such as 1:6.*

**advice**

*It's a good idea to brush up on adding/ subtracting fractions (with a calculator if necessary) so you can answer these questions more easily.*

### EXAMPLE

James owns 50 Xbox games, 30 PS4 games and 20 Wii games. When one game is selected at random, work out the probability that it is:

**a.** a Wii game     **b.** an Xbox game     **c.** not a PS4 game

### SOLUTION

In total there are 50 + 30 + 20 = 100 games. We need to know this in order to answer each question.

**a.** There are 20 Wii games, so $P(\text{Wii game}) = \frac{20}{100} = \frac{1}{5}$.

**b.** There are 50 Xbox games, so $P(\text{Xbox game}) = \frac{50}{100} = \frac{1}{2}$.

**c.** There are 30 PS4 games, so $P(\text{PS4 game}) = \frac{30}{100} = \frac{3}{10}$.

So, P(not PS4 game) = 1 − P (PS4 game).

$$P(\text{not PS4 game}) = 1 - \frac{3}{10} = \frac{10}{10} - \frac{3}{10} = \frac{7}{10}.$$

## EXERCISE 2

1. In a bag of 5 green, 8 red, and 2 black dice, work out the probability that when one dice is chosen at random it is:

    **a.** red        **b.** green        **c.** not red

2. Freya put the letters of the word LANCASHIRE into a bag and pulled one out at random. Work out the probability that the letter was:

    **a.** a vowel        **b.** a consonant        **c.** not the letter A

    **d.** what do you get if you add together your answers to parts a and b? Why is this?

3. A fair, normal dice is thrown. What is the probability of it landing on:

    **a.** 3        **b.** a prime number

    **c.** a factor of 4        **d.** 9

**advice**

*If you need to give a numerical answer for something which is "impossible", you simply answer 0, not $\frac{0}{10}$ or $\frac{0}{23}$ etc.*

4. This fair spinner has equal sized sectors and is spun. Find the probability that the spinner lands on:

    **a.** blue

    **b.** yellow

    **c.** not yellow

    **d.** red

5. This is a prize spinner at a fair. Each entrant gets one spin to try and win a prize.

    What is the probability that the spinner lands on:

    **a.** cuddly toy        **b.** spin again        **c.** no prize

    **d.** a section that does not give a prize

6. On Shaun's iPod, the probability of a track *not* being by Marillion is 85%. What is the probability of the next track, playing on shuffle, being by Marillion?

7. In a box, there are green socks, red socks and blue socks.

    P(green sock) = 0.5

    P(not red sock) = 0.8

    Work out the probability that a sock, chosen at random, is

    **a.** red        **b.** blue

# Working with probability for more than one event

Sometimes you will need to establish all the possible outcomes of an event before you can answer any questions. You may be asked about a combined event that involves flipping a coin and rolling a dice. You will need to be working with a **sample space diagram** in those situations.

Imagine you are asked about a coin and a fair, 6-sided dice. What are all the possible combinations of these two things? How can you present the information?

It is best to work systematically so that you don't miss a combination. For example, you may choose to write a list:

| | |
|---|---|
| H1 | T1 |
| H2 | T2 |
| H3 | T3 |
| H4 | T4 |
| H5 | T5 |
| H6 | T6 |

Or you may choose to present the information in a table:

| | | DICE | | | | | |
|---|---|---|---|---|---|---|---|
| | | 1 | 2 | 3 | 4 | 5 | 6 |
| COIN | Head | H1 | H2 | H3 | H4 | H5 | H6 |
| | Tail | T1 | T2 | T3 | T4 | T5 | T6 |

## EXAMPLE

Two fair normal dice are rolled and their scores are added to give a total. What is the probability of scoring a total of 8?

## SOLUTION

We need to create a sample space diagram in order to answer this question.

| | | DICE 1 | | | | | |
|---|---|---|---|---|---|---|---|
| | | 1 | 2 | 3 | 4 | 5 | 6 |
| DICE 2 | 1 | 2 | 3 | 4 | 5 | 6 | 7 |
| | 2 | 3 | 4 | 5 | 6 | 7 | (8) |
| | 3 | 4 | 5 | 6 | 7 | (8) | 9 |
| | 4 | 5 | 6 | 7 | (8) | 9 | 10 |
| | 5 | 6 | 7 | (8) | 9 | 10 | 11 |
| | 6 | 7 | (8) | 9 | 10 | 11 | 12 |

We can now see that there are 5 ways to score 8 and there are 36 possible combinations, so the probability of scoring 8 is $\frac{5}{36}$.

Two events can be said to be **mutually exclusive** if they cannot both happen at the same time. If you roll a fair, 6-sided dice then the result cannot be odd and even at the same time, it has to be one or the other. This means that the events "odd" and "even" are mutually exclusive. Compare this to the result being prime or odd. These events are not mutually exclusive because 3 and 5 are both odd and prime.

For mutually exclusive events, you find the probability of one event **or** the other event happening by adding together the probability of each event.

$$P(A \text{ or } B) = P(A) + P(B)$$

This is only true for mutually exclusive events when there is no overlap between the two events.

## EXAMPLE

Which of these pairs of outcomes are mutually exclusive?

  **a.** Getting a prime number from a fair, 6-sided dice.
  Getting an even number from a fair, 6-sided dice.

  **b.** Throwing a head on an unbiased coin.
  Throwing a tail on an unbiased coin.

  **c.** Turning left at a roundabout.
  Turning right at a roundabout.

> **advice**
>
> *Whilst the table takes a little longer to set up, you are less likely to miss a combination this way.*

> **advice**
>
> *This is sometimes called the Addition Rule for probability. You may still see it referred to in this way in other sources.*

## SOLUTION

**a.** Not mutually exclusive. The number 2 is both prime and even.

**b.** Mutually exclusive. It's not possible for the coin to land on heads and tails simultaneously.

**c.** Mutually exclusive. It's not possible to turn both left and right at the same time.

## EXERCISE 3

**1.** Winston has a fair coin and a spinner with equal sized sections showing the numbers 1, 2, 3, 4. Draw a sample space diagram to show all combinations when the coin is flipped and the spinner spun. Use your diagram to work out the probability of getting:

**a.** A head and an even number

**b.** A tail and a prime number

**c.** A number less than 4 and a head

**2.** A café offers a vegetarian breakfast choice of either mushrooms, tomatoes or beans on toast with either orange, cranberry or apple juice. Work out the probability that Sasha gets mushrooms on toast with apple juice when she asks the waitress to bring her a surprise vegetarian breakfast.

**3.** Keeley has this spinner and a fair normal dice. She adds together what each lands on to make her score. Work out the probability that she scores:

**a.** 12

**b.** a number greater than 12

**c.** an odd number

**d.** a square number

**4.** Livvi watches a tv show from 6pm to 7pm. The probability that she watches *Pretty Little Liars* is 0.3. The probability that she watches *Gilmore Girls* is 0.4.

**a.** Why can we not say that the probability that she watches *Shadow Hunters* is 0.3?

**b.** Explain why the probability that she watches *Pretty Little Liars* or *Gilmore Girls* is 0.7.

**advice**

*Write down all the combinations before you begin.*

**5.** Nathan has these cards that spell out his name.

Nathan chooses a card at random. Work out the probability that it is:

    **a.** a letter A      **b.** not a letter N      **c.** not yellow

    **d.** a blue T      **e.** a blue card or the letter A

# Independent events

If the outcome of an event does not affect the outcome of a different event, they are said to be **independent events**. When you throw a coin and get a head, this will not affect the score on a dice being rolled. Flipping a coin and rolling a dice are independent events.

For independent events,

    P(A and B) = P(A) × P(B)

This multiplication law is sometimes called the AND rule because you are working out the probability of one event AND another event happening.

### EXAMPLE

A fair coin is flipped and a fair, 6-sided dice is thrown. What is the probability that:

    **a.** a 3 is thrown      **b.** the coin lands on tails

    **c.** a 3 is thrown and the coin lands on tails

### SOLUTION

    **a.** There are 6 numbers on the dice and only one three, so the probability is $\frac{1}{6}$.

    **b.** There are two sides to the coin, so the probability of it landing on tails is $\frac{1}{2}$.

    **c.** These events are independent, so the probability of them both happening is $\frac{1}{6} \times \frac{1}{2} = \frac{1}{12}$.

**advice**

*It's a good idea to brush up on multiplying fractions for these questions. Cancelling fractions before multiplying may make the calculations easier to manage though you can use a calculator in statistics.*

## EXERCISE 4

1. Julia has these two bags with tokens in.

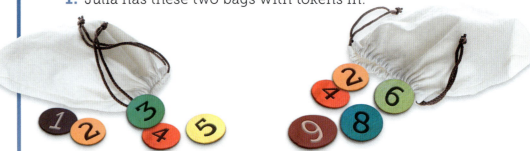

   She pulls one counter from each bag at random. What is the probability that the counters are:

   **a.** 1 and 8    **b.** 2 and 2

   **c.** 5 and an even number

2. The biscuit tin contains 5 Custard Creams, 3 Bourbons and 2 Jammie Dodgers.

   The chocolate box contains 8 strawberry creams, 5 nut surprise and 3 caramel.

   Elijah chooses one biscuit and one chocolate, each at random. What is the probability he chooses:

   **a.** Bourbon and caramel

   **b.** Custard Cream and strawberry cream

   **c.** Bourbon and nut surprise

3. Two fair, 6-sided dice are thrown. One is black and one is white. Work out the probability that they land:

   **a.** white 6 and black 2

   **b.** white even and black odd

   **c.** white even and black even

   **d.** white 2 or 3 and black 5

4. CEELEY BRENNAN picks, at random, one letter from his first name and one from his last name. Work out the probability he picks:

   **a.** E from both names

   **b.** C from first name and N from last name

   **c.** C or L from first name and vowel from last name

5. The team mascot always calls "tails" when the coin is thrown at the start of a football match. Calculate the probability that he made the right call at three consecutive matches.

# Probability tree diagrams

You can draw a **probability tree diagram** to help you see possible outcomes of combined events and their probabilities. These will work for you whether you have independent events or not, so they are very useful.

The "tree" is a very basic structure and tells you the probability of each event happening along the branches. As you move along each branch to combine events, you should multiply the probabilities to get the overall probability of the combined event.

### EXAMPLE

Draw a probability tree to show the outcomes and probabilites when two fair coins are flipped.

### SOLUTION

Firstly, draw the set of branches for the first coin and write on the probabilities.

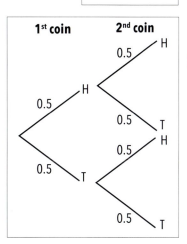

Next, we need to draw on the branches for the second coin, with probabilities.

**advice**

*For every set of branches, the total probability must equal 1.*

We can then include the final probabilities of the combined outcomes.

You can see that it is equally likely you will get HH, HT, TH, or TT when two fair coins are flipped.

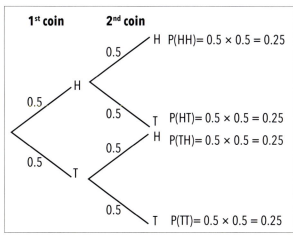

## EXAMPLE

Aditya has some tinned food in a cupboard, but all the labels came off when his bath water flooded through the ceiling last week, so now all the tins look identical! Fortunately he had the meat/fish tins on one side of the cupboard and the tinned vegetables on the other side. He can easily make a meal from meat/fish and vegetables but he has no idea what he will be getting until he opens the tin. He knows that he had:

2 tins of stewed steak, 3 tins of chicken supreme, 5 tins of bbq pork, and one tin of pilchards

5 tins of peas, 3 tins of carrots, and 2 tins of potatoes

**a.** Draw the probability tree diagram to show what combinations he may end up with.

**b.** Use your tree to help you work out the probability that he ends up with either chicken supreme or bbq pork with carrots as his first meal.

## SOLUTION

**1** Firstly, draw up the meat/fish branches and put the probabilities on.

**2** Then add on the extra branches for the vegetables from <u>each</u> of the first outcomes.

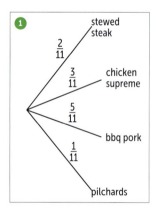

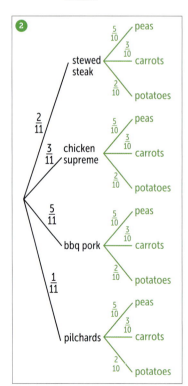

You can see from these highlighted branches which paths would lead to answering part (b).

For chicken supreme and carrots, we need to multiply their probabilities together:

$$\frac{3}{11} \times \frac{3}{10} = \frac{9}{110}$$

For bbq pork and carrots, we need to multiply their probabilities together:

$$\frac{5}{11} \times \frac{3}{10} = \frac{15}{110}$$

Now to get the "or" part of the question, we add together the two probabilities we have found. This is because these outcomes are mutually exclusive and cannot both happen at the same time.

$$\frac{15}{110} + \frac{9}{110} = \frac{24}{110} = \frac{12}{55}$$

The probability that Aditya picks bbq pork or chicken supreme with carrots for his first meal is $\frac{12}{55}$.

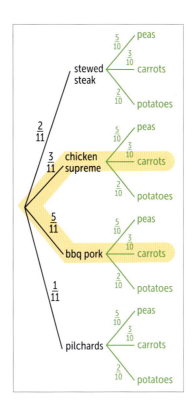

advice

*Don't be in too much of a hurry to cancel down these initial probabilities. They are likely to all have the same denominator and keeping that figure will make them easier to add at the end.*

# Introduction to conditional probability

In other tree diagrams you will need to consider "replacement". This is where once you pull a counter out of the bag, you have to think whether or not the counter is replaced before a second counter is pulled from the bag.

When you replace the item back in the bag, the probabilities on the second set of branches will be identical to those on the first set. However, if you pull for a second time "without replacement" the probabilities will have to be adjusted to take into consideration that which has left the bag. If a probability has to be adjusted because of something that has already happened or because we know some extra information, this is called **conditional probability**.

There will be a lot more on conditional probability in the chapter Probability 2.

## EXAMPLE

There are ten balls in a bag, three white and seven pink. Explore the differences in the probability of choosing two pink balls, when choosing at random with or without replacement of the first ball.

## SOLUTION

Firstly, we need to set up a tree diagram for each. Here is the tree diagram with replacement; once selected and noted, the ball goes back into the bag for the second draw. In this way, there are 10 balls in the bag each time.

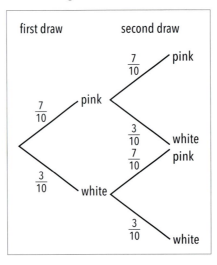

$P(\text{pink, pink}) = \frac{7}{10} \times \frac{7}{10} = \frac{49}{100} = 0.467$ (to 3dp which is lower than with replacement)

Now we need to set up the tree diagram for the set without replacement. Here, once the ball has been selected, it stays out of the bag. This means that if a white ball is selected first then there will only be 6 white balls to choose from in the second draw. Overall, there will only be 9 balls in the second draw.

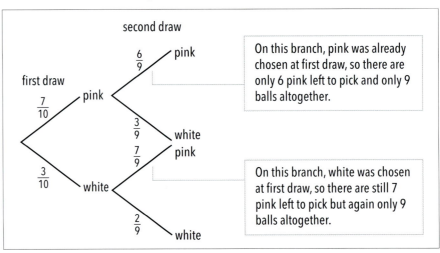

On this branch, pink was already chosen at first draw, so there are only 6 pink left to pick and only 9 balls altogether.

On this branch, white was chosen at first draw, so there are still 7 pink left to pick but again only 9 balls altogether.

Here, $P(\text{pink, pink}) = \frac{7}{10} \times \frac{6}{9} = \frac{42}{90} = 0.467$ (to 3dp) which is lower than with replacement.

**advice**

*On this type of tree, you should check that each set of branches still has probabilities totalling 1 as a way to guard against small errors creeping in.*

You can see that the probabilities with/without replacement are similar but definitely not the same, highlighting that the probability of something happening often changes when we have additional, prior information.

## EXERCISE 5

1. Lorretta has a biased coin. The probability of the coin landing heads is 0.7.

   She flips the coin twice. Calculate the probability of it landing:

   **a.** at least one head       **b.** both heads

   **c.** both tails

2. In a bag there are 5 red discs and 3 yellow discs. One disc is taken at random from the bag and then replaced. A second disc is then taken from the bag. Calculate the probability that the discs were:

   **a.** exactly one yellow   **b.** both red

   **c.** red then yellow       **d.** not both yellow

3. Sam plays football for a team and swims in a club. He has a football match on Saturday and a swimming gala on Sunday. The probability of his team winning the football match is 0.35 and the probability of his club winning the swimming gala is 0.72.

   Work out the probability that Sam:

   **a.** wins both events     **b.** wins neither event

   **c.** loses exactly one event

4. In a bag of jelly babies, there are 5 black, 4 red, and 1 orange sweets.

   Lou eats one jelly baby, at random, and then eats a second jelly baby at random.

   Calculate:

   **a.** the probability that both jelly babies are red

   **b.** the probability that she eats exactly one black and one red jelly baby

   **c.** the probability that she eats 2 orange jelly babies

5. In a tin of biscuits, there are 8 Custard Creams, 5 Bourbons, and 3 digestives.

Arthur then Bea each take a biscuit at random from the box and eat it.

Work out the probability that:

   a. Arthur gets a Custard Cream and Bea gets a digestive

   b. Arthur gets a Bourbon and Bea gets a Custard Cream

   c. They each get a digestive

6. Yousef is testing matches to see if they are damp. He has 500 in a box. The probability that a match lights is 0.15. Yousef tests two matches at random. What is the probability that:

   a. both matches light

   b. exactly one match lights

   c. at least one match lights

## You should now know how to:

**Use standard probability words**

**Use the probability scale**

**Calculate probabilities**

**Set up and use probability tree diagrams with and without replacement**

**Work with mutually exclusive events**

**Use sample space diagrams**

**Use formal notation for independent events**

**Work with basic conditional probability**

# Exam Practice Questions

**1.** Here is a list of probability words.

*impossible*    *unlikely*    *evens*    *likely*    *certain*

Write down the word from the list above that **best** matches the chance of each event.

a 5 is rolled on a fair, ordinary, 6-sided dice

a fair coin lands heads up when it is flipped

it will rain in London sometime in 2027

a student will get 200 marks on a paper out of 100

a person will live to be at least 20 years old

© AQA 2016

**2.** 200 people have been chosen as winners of a competition.

Each winner is given one of four types of prize.

The table shows the probability of winning each type of prize.

| TYPE OF PRIZE | PROBABILITY |
|---|---|
| Car | 0.03 |
| Holiday | 0.12 |
| £1000 | 0.25 |
| Television | 0.6 |

Ernie is one of the 200 winners.

**(a)** Which of the four prizes is he least likely to win?

**(b)** Write down the probability that he wins a washing machine.

**(c)** Work out the probability that he wins a holiday or £1000.

© AQA 2017

**3.** Kendra and Liam are in a high jump competition.

They each have one chance to jump a height of 170 cm.

The probability that Kendra can jump this height is 0.75.

The probability that Liam can jump the height is 0.8.

**(a)** Copy and complete the tree diagram.

Assume that the jumps of Kendra and Liam are independent.

**(b)** Work out the probability that **both** Kendra and Liam jump the height.

© AQA 2015

**4.** In a game at a fair you always win one of four prizes.

The table shows the probability of winning each type of prize.

| PRIZE | PROBABILITY |
|---|---|
| Toy | 0.65 |
| Sweet | 0.20 |
| Pen | 0.10 |
| Pack of stickers | 0.05 |

**(a)** Which prize are you most likely to win?

**(b)** Work out the probability that you win a toy or sweets.

**(c)** Work out the probability that you do **not** win a pen.

© AQA 2013

**5. (a)** Circle the **three** values which could be probabilities.

    1.3       0.4      0      −0.5      1

**(b)** A fair coin is thrown.

Write down the probability it lands on heads.

**(c)** A weather forecaster says,

"There is a 90% chance it will rain today."

What is the chance it will **not** rain today?

© AQA 2014

**6.** A bag contains 7 green balls and 3 red balls.

A ball is selected at random and the colour of the ball is recorded.

The ball is put back in the bag.

A second ball is selected at random and the colour of the ball is recorded.

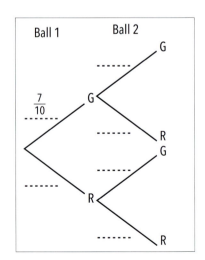

**(a)** Complete the tree diagram to represent the information.

**(b)** Work out the probability of selecting two red balls.

**(c)** Work out the probability of selecting one ball of each colour.

© AQA 2017

**7.** A fish tank has different varieties of tropical fish .

| VARIETY OF TROPICAL FISH | NUMBER |
|---|---|
| Tetra | 10 |
| Guppy | 4 |
| Catfish | 5 |
| Molly | 8 |
| Loach | 3 |

Carolyn catches a fish at random.

**(a)** Which variety of fish is she least likely to have caught?

**(b)** What is the probability of catching a Catfish?

**(c)** What is the probability of catching a Goldfish?

**(d)** What is the probability of catching a Tetra or a Molly?

**(e)** What is the probability she doesn't catch a Guppy?

# 5 | Averages 1

## In this chapter you will learn to:

Calculate averages for discrete data

Calculate averages for grouped data

Know when to use which average

Recognise formal notation for calculating the mean

Compare two data sets using an average value

Calculate a moving average

Plot moving averages

Draw and interpret a trend line

Averages are something that are thought about in everyday real life, not just in statistics. Before you buy a new games console, you may wonder what the **average** price is for a game or before you buy a new tablet, you may research the average battery life. This means we have a feeling for "averages", even if we aren't too sure yet of the specifics; we tend to think of it as being a number, somewhere around the middle. There are quite a few different ways to calculate an average, each of them useful in different situations. It's good to be aware which one to use in which situation.

## New Vocabulary

Average

Mode

Modal

Bimodal

Median

Mean

Arithmetic mean

Geometric mean

Grouped frequency distribution

Trend

Moving average

Trend line

# Mode

To find the **mode** (or **modal**) value or item you do not need to do any calculations. You simply need to identify the value (or values) in the group that occur most frequently, which means it will always be a value from the original data set. It may be easier to list the values in numerical order first, so that you don't miscount.

### EXAMPLE

Find the mode of:    1, 3, 4, 5, 3, 7, 4, 6, 3, 3

### SOLUTION

Writing the numbers in numerical order, we get:

1, 3, 3, 3, 3, 4, 4, 5, 6, 7

It's now easy to see that 3 occurs the most (there are four 3s and two 4s), so the mode is 3.

Sometimes, there will be two values that occur most frequently. When that happens, the data set is said to be **bimodal**. There can also be more than two modes in some data.

If a set of data has no value appearing the most, it is said to have no mode.

**advice**

*You can remember how to find the mode by thinking MOde appears the MOst.*

**advice**

*A data set with no mode does not have a mode of 0. It simply has "no mode".*

# Median

The **median** is the middle value from a set of *ordered* values. Since we are only looking at the middle values of a data set, extreme values at either end will not affect the median as they are not part of the calculation.

If there are $n$ values in the set, the middle one will be the $\frac{(n+1)}{2}$ value... so for 105 values, it'll be the $\frac{(105+1)}{2} = 53^{rd}$ value. You then need to count along the set until you find the $53^{rd}$ value. (Remember you need the $53^{rd}$ value......53 is not the answer.)

If you have an even number of items in the list, there will not be a middle value to find. In this case, you have to find the value exactly half way between the two middle values. Because of this, the median will not always be a value from the original data set.

**advice**

*You can remember how to find the median by thinking meDian is miDdle value when in orDer.*

**EXAMPLE**

Find the median of:

2     7     3     9     4     8     5     7

**SOLUTION**

Written in numerical order, the values are:

2     3     4     5     7     7     8     9

There are 8 values, so we need to find the $\frac{(8+1)}{2}$ = 4.5th value – this is the value exactly half way between the 4th and 5th values.

2     3     4     5     7     7     8     9

Exactly half way between 5 and 7 is 6, so the median is 6.

Notice that 6 was not a value originally in the list.

If the half way value is not so obvious, you can calculate it by adding the two values and then halving the result. It will work for our values in the last example: 5 + 7 = 12, 12 ÷ 2 = 6.

# Mean

The **mean** is the average that people usually refer to when they ask someone to work out an average. There are actually two types of mean that are studied for GCSE Statistics; this one has the full name of **arithmetic mean** (but we will just refer to it as the mean). Every value in the data set goes in to calculating the mean so if you have any extremely low or extremely high values, they will affect the mean. The other one is called the **geometric mean** and is covered in Averages 2.

**advice**

*You will not always have a whole number as your answer. This is not a problem, but do consider the type of data you are working with – does a decimal make sense?*

To calculate the mean, you first add up all the values in the data set, then divide that total by how many values there are.

**EXAMPLE**

Find the mean of:    7     8     3     9     3

**SOLUTION**

First, we need to add up all the values: 7 + 8 + 3 + 9 + 3 = 30

Now, we divide by how many values there are. There are five values, so 30 ÷ 5 = 6. The mean of the data set is 6.

You probably also know about the range. This is not an average (it measures spread) but is often calculated alongside averages. Range = highest value - lowest value. So in the example above range 9 – 3 = 6.

## EXERCISE 1

**advice**

*Remember to order the data before you find the middle value.*

1. Find the mode, median, mean, and range of:

   a. 1   2   7   4   6   8   2   9   3

   b. 3   7   1   9   4   6   8   10   1

   c. 21   22   24   22   26   28   22   24   23

2. Tim works on a farm. During May, 10 sows give birth. Tim records the size of each litter:

   5      14      17      14      16      10      9      14      10      7

   What is:

   a. The modal size of a litter?

   b. The median size of a litter?

   c. The mean size of a litter?

3. These are the colours of 15 colouring pens left on the classroom floor after school one day:

   | Green | Blue  | Black | Orange | Red    |
   |-------|-------|-------|--------|--------|
   | Red   | Red   | Green | Blue   | Yellow |
   | White | Green | Green | Black  | Green  |

   Which colour is the modal colour?

4. Avtar wants to be accepted into a walking group. She needs to have an average of at least 5 km per day, over 10 days, and will use the mode as the average. These are her distances for the first 8 days:

   3.5      2.5      4      6      4      3.5      4      6

   What is the minimum distance she can walk altogether on the penultimate day in order to be accepted?

5. Tilly drives a modal distance of 400 km per day. Tessa drives a modal distance of 30 km per day. Compare the two drivers' average distances per day.

6. Write down a set of 5 whole numbers where the mode is double the median.

7. Write down a set of 8 numbers that is bimodal and where the median is exactly half way between the modes.

8. Ciaron has a median test score of 69. Three of his scores, in numerical order, are 66, 67, and 71. Give one possible value for the missing test score.

9. Jody works in a dress shop. The prices of the black dresses they sell are:

   £14   £32   £27   £25   £35   £20   £28   £25   £30

   a. What is the mean price of a black dress?

   b. Use your answer to a) to estimate the mean price of the population of dresses in her shop.

10. The average mass of a runner in a 5 km race is 75 kg. There are 30 female and 50 male runners. If the mean mass of a female runner is 68 kg, what is the mean mass of a male runner?

11. Write a set of 6 whole numbers, each number less than 10, so that there is one mode and the mean is equal to the median.

12. Write a set of 5 whole numbers so that there is one mode and the mean is double the median.

13. Polly breeds and sells Labrador puppies. She calculated there to be a mean of 4 pups per litter, from the last 7 litters. If the 8th litter has 6 pups, and Polly makes £450 profit per pup, how much profit has she made in total from the 8 litters?

# Averages from data in frequency tables

Sometimes the data we have is presented in an ungrouped frequency table, rather than as a list. We are still able to find exact values for the mode, median, and mean, as long as the data is discrete, but should just take a little extra care. If the data is grouped, we can estimate the median and mean, and find the group in which the true median lies, as well as finding the modal group.

## EXAMPLE

The table shows information about how many tablets are in 30 households. Find the:

a. mode      b. median      c. mean

| NUMBER OF TABLETS | FREQUENCY |
| --- | --- |
| 0 | 2 |
| 1 | 5 |
| 2 | 10 |
| 3 | 11 |
| 4 | 1 |
| 5 | 1 |

## SOLUTION

**a.** The highest frequency is 11; which is for 3 tablets. So the mode is 3 tablets (not 11).

**b.** We have 30 households, so the median will be the $\frac{(30+1)}{2} = 15.5$th household.

We need to make a note of the number of households as we go down the list:

| NUMBER OF TABLETS | CUMULATIVE NUMBER OF HOUSEHOLDS |
|---|---|
| 0 | 2 |
| 1 | 2 + 5 = 7 |
| 2 | 7 + 10 = 17 |
| 3 | 17 + 11 = 28 |
| 4 | 28 + 1 = 29 |
| 5 | 29 + 1 = 30 |

We can stop once we have gone past the 15.5th household. At 7 households, we have not gone far enough. By 17 households, we have gone far enough, so the 15th and 16th households must have 2 tablets. Therefore the median is 2 tablets.

**c.** To find the mean, we need to think about the data we have. We are told that there are 2 households with 0 tablets, 5 households with 1 tablet, 10 households with 2 tablets, etc.

If we were to rewrite the data as a list, we would get:

0, 0, 1, 1, 1, 1, 1, 2, 2, 2, 2, 2, 2, 2, 2, 2, 3, 3, 3, 3, 3, 3, 3, 3, 3, 3, 3, 4, 5

We could then proceed to add these and divide by 30.

If the data were about 300 households though, that would take a long time and leave a lot of room for error! Let's look at a better way to perform the calculation.

We have two 0s, five 1s, ten 2s, eleven 3s, one 4, and a 5 to add. If we put an extra column onto the original table, we can use this to multiply each row across:

| NUMBER OF TABLETS | FREQUENCY | ROW TOTAL |
|---|---|---|
| 0 | 2 | 0 x 2 = 0 |
| 1 | 5 | 1 x 5 = 5 |
| 2 | 10 | 2 x 10 = 20 |
| 3 | 11 | 3 x 11 = 33 |
| 4 | 1 | 4 x 1 = 4 |
| 5 | 1 | 5 x 1 = 5 |
| Grand total | 30 | 67 |

This total of all the rows is our grand total of all values that we will divide by 30 (remember there were 30 households).

$67 \div 30 = 2.23$, so the mean is 2.23 tablets.

### EXAMPLE

Heather and Gillian run a hair salon. The table shows information about the duration of appointments they each had last week.

| Duration of Appointment, $t$ (Mins) | FREQUENCY | |
| --- | --- | --- |
| | Heather | Gillian |
| $0 < t \leq 15$ | 3 | 8 |
| $15 < t \leq 30$ | 7 | 9 |
| $30 < t \leq 45$ | 12 | 5 |
| $45 < t \leq 60$ | 6 | 15 |
| $60 < t \leq 90$ | 4 | 2 |
| $90 < t \leq 180$ | 5 | 0 |

Heather thinks that her average appointment is longer than Gillian's, but Gillian thinks hers is longer. Which of them is correct?

### SOLUTION

We can use the modal class, the class the median falls in, an actual estimate of the median, or an estimate of the mean as the statistical measures.

The modal class for Heather is $30 < t \leq 45$ mins and for Gillian is $45 < t \leq 60$ mins. So, using the modal class, on average, Gillian's appointments last longer than Heather's.

Heather has had 37 appointments, so the median will be the $\frac{(37+1)}{2} = 19^{th}$ value. This falls in the $30 < t \leq 45$ mins class.

Gillian has had 39 appointments, so the median will be the $\frac{(39+1)}{2} = 20^{th}$ value. This falls in the $30 < t \leq 45$ mins class.

Therefore, using the median, on average, Gillian's appointments last the same length of time as Heather's.

If you want a more specific estimate of the median, look at the final example.

In order to find the mean, we need to multiply and total each row. Here, we have no single figure on each row, so we assume that each value is the midpoint of each class in order to do the multiplications. This means we end up with an estimate for the mean as we don't know what the exact values are.

| HEATHER | | | |
|---|---|---|---|
| Duration of appointment *t* (Mins) | Midpoint | Frequency | Midpoint x Frequency |
| $0 < t \leq 15$ | 7.5 | 3 | 7.5 x 3 = 22.5 |
| $15 < t \leq 30$ | 22.5 | 7 | 22.5 x 7 = 157.5 |
| $30 < t \leq 45$ | 37.5 | 12 | 37.5 x 12 = 450 |
| $45 < t \leq 60$ | 52.5 | 6 | 52.5 x 6 = 315 |
| $60 < t \leq 90$ | 75 | 4 | 75 x 4 = 300 |
| $90 < t \leq 180$ | 135 | 5 | 135 x 5 = 675 |
| | Grand total | | 1920 |

Estimate of the mean for Heather is therefore 1920 ÷ 37 = 51.89 mins.

**advice**

*Remember here that you must divide by the total of the frequencies, not by 6 simply because there are 6 rows. You must add the frequencies if you are not given the total in the question.*

| GILLIAN | | | |
|---|---|---|---|
| Duration of appointment *t* (Mins) | Midpoint | Frequency | Midpoint x Frequency |
| $0 < t \leq 15$ | 7.5 | 8 | 7.5 x 8 = 60 |
| $15 < t \leq 30$ | 22.5 | 9 | 22.5 x 9 = 202.5 |
| $30 < t \leq 45$ | 37.5 | 5 | 37.5 x 5 = 187.5 |
| $45 < t \leq 60$ | 52.5 | 15 | 52.5 x 15 = 787.5 |
| $60 < t \leq 90$ | 75 | 2 | 75 x 2 = 150 |
| $90 < t \leq 180$ | 135 | 0 | 135 x 0 = 0 |
| | Grand total | | 1387.5 |

Estimate of the mean for Gillian is therefore 1387.5 ÷ 39 = 35.58 mins.

Therefore, using an estimate of the mean, on average Heather's appointments last longer than Gillian's.

Both Heather and Gillian are correct! Depending on which average you use, Heather or Gillian has the longer appointment time. This is an important aspect of statistics – the measure you use can determine the outcome you get!

You might see the formula for the mean written as $\overline{x} = \dfrac{\sum fx}{\sum f}$.

The symbol $\overline{x}$ (read as *x* bar) just stands for "the mean".

$\sum$ is the Greek letter capital Sigma (their letter S) and in maths it is used to mean "sum of".

$\sum fx$ you multiply each frequency by the corresponding data value and add them all up, so in the above example, for Gillian $\sum fx$ was 1387.5.

$\sum f$ you have to add up all the frequencies to find out how many data values there are above for Gillian $\sum f$ was 39.

Using notation such as this becomes more important when we look at how to calculate standard deviation in Chapter 12.

## EXAMPLE

A group of students were asked to guess the length of a line drawn on a piece of A4 paper. The **grouped frequency distribution** (the table) shows the results.

| LENGTH, $L$ (CM) | FREQUENCY |
|---|---|
| $0 \leq L \leq 10$ | 7 |
| $10 < L \leq 20$ | 8 |
| $20 < L \leq 25$ | 16 |
| $25 < L \leq 35$ | 5 |
| $35 < L \leq 45$ | 3 |

Calculate an estimate of the median.

## SOLUTION

There are 39 values, so the median value will be the $\frac{(39+1)}{2} = 20^{th}$ value.

There are 7 + 8 = 15 values in the first two classes and the third class takes us to the 31$^{st}$ value, so contains the 20$^{th}$ value. The 20$^{th}$ value is 5 values into the third class, so $\frac{5}{16}$ of the way through the class. The class is 25 − 20 = 5 cm wide. So $\frac{5}{16} \times 5 =$ 1.5625 cm. The estimated median therefore will be at 21.6 cm.

**advice**

*This method is known as interpolation.*

## EXERCISE 2

1. Russell is a car mechanic and needs to keep records of the costs of parts he uses. From the data in the table, work out:

   **a.** an estimate of the mean cost

   **b.** an estimate of the median cost

| COST PER PART, $C$ (£) | FREQUENCY |
|---|---|
| $0 < C \leq 5$ | 45 |
| $5 < C \leq 10$ | 21 |
| $10 < C \leq 20$ | 38 |
| $20 < C \leq 50$ | 49 |
| $50 < C \leq 100$ | 11 |

**2.** Sarah and Ed have the costs for the guests' meals at their wedding.

| TYPE OF MEAL | COST (£) |
|---|---|
| Vegetarian | 6 |
| Chicken | 9 |
| Lamb | 11 |
| Salmon | 8.50 |

They have received replies from their guests about who would like which option and they need to pay for 15 vegetarian, 73 chicken, 20 lamb, and 42 salmon meals.

Vicky uses Sarah and Ed's figures to work out an estimate of the average cost per person in order to plan for her own wedding. She has a budget of £1000 to pay for the meals. How many guests should she plan to invite?

**3.** Lizzie sells make-up. She has 80 regular customers and the table shows information about their last orders.

| COST OF ORDER, $C$ (£) | FREQUENCY |
|---|---|
| $0 < C \le 5$ | 12 |
| $5 < C \le 10$ | 9 |
| $10 < C \le 15$ | 43 |
| $15 < C \le 20$ | 11 |
| $20 < C \le 30$ | 4 |
| $30 < C \le 50$ | 1 |

    **a.** Which is the modal class?

    **b.** Calculate the group in which the median lies.

HIGHER TIER    **c.** Calculate an estimate for the mean cost.

**4.** The table shows information about the masses of lambs born on a farm last week.

| MASS, $m$ (GRAMS) | FREQUENCY |
|---|---|
| $0 < m \le 2000$ | 14 |
| $2000 < m \le 3500$ | 30 |
| $3500 < m \le 4000$ | 38 |
| $4000 < m \le 4500$ | 11 |
| $4500 < m \le 5000$ | 5 |
| $5000 < m \le 7000$ | 2 |

    **a.** What is the modal class mass?

    **b.** Calculate an estimate of the mean mass.

HIGHER TIER    **c.** In which group does the median lie?

HIGHER TIER    **d.** Calculate an estimate of the median mass.

*Remember when we use class intervals, we can only end up with estimates of means or medians. This is because we have no actual values for the data, so we assume each value in the class to have the value of the midpoint.*

**advice**

*When you are comparing two or more data sets you need to think about the real context. It's not enough to say that one has a higher median, you have to interpret that in context.*

**5.** Gary organises a running club who want to take part in a sprint for charity. Only the clubs with the fastest sprinters can take part. The table shows information about the times of the 200 club sprinters over 400 m.

| TIME, $t$ (secs) | FREQUENCY |
| --- | --- |
| $50 < t \le 54$ | 14 |
| $54 < t \le 58$ | 87 |
| $58 < t \le 62$ | 73 |
| $62 < t \le 66$ | 11 |
| $66 < t \le 80$ | 15 |

Which average value will Gary send off to the charity board to ensure he has the best chance of his club being selected? Explain your choice.

**6.** In Downberry, there are two driving instructors. The median number of lessons needed to pass with chLoe is 22 whilst the median number of lessons needed to pass with Vroom is 19. Compare the two driving instructors.

**7.** For a set of data $\sum f = 50$ and $\sum fx = 775$, calculate the value of $\bar{x}$.

**HIGHER TIER**

**8.** Bradly builds conservatories. This table shows information about some of his recent builds.

| COST, $C$ (£) | FREQUENCY |
| --- | --- |
| $0 < C \le 5000$ | 1 |
| $5000 < C \le 8000$ | 3 |
| $8000 < C \le 10\,000$ | 4 |
| $10\,000 < C \le 12\,000$ | 2 |
| $12\,000 < C \le 20\,000$ | 5 |

He has been asked to quote his average price to build a conservatory. He wants to quote the lowest possible price whilst still being truthful. What value should Bradly quote? Give a reason for your answer.

## Moving averages

Now that you are confident in finding the mean, we can use this skill to predict future values by looking at **trends** in data. To do this, we use a **moving average** which smooths out any variations in the data. It's often used for seasonal data, such as quarterly gas bills where some bills will be much less than others. For quarterly data, it is sensible to use a 4-point moving average, where we take the average of data points 1, 2, 3, and 4 firstly, then the average of data points 2, 3, 4, and 5, then 3, 4, 5, and 6 etc. This means we are averaging a whole year at a time, moving with the seasons. At Foundation Tier, only 4-point moving averages are required. At Higher Tier, other data sets may require a $n$-point moving average.

**advice**

*It would be sensible to use a 7-point moving average when looking at week-long data sets.*

## EXAMPLE

Laura's last 8 gas bills are: £124, £99, £144, £191, £177, £105, £151, £200

Calculate the 4-point moving averages.

## SOLUTION

The first 4-point moving average is:
$$\frac{(124 + 99 + 144 + 191)}{4} = \frac{558}{4} = 139.5$$

The second 4-point moving average is:
$$\frac{(99 + 144 + 191 + 177)}{4} = \frac{611}{4} = 152.75$$

The third 4-point moving average is:
$$\frac{(144 + 191 + 177 + 105)}{4} = \frac{617}{4} = 154.25$$

The fourth 4-point moving average is:
$$\frac{(191 + 177 + 105 + 151)}{4} = \frac{624}{4} = 156$$

The fifth 4-point moving average is:
$$\frac{(177 + 105 + 151 + 200)}{4} = \frac{633}{4} = 158.25$$

(We cannot do a sixth 4-point moving average as there are not 4 more points to average.)

We can see from the moving averages that the gas bills show a gradually increasing trend.

Sometimes we show the moving averages on the same table as the original data. Each moving average must be centred below the period it covers.

| | YEAR 1 | | | | YEAR 2 | | | |
|---|---|---|---|---|---|---|---|---|
| Quarter | 1 | 2 | 3 | 4 | 1 | 2 | 3 | 4 |
| Gas bill (£) | 124 | 99 | 144 | 191 | 177 | 105 | 151 | 200 |
| 4-point moving average (£) | | 139.50 | 152.75 | 154.25 | 156.00 | 158.25 | | |

You can see that the first 4-point moving average which uses the data from quarters 1, 2, 3, and 4 is centred between quarters 2 and 3, as this is the centre of the data being averaged.

All of these data (original data points and moving averages) can be plotted on a graph, called a time series graph. Once the moving averages are plotted, we draw a line of best fit through them that we call a **trend line** and we use it to see the general trend of the data that gets lost in all the ups and downs.

First of all, we draw the graph of the original data values:

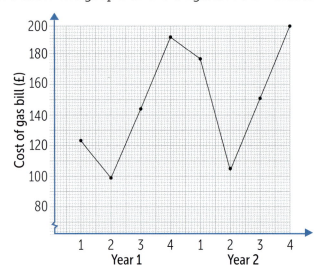

Next, we plot the moving average values – remembering to centre them in the middle of the data used to calculate them.

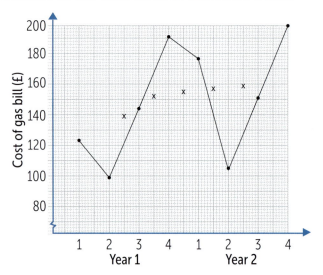

Now we can draw on a trend line by eye – remembering that this is a line of best fit and has roughly equal numbers of point either side of it.

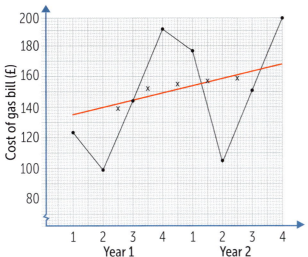

From the trend line, we can see that the general trend is for the gas bill to be increasing over the 8 quarters. We can also see from the graph or from the original data that in both years, Q4 had the most expensive gas bill and Q2 had the cheapest gas bill. This is to be expected as more heating will be required in the colder months and much less in the warmer months. We could predict from this, that during the cycle of one year, Q4 is likely to have the largest gas bill next year. Using time series for predictions is shown in Chapter 7.

## EXERCISE 3

1. Find the 4-point moving averages of:

   a. 23, 25, 26, 22, 24, 26, 26, 22, 25, 28, 29, 25, 30

   b. 123, 132, 145, 106, 144, 133, 165, 138

   c. 2.4, 0.7, 1.3, 4.9, 2.2, 3.2, 1.6, 4.8, 4.0, 3.4, 3.9

   d. 184, 142, 90, 125, 230, 160, 95, 144, 295, 201, 120, 188

2. These are the visitor figures to a wool museum for a year. Calculate the 4-point moving averages and comment upon any trend you notice.

| Month | Jan | Feb | Mar | Apr | May | Jun |
|---|---|---|---|---|---|---|
| Number of Visitors | 355 | 468 | 401 | 598 | 544 | 601 |

| Month | Jul | Aug | Sept | Oct | Nov | Dec |
|---|---|---|---|---|---|---|
| Number of Visitors | 555 | 468 | 401 | 378 | 211 | 78 |

**advice**

*Remember that the trend line will not go through all of the points. It is a line of best fit, and you should try to fit approximately an equal number of points above and below the line.*

**advice**

*These questions have all been suitable for students taking the foundation or the higher tier. Those taking the higher tier should be prepared to calculate appropriate n-point moving averages – which is covered in the Averages 2.*

**3.** The table shows the number of fish in a lake, each quarter for three years.

| | | YEAR | | |
| --- | --- | --- | --- | --- |
| | | 2016 | 2017 | 2018 |
| QUARTER | 1 | 800 | 825 | 830 |
| | 2 | 750 | 725 | 740 |
| | 3 | 950 | 930 | 945 |
| | 4 | 900 | 910 | 915 |

   **a.** Draw a time series graph to show the data.

   **b.** Calculate 4-point moving averages.

   **c.** Explain why a 4-point moving average is used for this data.

   **d.** Plot the moving averages on your graph.

   **e.** Draw on a trend line.

   **f.** Comment on the trend shown by the trend line.

**4.** The table shows information about the numbers of students attending Retfield College over the past ten years.

| YEAR | NUMBER OF STUDENTS | YEAR | NUMBER OF STUDENTS |
| --- | --- | --- | --- |
| 2009 | 4871 | 2014 | 5436 |
| 2010 | 4903 | 2015 | 5614 |
| 2011 | 4898 | 2016 | 5547 |
| 2012 | 5244 | 2017 | 5373 |
| 2013 | 5235 | 2018 | 5488 |

   **a.** Draw a time series graph for the data.

   **b.** Calculate and plot the 4-point moving averages.

   **c.** Draw on a trend line.

   **d.** Comment on any trend you can see from the data or graph.

# Appropriate average

Now that you have seen the mean, mode, and median in action, let's think about when it is best to use each one. There are advantages and disadvantages to each.

| AVERAGE | ADVANTAGES | DISADVANTAGES |
|---|---|---|
| **Mean** | The mean is the only average to use every value in the original data set. | It can be time consuming as you have two calculations to perform. There are also more chances for human error to occur.<br><br>The answer is highly unlikely to be a value from the original data set and you shouldn't be surprised if you do not get a whole number – you should be prepared to round to a sensible number of decimal places.<br><br>If you have extreme values at either end of the data set, these will distort the mean. |
| **Median** | A good average to use when you have a data set that has extremely high or extremely low values that are set away from the other values in the set. The median only considers the middle of the set and so these extreme values will not affect the answer you give. | You need to be aware that if you have an even number of data items, your answer may well not be a value from the original set. This is not a problem but can't expect your answer always to be one of the values you started with.<br><br>Data needs ordering before you can find the median. This can produce errors when handling large data sets. |
| **Mode** | Easy to spot if you've made a mistake as it will always be a value from the original data set.<br><br>The only average you can use if you have non-numerical data – you can still find the most frequent colour/manufacturer of car, for example. | Many data sets do not have a mode or will return more than one mode which makes giving an average quite tricky.<br><br>Sometimes the mode might happen to the biggest or smallest value which doesn't represent the data very well. |

## EXAMPLE

Prableen records the number of miles she drives in her car each day for 10 days. She has:

12    8    12    34    23    12    12    5    12    135

Calculate the mean, median, and mode and determine which average best represents the data.

## SOLUTION

Mean: $\frac{(12 + 8 + 12 + 34 + 23 + 12 + 12 + 5 + 12 + 135)}{10} = \frac{265}{10} = 26.5$ miles

Median:

The ordered data is  5    8    12    12    12    12    12    23    34    135

The median value is the $\frac{(10+1)}{2} = 5.5$th value, so it lies half way between the 5th and 6th values.

Half way between 12 and 12 is 12 - the median is 12 miles.

Mode: we can see from the ordered list that the most frequently occurring value is 12, so the mode is 12 miles.

The mode is the best average to use as this appears 5 times out of 10 so is most likely her most common journey (maybe to work or college each day). The mean is not a good average to use here as the value of 135 miles distorts the calculation. The median would also be appropriate as the median lies in the middle of several of the same values.

## EXAMPLE

Vlad sells figurines at gaming conventions. These are his profits for the last 10 conventions:

£123   £154   £133   £145   £136   £546   £163   £120   £131   £144

Which average is the best measure for him to use? Give reasons for your answer.

## SOLUTION

The data set has no mode, so he can't use that. There is one extreme value at £546 that's a long way away from the rest of the data, so it's best not to use the mean, as this value would distort the figure. Vlad is best to use median as it ignores the extreme value and will produce an answer in the middle of the data.

## EXAMPLE

In the 2016 Rio Olympic Games, the 8 finalists in the 100 m butterfly had finishing times of:

50.39s   51.14s   51.14s   51.14s   51.26s   51.58s   51.73s   51.84s

Which average is the best measure of these times?

## SOLUTION

There are no outlying values so it is appropriate to use the mean. As there are three instances of 51.14 s, it would also be acceptable to use the mode, but since this does not use all the data, it would not be quite as good as using the mean.

## EXERCISE 4

1. These are the favourite football teams of 14 people:

| Arsenal | Manchester United | Chelsea | West Ham | West Ham |
| Arsenal | Manchester United | Chelsea | West Ham | West Ham |
|---|---|---|---|---|
| West Ham | Charlton Athletic | Arsenal | Queens Park Rangers | |
| Arsenal | Arsenal | Crystal Palace | Manchester United | Arsenal |

   a. Explain why you cannot use the mean to find the average of these favourite football teams.

   b. Explain which average would be appropriate to use.

2. Give one advantage and one disadvantage of using the median instead of the mean.

3. These are the daily takings at Dolly's Diner over two weeks:

   £305   £310   £265   £280   £345   £330

   £290   £310   £250   £400   £340   £975

   a. Calculate the mean of the daily takings.

   b. Calculate the median of the daily takings.

   c. Explain which average is better to use for these daily takings.

4. Katharine runs a clothes shop. She stocks jumpsuits in sizes 8, 10, 12, 14, 16, 18, and 20. The table shows how many she sold last week:

| SIZE | NUMBER OF JUMPSUITS SOLD |
|---|---|
| 8 | 3 |
| 10 | 2 |
| 12 | 5 |
| 14 | 3 |
| 16 | 17 |
| 18 | 9 |
| 20 | 1 |

Katharine is going to stock a new tunic dress and wants to buy plenty of the average size.

She calculates the mean to be a size 15.

   a. Explain why this average is no use to her.

   b. Which average should she use? Give a reason for your answer.

5. Here are the costs of a brand of tea at 8 different shops:

   £3.50   £3.30   £3.79   £4.00   £4.25   £6.39   £6.39   £6.55

   Ben would like to work out the average price.

   Suggest which average is best for him to use. Give a reason for your answer.

6. Toni has a new fitband and has recorded the number of steps she has walked each day for a week:

   6185      10156      7571      3972      3255      6684      3395

   Which average is the best measure for her to use? Give reasons for your answer.

# You should now be able to:

Calculate averages for discrete data

Calculate averages for grouped data

Know when to use which average

Recognise formal notation for calculating the mean

Compare two data sets using an average value

Calculate a moving average

Plot moving averages

Draw and interpret a trend line

# Exam Practice Questions

**1. (a)** Andrew has three number cards.

| | | |
|:---:|:---:|:---:|
| ................... | ................... | ................... |

The **mode** of Andrew's numbers is 10.

What could they be?

**(b)** Here are some numbers.

6    9    7    8    6

Sarah says, "The mode is double the range."

Is Sarah correct?

Show your working.

© AQA 2014

**2. (a)** In a game you have to knock down skittles.

Dan plays the game 8 times.

The number of skittles he knocks down each time is

10    6    8    8    7    4    5    8

Work out the mean number of skittles he knocks down.

**(b)** Erin also plays the game 8 times.

The mean number of skittles she knocks down is 7.5.

How many skittles does Erin knock down altogether?

**(c)** Look at the information in parts (a) and (b).

Who do you think is the better player? Give a reason for your answer.

**(d)** Name one other measure you might use to compare the players' results.

© AQA 2014

**3.** Six lifeguards work at a swimming pool.

The table shows the number at the swimming pool each day for three weeks.

| NUMBER OF LIFEGUARDS | FREQUENCY |
|---|---|
| 1 | 0 |
| 2 | 5 |
| 3 | 4 |
| 4 | 5 |
| 5 | 6 |
| 6 | 1 |
| | TOTAL = 21 |

**(a)** How many days per week is the swimming pool open?

**(b)** Work out the median number of lifeguards working. You **must** show your working.

**(c)** The manager claims that, on average, more than half the lifeguards work on a given day.

Does your answer to (b) support this? You **must** explain why.

© AQA 2014

**4.** Eight dancers take part in a competition.

Each dancer performs a dance which is marked by two judges.

The table shows the scores (out of 10) the judges gave to each dancer.

| | ALEX | NINA | TANYA | RACHEL | SAM | CRUZ | JESS | MIRA |
|---|---|---|---|---|---|---|---|---|
| Judge A | 6 | 5 | 10 | 3 | 9 | 3 | 7 | 7 |
| Judge B | 7 | 7 | 9 | 5 | 7 | 6 | 7 | 6 |

**(a)** Work out the median of the scores given by **Judge A**.

**(b)** Work out the median of the scores given by **Judge B**.

**(c)** Which judge gave higher marks on average? You **must** support your answer with calculations.

© AQA 2015

**5.** Sam and Tom have both taken the same five tests.

Each test is out of 50 marks.

These are the results.

| | | | | | |
|---|---|---|---|---|---|
| Sam | 30 | 24 | 48 | 13 | 25 |
| Tom | 36 | 20 | 25 | 39 | 20 |

**Compare** how Sam and Tom did overall.

You must support your answer with calculations.

© AQA 2013

**6.** Sarah works as a receptionist at a doctor's surgery.

Each day she records the number of missed appointments.

The table shows the number of missed appointments for a 90-day period.

| Number of missed appointments ($x$) | 0 | 1 | 2 | 3 | 4 | 5 | 6 | 7 | 8 |
|---|---|---|---|---|---|---|---|---|---|
| Number of days ($f$) | 5 | 7 | 21 | 18 | 15 | 7 | 6 | 7 | 4 |

   **(a)** Write down the mode.

   **(b)** You are given that

   $$\sum fx = 315$$

   **(i)** Calculate the mean number of missed appointments.

   **(ii)** Is the mean a suitable measure of average in this case?
      Give a reason for your answer.

© AQA 2013

**7.** In May 2001, an estate agent sold nine three-bedroom houses. The sale price in pounds were:

| | | |
|---|---|---|
| 59200 | 65000 | 52000 |
| 129500 | 52000 | 62500 |
| 54500 | 57900 | 56000 |

   **(a)** Write down the mode of these prices.

   **(b)** Calculate the mean of these prices.

   **(c)** Give a *disadvantage* of using the mean to represent these prices.

**8.** The frequency table shows the number of times members of a club attended monthly meetings in one year.

| NUMBER OF MEETINGS ATTENDED | FREQUENCY |
|:---:|:---:|
| 0 | 1 |
| 1 | 3 |
| 2 | 6 |
| 3 | 2 |
| 4 | 13 |
| 5 | 11 |
| 6 | 17 |
| 7 | 15 |
| 8 | 19 |
| 9 | 16 |
| 10 | 8 |
| 11 | 4 |
| 12 | 10 |

**(a)** What is the modal number of meetings attended by the members?

**(b)** How many members does the club have?

**(c)** The total attendance for the year was 875. Use this fact and your answer to part (b) to work out the mean number of meetings attended by each member.

**9.** A local firm makes cheese.

The table shows the sales of cheese, in tonnes per quarter, from Quarter 1 of 2011 to Quarter 2 of 2013.

The first four moving average values have been calculated and entered in the table.

| Year | Quarter (Q) | Sales (tonnes) | Moving Averages |
|:---:|:---:|:---:|:---:|
| 2011 | 1 | 8.0 | |
| | 2 | 12.0 | 10.8 |
| | 3 | 14.2 | 11.4 |
| | 4 | 9.0 | 12.3 |
| 2012 | 1 | 10.4 | 13.5 |
| | 2 | 15.6 | ------- |
| | 3 | 19.0 | ------- |
| | 4 | 11.8 | ------- |
| 2013 | 1 | 15.2 | |
| | 2 | 19.2 | |

(Note: The figure of 19.2 tonnes for Quarter 2 of 2013 represents expected sales for that quarter).

(a) Calculate the missing moving average values. Write your answers in the table.

(b) The sales data, together with the first four moving averages, are plotted on the grid. Plot the remaining moving averages on this grid.

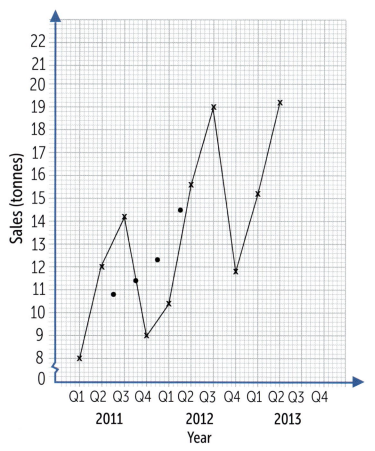

(c) Draw the trend line.

HIGHER TIER

(d) The seasonal effects for Quarter 3 and Quarter 4 are

| Quarter 3 | Quarter 4 |
|-----------|-----------|
| +3.65 | -3.49 |

Use these and your trend line to predict the likely sales for Quarter 3 and Quarter 4 of 2013.

(e) The owners plan to close the business if they do not reach total sales of at least 85 tonnes during 2013.

Advise the owners whether they are likely to achieve this level of total sales.

You must show your working.

© AQA 2013

# 6 Charts and Diagrams 2

## In this chapter you will learn to:

Create and interpret choropleth maps

Create and interpret box plots

Determine the skew of a data set from a box plot

Create and interpret stem and leaf diagrams

Determine the skew of a data set from a stem and leaf diagram

Complete and interpret a population pyramid

We have already looked at creating basic statistical charts and diagrams in Charts and Diagrams 1. In this chapter, we will see how to work with different charts and diagrams.

## New Vocabulary

Choropleth map

Box plot

Lower quartile

Upper quartile

Skewness

Interquartile range

Outlier

Stem and leaf

Population pyramid

# Choropleth maps

A **choropleth map** is something you possibly haven't worked with before. They are sometimes referred to as a "shading diagram" which does describe them quite well. The diagram is divided into different sections which are shaded differently according to the density of the distribution in each section. They can be seen on TV and in newspapers around election time, where they show how each ward has voted and in geography, to show distribution of different features.

This choropleth map shows how people in Lancashire voted in the 2017 Council Election.

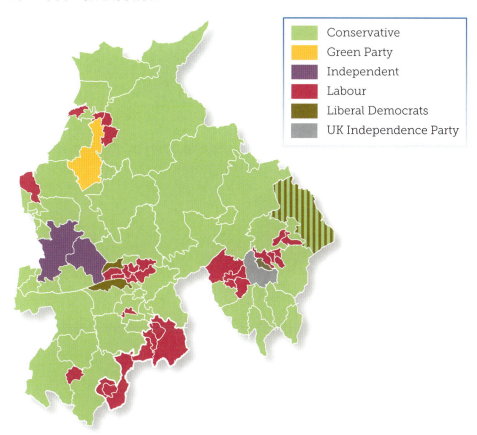

Conservative
Green Party
Independent
Labour
Liberal Democrats
UK Independence Party

**advice**

*You can see that it is essential to provide a key to the shading so that readers can identify each section.*

Source: http://www3.lancashire.gov.uk/elections/results/2017/map.asp

We can see that two areas voted for an Independent candidate, one area was equally split between Conservative and Liberal Democrat, and one area voted for the Green Party.

On a voting map, the boundaries are set before voting takes place. Each section is one voting area and there can be no movement between sections. In other examples, you may have to set up the map for yourself and choose your own boundaries. A grid system will be perfectly acceptable for this.

## EXAMPLE

A biologist may use a choropleth map to see if she can spot patterns about where a particular flower grows in a field. Create a choropleth map to illustrate the data.

To do this, the field has been split into sections and the numbers of the flower in each section recorded.

| | | | | |
|---|---|---|---|---|
| 2 | 4 | 5 | 8 | 9 |
| 1 | 3 | 5 | 6 | 6 |
| 1 | 3 | 4 | 5 | 6 |
| 0 | 2 | 3 | 3 | 3 |
| 1 | 2 | 2 | 0 | 1 |

## SOLUTION

Now that we can see the distribution of the flowers, we can shade the diagram. It's a little bit like doing a "colour by numbers" work.

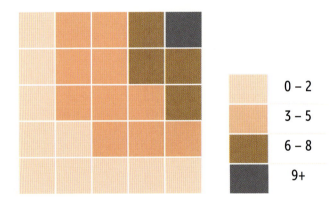

advice

*The shading takes the place of the numbers, so you don't have both shading and numbers on the choropleth map.*

It's easy to see from the shading that the most flowers are in the top right hand corner. It's possible that there is a water source (stream or leaky pipe) near there or something else that helps that flower to grow.

## EXERCISE 1

1. Chris has gone to the beach to pick up plastic so that it doesn't harm the wildlife. The grid represents the beach and the numbers show how many pieces of litter she collected in each section.

| | | | | | | | | | |
|---|---|---|---|---|---|---|---|---|---|
| 15 | 13 | 9 | 10 | 8 | 7 | 5 | 3 | 4 | 2 |
| 16 | 17 | 14 | 12 | 9 | 5 | 3 | 4 | 1 | 3 |
| 19 | 18 | 15 | 12 | 10 | 2 | 6 | 1 | 3 | 4 |

**advice**

*Choose your shading carefully so that sections are easy to tell apart.*

   a. Draw a choropleth map to represent the data in the grid.

   b. Chris thinks that a lot of the plastic is dropped by people sitting on the bench. Write a B on your map to show where you think the bench is. Explain why you think the bench is there.

2. This map shows the temperature one day at noon, in different areas, in °C.

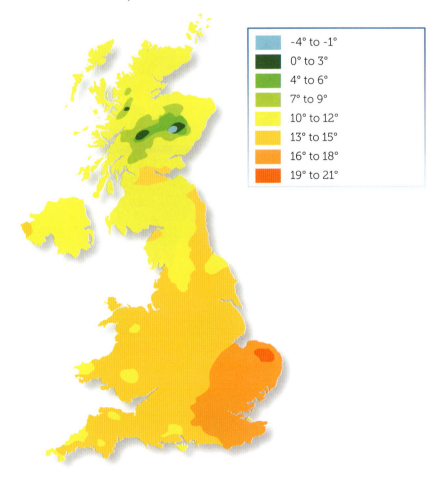

| | |
|---|---|
| | -4° to -1° |
| | 0° to 3° |
| | 4° to 6° |
| | 7° to 9° |
| | 10° to 12° |
| | 13° to 15° |
| | 16° to 18° |
| | 19° to 21° |

Source: Met Office

**113**

a. Give the range for the lowest temperature shown on the map.

b. What is the maximum possible temperature shown on the map?

c. In which country is the coldest section of this map?

3. This choropleth map shows the life expectancies for different areas of London in the past.

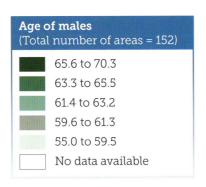

| Age of males (Total number of areas = 152) | |
| --- | --- |
| | 65.6 to 70.3 |
| | 63.3 to 65.5 |
| | 61.4 to 63.2 |
| | 59.6 to 61.3 |
| | 55.0 to 59.5 |
| | No data available |

Males in England can expect to live **63.2 years** in a state of "good" health

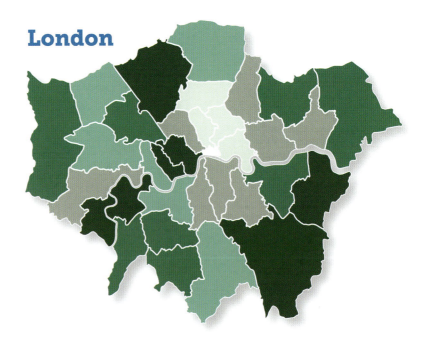

London

Source: https://www.ons.gov.uk/peoplepopulationandcommunity/
healthandsocialcare/healthandlifeexpectancies/bulletins/
healthylifeexpectancyatbirthforuppertierlocalauthoritiesengland/2015-09-18

a. Richmond had the highest life expectancy. Circle one area of London that Richmond may be in.

b. For how many areas were there no data available?

c. How many areas show as having the lowest life expectancy?

4. These maps come from an article about the health divide around the UK for males and females.

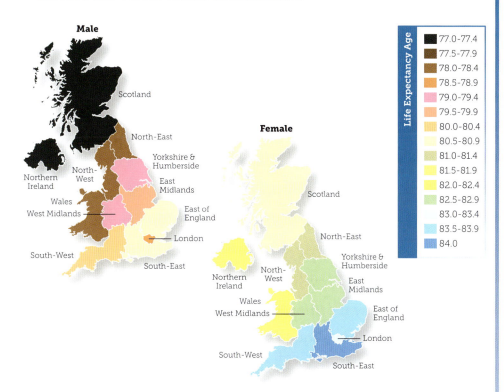

Use the maps to make two comparisons about males and females or north and south.

5. The number of students on the school field is shown on the grid.

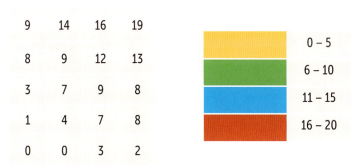

   a. Create a choropleth map using the key.

   b. There is a stray dog in the field. Suggest where you think the dog is. Give a reason for your answer.

6. Many years ago, Ericka's gran buried a metal box in her garden. Ericka would like to dig up the box but has no idea where to start digging to look for it. She thinks she will have to dig the garden over, one patch at a time, when Patryck says he will help her find where to start if she can send a diagram of where the wildflowers have grown in the lawn, so that he can construct a choropleth map.

Ericka sends this diagram.

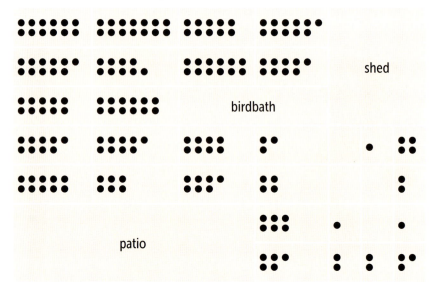

shed

birdbath

patio

a. Explain how Patryck thinks this will help to find the box.

b. Draw the choropleth map for Patryck.

c. Circle the square you would suggest they start digging in. Give a reason for your choice.

7. This choropleth map shows the heart transplant operations per 100 000 residents for each state of the USA. Each state has its own code, as shown on the map.

Heart transplant operations per 100000 residents by U.S. state, 2007-2016

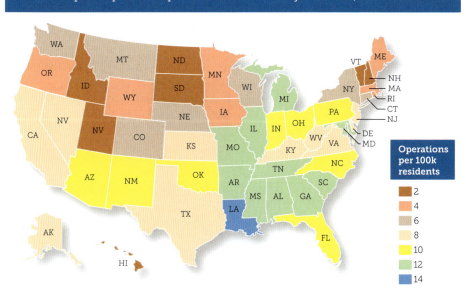

a. Give the code of the state that has the highest number of heart transplant operations per 100000 residents.

b. Suggest an improvement that could be made to this map.

**8.** Use the Internet to gather data on the maximum temperature reached in at least 25 UK locations yesterday. Use a blank map of the UK, and divide it into regions, in order to draw a choropleth map of temperatures. Decide upon the ranges for each colour before you begin. Write a few comments noting any patterns you identify.

# Box plots

A **box plot** (also known as a box-and-whisker plot) is a great way to show the range of a data set by plotting the maximum and minimum points along with the median and upper/lower quartiles. We can also see from a box plot whether the data is skewed.

In order to create a box plot, we will need to calculate the median of the data set and the upper and lower quartiles.

In order to find the **lower quartile**, we need to order the data. Once ordered, we need to find the value that is $\frac{1}{4}$ of the way through the data. The easiest way to calculate this is to find the $\frac{(n+1)}{4}$th value (just as we found the $\frac{(n+1)}{2}$nd value for the median).

The **upper quartile** is found in a similar way, it's the $\frac{3(n+1)}{4}$th value in the list i.e. $\frac{3}{4}$ of the way through the ordered list.

Once we have those values, each box plot will take the same form – some will look more stretched than others, but will have the same basic shape. You can see that we join the lines drawn for lower quartile, median and upper quartile to create the "box".

**advice**

*Remember that the median value is the middle value, once the data is in order. You can recap by looking in Averages 1.*

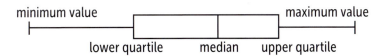

minimum value        maximum value

lower quartile    median    upper quartile

Every box plot will need to be plotted onto a scale, so it's usual to use graph paper to do this. If you are presented with a box plot that is not on a scale, you can determine the **skewness** of the data, by examining the shape of the box plot.

| This box plot shows a symmetrical distribution – the median is equally positioned between the lower and upper quartiles. | This box plot shows positive skew – the median is nearer to the lower quartile. | This box plot shows negative skew – the median is nearer to the upper quartile. |
|---|---|---|

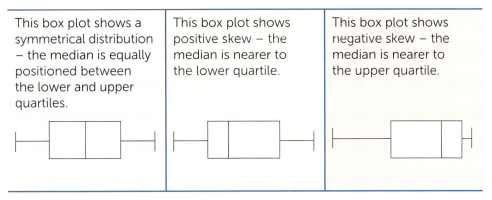

The box plot neatly sections the data into chunks that are each one quarter of the data. This means that between the lower and upper quartile, lies 50% of the data (just as does between the minimum and median or median and maximum). This will always be the case, no matter how tightly packed the values are to each other.

### EXAMPLE

Draw a box plot to illustrate the data set:

5  14  17  14  16  10  9  14  10  7  12

### SOLUTION

In order to draw a box plot, we need to be plotting the minimum, the maximum, the median, the lower quartile and the upper quartile.

minimum = 5                    maximum = 17

To find the other three values, we need to order the data set:

5    7    9    10    10    12    14    14    14    16    17

There are 11 values in the data set, so the median value is the $\frac{(11+1)}{2}$th value, or the 6th value = 12.

The lower quartile value is the $\frac{(11+1)}{4}$th value, or the 3rd value = 9.

The upper quartile value is the $\frac{3(11+1)}{4}$th value, or the 9th value = 14.

Now we can plot the values onto a scale. The scale needs to cover everything from 5 to 17.

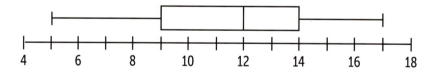

Once we have the lower and upper quartiles, we can use them to calculate the **interquartile range (IQR)**. You've met "range" before, where you subtract the minimum from the maximum, this works in a similar way. We simply subtract the lower quartile from the upper quartile.

### EXAMPLE

Find the interquartile range from the data above.

### SOLUTION

From our previous calculations, we know that:

The lower quartile = 9 and the upper quartile = 14.

Therefore the interquartile range must be 14 − 9 = 5.

**advice**

*There is no need to label the median, lower quartile, upper quartile, etc., because on any box plot, each of them will be in the same order.*

Sometimes there may be a data point (or a few) that lay apart from the rest of the set. They may be much lower than the lower quartile, or much higher than the upper quartile. These are usually referred to as **outliers** and are quite easy to spot.

**HIGHER TIER**

The outliers are not included in the box plot itself, but shown as crosses at the end of the box plot.

Outliers can be judged by inspecting the data, but this method would mean that one person could deem a data point to be an outlier where another person may not judge it so. It's better to have a proper definition that everyone can follow. The definition we use is this:

An outlier is less than: lower quartile − 1.5 × interquartile range.

or

An outlier is more than: upper quartile + 1.5 × interquartile range.

## EXAMPLE

Angus plays golf and these are his most recent scores:

| 81 | 82 | 78 | 83 | 86 | 77 | 94 | 87 | 85 | 80 |
|----|----|----|----|----|----|----|----|----|----|
| 79 | 78 | 83 | 83 | 83 | 80 | 77 | 81 | 74 |    |

**a.** Identify any outliers in the data.

**HIGHER TIER**  **b.** Draw a box plot for the data.

## SOLUTION

**a.** ordering the data gives:

| | | 74 | 77 | 77 | 78 |
|---|---|---|---|---|---|
| 78 | 79 | 80 | 80 | 81 | 81 | 82 | 83 |
| 83 | 83 | 83 | 85 | 86 | 87 | 92 |

To check for an outlier, we need to do 1.5 × IQR. IQR = UQ − LQ, so IQR = 83 − 78 = 5.

Therefore: outliers are > 83 + 1.5 × 5, i.e., outliers are > 90.5

or

outliers are < 78 − 1.5 × 5, i.e. outliers are < 70.5 (no values are < 70.5)

So the only outlier of this data set is 94.

**b.**

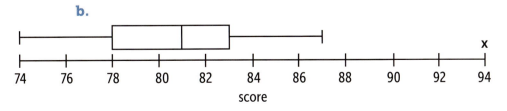

score

119

## EXERCISE 2

**advice**

*Remember that when you are asked to compare two data sets, one comment should be about an average and one comment about a measure of spread. Here you can choose to discuss the range or the interquartile range.*

1. Here is a box plot.

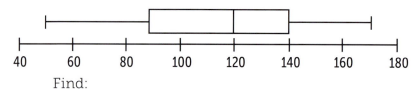

Find:

a. the median

b. the range

c. the interquartile range

2. Here is a data set.

7, 9, 13, 14, 18, 3, 9, 10, 2, 8, 5, 16, 14, 7, 11

a. Do you think there are any outliers in this data set? Explain why you think this.

b. Draw a box plot to represent the data.

3. Murphy and Bruno are two dogs that are run in a dog fun run each month. Their owners have been keeping a record of their recent times (to the nearest tenth of a second). This is a summary of the data for Murphy and raw data for Bruno:

| MURPHY | |
| --- | --- |
| Median | 25.4 |
| Lower quartile | 25.2 |
| Upper quartile | 25.8 |
| Maximum | 25.9 |
| Minimum | 25.1 |

| BRUNO | 25.9 | 24.2 | 24.8 |
| --- | --- | --- | --- |
| | 25.4 | 26.2 | 24.7 | 25.8 |

a. Draw a box plot for Murphy's data.

b. On the same scale, draw the box plot for Bruno's data.

c. Make two comparisons about Murphy's and Bruno's times.

4. The box plot shows information about the heights (in centimetres) of people at a gym.

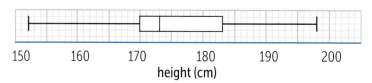

height (cm)

Which of these statements are true?

a. The average height is 175 cm.

b. One quarter of people are over 180 cm.

**c.** The shortest person is 152 cm.

**d.** The range is 175 cm.

**e.** The interquartile range is 13 cm.

**f.** Half of the people are under 173 cm.

**g.** The data shows negative skew.

HIGHER TIER **h.** The minimum given is actually an outlier.

**5.** The two box plots show data about the heights (in centimetres) of runner beans grown with and without fertiliser.

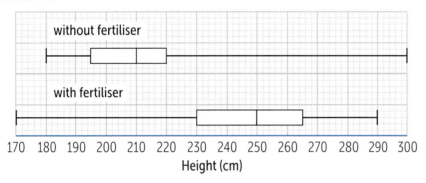

**a.** Write down the median length of a runner bean plant grown with fertiliser.

**b.** Calculate the range of the plants grown without fertiliser.

**c.** Make two comparative statements about the runner beans grown with and without fertiliser.

**d.** Comment upon the skewness of each data set.

**6.** The table and the box plot each show some information about the scores in a quiz.

| | SCORE |
|---|---|
| Lowest score | |
| Lower quartile | |
| Median | 49 |
| Upper quartile | |
| Highest score | 85 |

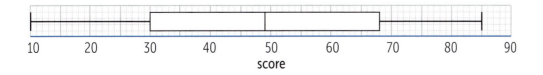

**a.** Use the information in the table to complete the box plot.

**b.** Use the information in the box plot to complete the table.

**c.** Comment on the skewness of the data.

HIGHER TIER **d.** Calculate the scores that would represent statistical outliers for this quiz.

**7.** This table shows information about the marks of the boys in a class.

| Median | Lower quartile | Upper quartile | Minimum | Maximum |
|--------|----------------|----------------|---------|---------|
| 58 | 45 | 75 | 32 | 90 |

The maximum mark scored by a girl was 87. One quarter of the girls scored over 80.

The interquartile range is the same for boys and girls.

The median for girls lies exactly half way between the lower and upper quartiles.

The girl who scored the lowest mark scored 16 more than the boy who scored the lowest mark.

**a.** Draw a box plot for the boys' data.

**b.** On the same scale, draw the box plot for the girls' data.

**c.** Make two comparisons about the boys' and the girls' marks.

HIGHER TIER **d.** Martyn scored the lowest mark in the test. Francis says Martyn's score is an outlier. Explain how you know this cannot be true.

## HIGHER TIER

**8.** Henri makes a telephone call to his bank and has to wait 14 minutes before his call is answered. The median waiting time for telephone calls to the bank is 9 minutes, with an upper quartile of 11 minutes and a lower quartile of 8.5 minutes. Can Henri's telephone call be classed as an outlier? Give a reason for your answer.

**9.** These are the amounts (to the nearest £) that Jonas spent at the shop last week:

46  65  64  48  52  12  62  55  51  54  53

Draw a box plot for these amounts. You should be careful to highlight any outliers you find.

**10.** Mike asks 23 friends to record the number of steps they take one day. The numbers of steps are:

| | | | | |
|---|---|---|---|---|
| 5106 | 5927 | 2240 | 4216 | 5827 |
| 6453 | 7005 | 16009 | 7216 | 5992 |
| 6134 | 5432 | 8641 | 9521 | 8217 |
| 8216 | 8563 | 6798 | 7234 | 5068 |
| 6565 | 6318 | 7713 | | |

Create a box plot to represent these numbers of steps.

# Stem and leaf diagrams

A **stem and leaf** diagram is a great way to visually represent the data without losing any of the details. Each item of data is shown in full, whilst at the same time we can spot the mode easily and see the shape of the distribution and spot any skewness.

To construct a stem and leaf diagram, we split each item of data into a "stem" and a "leaf". The stem is usually the first part of the number, and the leaf is usually the last part. You will get to choose which you think are the best stems and leaves but often it will be obvious.

## EXAMPLE

These are the masses of some dogs (in kg):

25.2  26.8  26.9  33.4  30.4  27.6  29.1  27.9  31.2  28.3
26.4  26.8  27.1

Draw a stem and leaf diagram to illustrate the data.

## SOLUTION

It would seem sensible to have the stem as the part of the number before the decimal point, so we would start off the diagram like this:

Next we put on the leaves.

| | |
|---|---|
| 25 | |
| 26 | |
| 27 | |
| 28 | |
| 29 | |
| 30 | |
| 31 | |
| 32 | |
| 33 | |

The first number was 25.2 and we have a 25 in place on the left-hand side, so we just need |to place the .2. To do this, we just write a "2" in the 25 row. We will show the decimal point is there in the key later.

| 25 | 2 |
|----|---|
| 26 |   |
| 27 |   |
| 28 |   |
| 29 |   |
| 30 |   |
| 31 |   |
| 32 |   |
| 33 |   |

Now we put on all of the other leaves in the same way.

advice

*This is an unordered stem and leaf diagram. You need to order the data or the stem and leaf diagram is unfinished.*

We have two things left to do at this point; we need to order the data and put on a key so that readers can tell we have 25.2 and not 252.

| 25 | 2 |
|----|---|
| 26 | 8 9 4 8 |
| 27 | 6 9 1 |
| 28 | 3 |
| 29 | 1 |
| 30 | 4 |
| 31 | 2 |
| 32 |   |
| 33 | 4 |

Re-ordering the data and adding the key gives the stem and leaf diagram shown.

| 25 | 2 |
|----|---|
| 26 | 4 8 8 9 |
| 27 | 1 6 9 |
| 28 | 3 |
| 29 | 1 |
| 30 | 4 |
| 31 | 2 |
| 32 |   |
| 33 | 4 |

Key:  25|2 = 25.2kg

You can also use a stem and leaf diagram to compare two distributions; this is known as a back-to-back stem and leaf diagram. The stem goes down the middle and the leaves for each data set are on each side.

## EXAMPLE

The back-to-back stem and leaf diagram shows the amounts of time spent exercising yesterday (to the nearest minute) by 20 men and 18 women in a park.

| WOMEN | | | | | | | | | MEN | | | | | | |
|---|---|---|---|---|---|---|---|---|---|---|---|---|---|---|---|
| | | | | | | | 0 | 3 | 7 | | | | | | |
| | | 6 | 4 | 2 | 2 | 1 | 2 | 3 | 3 | 4 | 6 | 7 | 9 | | |
| 7 | 6 | 5 | 4 | 4 | 4 | 3 | 1 | 2 | 0 | 1 | 5 | 7 | 7 | 9 | |
| | | 9 | 9 | 9 | 4 | 3 | 3 | 1 | 6 | | | | | | |
| | | | | | | 0 | 4 | 3 | | | | | | | |
| | | | | | | | 5 | 5 | 6 | | | | | | |

Key: 1 | 2 | 0 represents 21 minutes for women and 20 minutes for men

**advice**

*The key for a back-to-back stem and leaf diagram must show how to read the diagram in each direction.*

a. What proportion of women spent longer than 30 minutes exercising yesterday?

b. What proportion of men spent less than 20 minutes exercising yesterday?

c. Compare statistically the exercise times for men and women.

## SOLUTION

a. There are 6 women who spent longer than 30 minutes exercising yesterday (their times are 33, 34, 39, 39, 39, and 40 minutes). So the proportion is $\frac{6}{18} = \frac{1}{3}$.

b. There are 9 men who spent less than 20 minutes exercising yesterday (their times are 3, 7, 12, 13, 13, 14, 16, 17 and 19 minutes). So the proportion is $\frac{9}{20}$.

c. To make statistical comparisons, we need to calculate a range (or interquartile range) and an average for men and for women.

Median for women is: $\frac{(18 + 1)}{2}$*th* value, so 9.5th value, i.e. half way between 9th and 10th values.

Median for women is: 24.5 minutes.

Median for men is: $\frac{(20 + 1)}{2}$*th* value, so 10.5th value, i.e. half way between 10th and 11th values.

Median for men is: 20.5 minutes.

Range for women is: 40 − 12 = 28 minutes.

Range for men is: 56 − 3 = 53 minutes.

Women, on average, exercised for a longer period of time yesterday than men.

The times that the women spent exercising were more consistent than the times men spent exercising in the park.

It's also possible to examine a stem and leaf diagram and determine the skew of the data. You need to imagine the diagram turned through 90°, then work out where the "tail" of the data is.

Here is a stem and leaf diagram:

| 0 | 1 1 2 4 7 8 |
| 1 | 2 2 3 5 6 9 9 |
| 2 | 1 5 6 6 9 |
| 3 | 2 3 3 4 |
| 4 | 0 0 1 2 |
| 5 | 5 6 7 |
| 6 | 9 |
| 7 | 1 |

When we rotate the diagram, we get:

Then we can draw the shape of the data over the top (with pen or in our imagination):

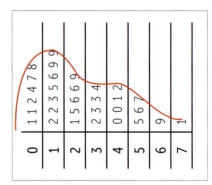

Where the "tail" slopes off to the right, we have positive skew.

| This stem and leaf diagram shows a symmetrical distribution – more or less equal tails on each side. | This stem and leaf diagram shows positive skew – the tail slopes to the right. | This stem and leaf diagram shows negative skew – the tail slopes to the left. |
|---|---|---|
| 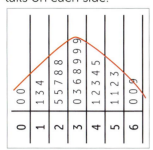 | 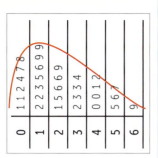 | 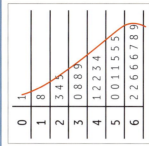 |

## EXERCISE 3

1. Draw a stem and leaf diagram to represent these numbers of birds seen in 15 gardens.

   7, 9, 13, 14, 18, 23, 29, 10, 32, 8, 5, 16, 14, 7, 11

2. Gavin and Tim each planted 19 seeds. Gavin used a fertiliser and Tim used compost from his garden. The table shows the heights that their plants (to the nearest cm) grew.

| Gavin | 0 | 14 | 24 | 22 | 30 | 28 | 41 | 25 | 21 | 22 | 22 | 65 | 0 | 31 | 38 | 40 | 12 | 33 | 58 |
|---|---|---|---|---|---|---|---|---|---|---|---|---|---|---|---|---|---|---|---|
| Tim | 14 | 9 | 22 | 0 | 17 | 12 | 14 | 23 | 0 | 13 | 21 | 18 | 11 | 15 | 20 | 30 | 24 | 0 | 67 |

   a. Draw a back-to-back stem and leaf diagram to show the data.

   b. What proportion of Gavin's seeds grew taller than 40 cm?

   c. What proportion of Tim's seeds grew taller than 40 cm?

   d. Compare the average plant height for Gavin and for Tim.

3. The masses (to the nearest 0.1 kg) of some first class and second class parcels are shown in the back-to-back stem and leaf diagram.

| FIRST CLASS | | | | | | | | SECOND CLASS | | | | | | |
|---|---|---|---|---|---|---|---|---|---|---|---|---|---|---|
| | | | | | | | 0 | 3 | 8 | | | | | |
| | | | 6 | 4 | 2 | 2 | 1 | 2 | 2 | 3 | 4 | 6 | 8 | 9 |
| 7 | 5 | 5 | 5 | 4 | 4 | 3 | 1 | 2 | 0 | 1 | 4 | 7 | 7 | 9 |
| | | | 9 | 9 | 7 | 4 | 2 | 3 | 1 | 9 | | | | |
| | | | | | | 1 | 4 | 3 | | | | | | |
| | | | | | | 5 | 4 | 6 | | | | | | |

Key: 1 | 4 | 3 represents 4.1 kg for first class and 4.3 kg for second class.

Decide whether each of these statements are true, false, or you cannot tell:

    **a.** The heaviest first class parcel is 56 kg.

    **b.** The median second class parcel is 10.5 kg.

    **c.** The modal mass for second class is heavier than the modal mass for first class.

    **d.** $\frac{7}{8}$ of the first class parcels were heavier than the median mass of a second class parcel.

    **e.** There were an equal number of first class and second class parcels with a mass of 1.2 kg.

    **f.** There were more first class than second class parcels with a mass of than 2 kg.

4. Liv goes to Park Run each Saturday morning. Her times (to the nearest minute) for the last 19 runs are:

| 45 | 42 | 44 | 38 | 40 | 38 | 39 | 38 | 37 | 35 |
| 40 | 38 | 35 | 36 | 35 | 33 | 32 | 33 | 29 | |

    **a.** Draw a stem and leaf diagram to represent the data.

    **b.** Find Liv's median time.

    **c.** Find the interquartile range for the times.

5.   **a.** Draw a back-to-back stem and leaf diagram to represent these amounts of money (in £) that some men and some women had in their pockets.

    Men:    3.48  9.64  4.53  7.82  4.22  5.87  3.96
                6.05  5.19  4.58  6.42  3.15  4.61  6.09  4.73

    Women:  0.77  2.33  5.44  1.98  6.21  7.14  5.36  3.22
                1.57  4.21  4.62  0.80  5.00  2.66  3.71

    **b.** Compare the average amount of money that men and women had in their pockets.

6. This stem and leaf diagram shows the lengths (in inches) of some scarves for sale in shops.

| 5 | 0 0 4 5 |
|---|---|
| 6 | 5 5 5 5 5 6 6 |
| 7 | 0 0 0 2 2 2 2 2 2 2 |
| 8 | 1 1 5 5 5 |
| 9 | 0 0 0 |

Key: 5 | 0 represents 50"

    **a.** Find the median scarf length.

    **b.** Find the modal scarf length.

    **c.** Calculate the range of scarf lengths.

    **d.** Represent the data from the table as a box plot.

    **e.** Comment on the skewness of the data.

**7.** Here are the ages of 47 people on a coach.

| 55 | 58 | 22 | 28 | 60 | 44 | 14 | 65 | 74 |
|----|----|----|----|----|----|----|----|----|
| 45 | 17 | 30 | 46 | 49 | 87 | 32 | 56 | 85 |
| 79 | 71 | 19 | 85 | 25 | 24 | 38 | 57 | 49 |
| 60 | 20 | 17 | 33 | 25 | 84 | 23 | 27 | 41 |
| 22 | 86 | 63 | 40 | 37 | 81 | 19 | 68 | 59 |
| 15 | 85 | | | | | | | |

    **a.** Draw a stem and leaf diagram to represent the data.

    **b.** Work out the range of ages.

    **c.** What percentage of people are aged 60 or over?

    **d.** Work out the median age.

    **e.** Find the modal age.

    **f.** Comment on the skewness of the data.

**8.** The stem and leaf diagram shows the speeds of some cars (in miles per hour), as they travel past a speed camera on Monday morning.

| 0 | 5 9 |
|---|-----|
| 1 | 9 |
| 2 | 4 5 5 6 8 8 9 9 9 9 9 |
| 3 | 0 0 0 0 0 1 2 4 5 6 6 6 7 |
| 4 | 0 0 1 2 |

Key: 0 | 5 represents 5 mph

    **a.** What is the average speed of a car travelling past the speed camera? Explain which average you chose and why.

    **b.** What do you think the speed limit is along the road? Why do you think this?

    Here are the speeds (in mph) of some cars travelling past the same speed camera, 12 hours later.

| 25 | 35 | 40 | 19 | 27 | 34 | 30 | 31 |
|----|----|----|----|----|----|----|----|
| 36 | 46 | 50 | 34 | 38 | 28 | 24 | 30 |
| 35 | 36 | 40 | | | | | |

c. Use these speeds to create a back-to-back stem and leaf diagram, showing the morning and evening speeds.

d. Compare statistically the two sets of speeds.

9. Use the Internet to research finishing times for men and women for the 100 m backstroke Olympic swimming race. Use your data to draw a back-to-back stem and leaf diagram for the finishing times. Comment on your findings.

# Population pyramids

Having just seen back-to-back stem and leaf diagrams, let's now look at a type of back-to-back histogram, known as **population pyramids**. A population pyramid gives a visual profile of the age distribution for a population, split by gender. There is a wealth of information to be taken from a population pyramid. We can see the general shape of the distribution, and we can see at a glance whether males or females generally live longer and which age group contains the most people.

## EXAMPLE

This population pyramid shows the age distribution for Dartford in 2015.

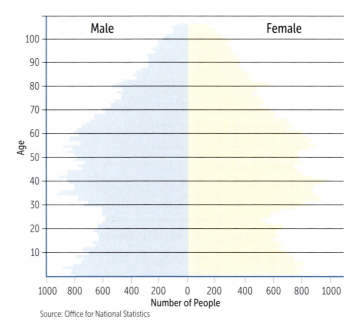

Source: Office for National Statistics

**advice**

*Sometimes the horizontal scale will be in percentages, other times in just ordinary numbers.*

a. In general do males or females tend to live longer?

b. Estimate the total number of people aged 10-19 years.

## SOLUTION

a. In both the 90-100 group and the 100+ group, the bars for females is much longer than the bars for males, so we can say that females live longer than males.

b. There are about 10 500 people ages 10-19 years in Dartford.

## EXERCISE 4

1. These two population pyramids show the age distributions for Nigeria and Norway in 2015.

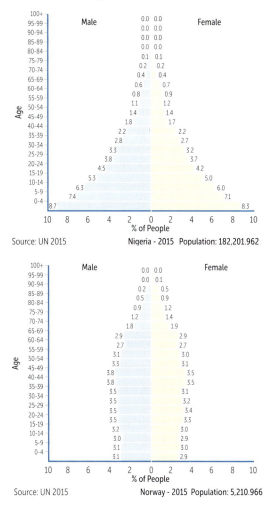

a. In Nigeria, what percentage of the population are aged 0-4?

b. Which age group has the most people in Norway?

c. In general, do people tend to live longer in Norway or Nigeria? Why do you think this might be?

d. What are the main differences you see between the two population pyramids?

131

**2.** The population pyramids show the age distributions for the United Kingdom in 1950 and in 2010.

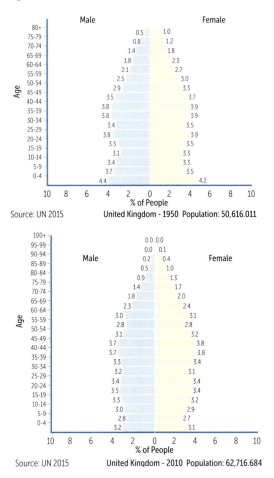

**a.** State two similarities between the two population pyramids.

**b.** State two differences between the two population pyramids.

**3.** These two population pyramids show the age distributions of Spain in 1950 and 2017.

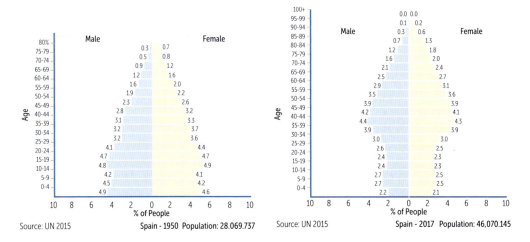

a. Explain how the pyramids support the idea that retired people from other countries are moving to Spain.

b. Explain how the pyramids support the idea that young people are moving abroad to study.

4. Explain how this population pyramid for Zambia in 1950 shows a high death rate.

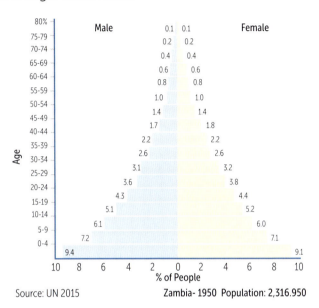

Source: UN 2015                    Zambia- 1950  Population: 2,316.950

5. One of these population pyramids shows the age distribution of a city in a wealthy country. The other shows the age distribution of a city in a developing country. Explain, giving details from the population pyramids, which pyramid belongs to which city.

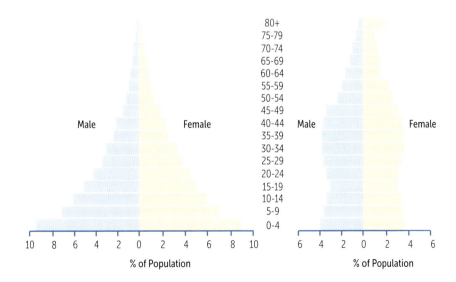

## You should now be able to:

Create and interpret choropleth maps

Create and interpret box plots

Determine the skew of a data set from a box plot

Create and interpret stem and leaf diagrams

Determine the skew of a data set from a stem and leaf diagram

Complete and interpret a population pyramid

## Exam Practice Questions

1.  The choropleth map shows the prices for concert tickets for different areas of a theatre.

    Four friends buy the **last** four tickets for a concert.

    One is in the front stalls and three are in the rear stalls.

    They decide to share the total cost equally.

    How much does each friend pay?

    © AQA 2016

| Balcony | | |
|---|---|---|
| Side Stalls | Rear Stalls | Side Stalls |
| | Front Stalls | |

☐ £45   ☐ £55   ☐ £75

HIGHER TIER

2.  Steve is a rowing coach. He trains three rowers, A, B, and C.

    The diagram summarises the times (seconds) of rower A and rower B in 30 practice races.

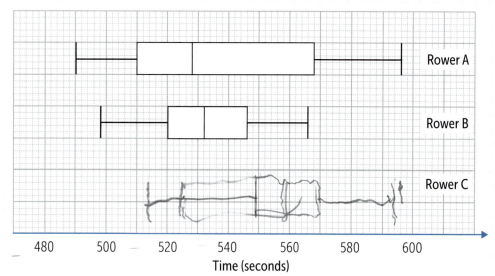

A summary of the times (seconds) for rower C in the practice races is shown in the table.

| | |
|---|---|
| Median time | 558 |
| Interquartile range | 20 |
| Upper quartile | 570 |
| Quickest two times | 517 and 524 |
| Slowest two times | 592 and 593 |

(a) Draw a box plot showing the times for rower C on the grid.

(b) Steve has to choose one of the three rowers for a competition.

He wants to choose a rower that meets these two conditions:

- has rowed faster than 540 seconds on at least 50% of practice races

- has practice times with an interquartile range less than 40 seconds

(c) Which rower meets both conditions?

Explain why Steve does **not** choose each of the other two rowers.

© AQA 2016

3. A population estimate was undertaken in 2018 to examine the age distribution by age and gender of Scotland's population.

(a) Use the table to copy and complete the drawing of the population pyramid for females. Assume that the age group 80+ covers the ages 80 – 89 years.

| Age (years) | Percentage of population (females) |
|---|---|
| 0 – 9 | 11.5 |
| 10 – 19 | 9.6 |
| 20 – 29 | 14.8 |
| 30 – 39 | 13.7 |
| 40 – 49 | 12.0 |
| 50 – 59 | 14.0 |
| 60 – 69 | 11.9 |
| 70 – 79 | 8.1 |
| 80+ | 4.4 |

(Source: Adapted from *Mid-Year Population Estimates Scotland*, Mid-2018)

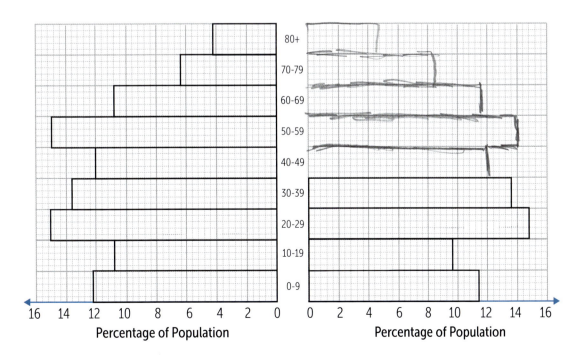

135

**(b)** What percentage of the population are males aged between 30 and 50 years?

**(c)** Which age group has the same percentage of population for both males and females?

**(d)** Compare the population of males aged 70 and over with females aged 70 and over.

4. Albina drives from work to home each evening.

   She takes either route A or route B.

   For each route, the times taken, in minutes, for a sample of 40 journeys are summarised in the box plot.

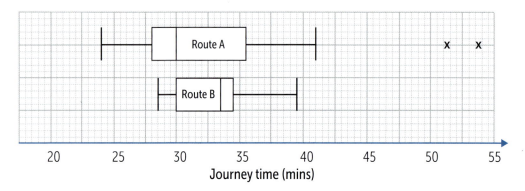

**(a)** Make three comparisons of journey times for both routes.

**(b)** In each case, state which route Albina should take and give a reason for your choice.

   **(i)** She needs to be at home within 30 minutes of leaving work.

   **(ii)** She needs to be at home within 40 minutes of leaving work.

© AQA 2013

5. The population pyramids below show the populations of India and Japan in 2018 for different age groups.

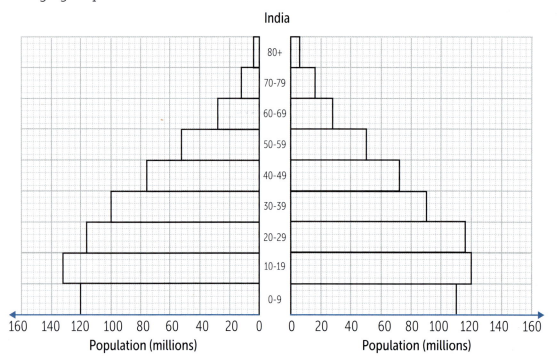

Japan

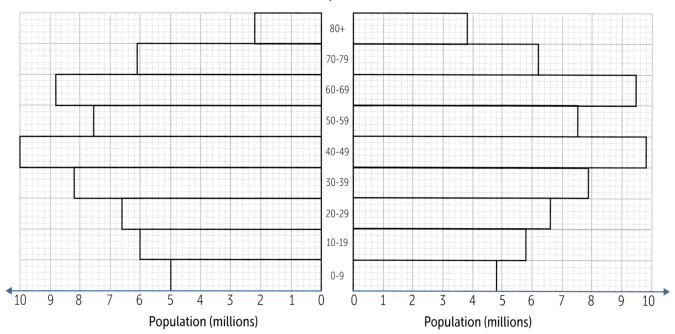

Population (millions)                     Population (millions)

(a) Write down the number of females aged 40 – 49 in India.

(b) Copy and complete this sentence:
*In Japan, there were* _____ *more females aged 80+*
*than males aged 80+.*

(c) Work out how many more 10 – 30 year olds there were in India compared to Japan.

(d) Explain how you can tell from the population pyramids that India has a lower age of life expectancy than Japan.

6. Heidi is planning to hold a charity collection at a local restaurant.

She will do this on either a Saturday evening or a Sunday evening.

To help her decide which evening to choose she finds out the number of people who visited the restaurant on these days.

Here are her results for the last 15 **Saturdays**.

113   101      87      94      126      128      111      96

89      102      106      89      105      119      88

(a) Show the data in an ordered stem-and-leaf diagram.

| 8  | 7 8 9 9 |
|----|---------|
| 9  | 4 6     |
| 10 | 1 2 5 6 |
| 11 | 1 3 9   |
| 12 | 6 8     |

Key: _9_|_7_ represents _97_ people

(b) Work out the median for the data.

**(c)** Show that the interquartile range for the data is 24 people.

**(d)** Data for the number of people visiting the restaurant over the last 15 **Sundays** is summarised below.

median = 110        interquartile range = 17

Give **two** reasons why Heidi should hold the collection on a Sunday rather than a Saturday.

© AQA 2014

**7.** The stem and leaf diagram shows the results of a test for the 23 students in class 11A.

| 2 | 0 3 5 8 |
|---|---------|
| 3 | 1 2 7 7 9 |
| 4 | 1 2 5 6 7 8 9 |
| 5 | 2 3 6 7 8 |
| 6 | 1 5 |

Key: 2|5 represents 25 marks

The pass mark for this test was 38 marks.

**(a)** How many students in class 11A passed the test?

**(b)** Work out the median mark.

**(c)** Work out the lower and upper quartiles.

The box and whisker plot shows the results of the same test for the students in class 11B.

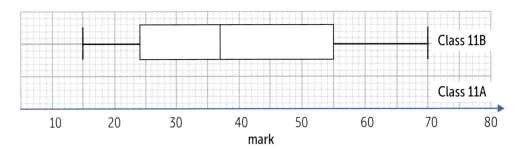

**(d)** On a copy of the grid, draw a box and whisker plot to show the results for class 11A.

**(e)** Use the box and whisker plots to compare the results of the two classes.

© AQA 2017

8. A farmer is choosing which vegetables to grow on his farm next year. He can either grow carrots, parsnips or cauliflowers.

The box plots show information about the different yields of vegetables in tons per hectare he could harvest.

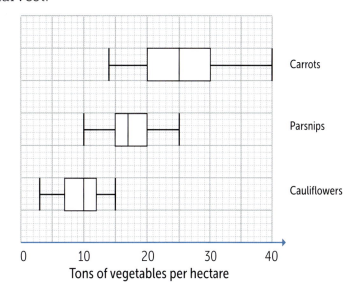

(a) The label on a sack of seeds gives the yield as 10 tons per hectare. Which vegetable seed is it? Give a reason for your answer.

(b) Which sort of vegetable should he choose to grow? Explain why.

9. Jon is on a school trip investigating the number of woodlice in a woodland. He divides the woodland into metre squares. He counts the number of woodlice in each square. This diagram shows his results.

| 6 | 9 | 5 | 7 | 2 |
|----|----|----|----|----|
| 8 | 12 | 13 | 8 | 4 |
| 16 | 14 | 12 | 12 | 4 |
| 18 | 17 | 14 | 13 | 7 |
| 23 | 19 | 13 | 12 | 11 |

(a) How can you tell by looking at the diagram that the median per square is more than 11?

(b) Use a grid to draw a choropleth map for the data.

(c) Part of the woodland has a pond in in it. Woodlice prefer damp areas. On your choropleth map put a P in the square metre most likely to be by the pond. Give a reason for your answer.

# 7 Averages 2 (HIGHER TIER)

## In this chapter you will learn to:

Calculate seasonal effect

Calculate mean seasonal variation

Calculate a weighted mean

Calculate a geometric mean

Understand a quality control situation

Plot and interpret a control chart

Plot and interpret action and warning lines

Everything in this chapter is used on the Higher Tier only, except index numbers and crude rates.

## New Vocabulary

Seasonal effect

Mean seasonal variation

Weighted mean

Quality control

Control chart

Action and Warning lines

# Seasonal variation

We saw in the previous chapter on averages how to calculate moving averages, and from them, spot general trends in data. We can also use those same time series graphs with the moving averages and trend lines to predict future values.

Let's look again at the gas bill data from Chapter 5.

**advice**

*You can find the first part of moving averages in Averages 1 if you would like a quick recap.*

|  | YEAR 1 | | | | YEAR 2 | | | |
|---|---|---|---|---|---|---|---|---|
| Quarter | 1 | 2 | 3 | 4 | 1 | 2 | 3 | 4 |
| Gas bill (£) | 124 | 99 | 144 | 191 | 177 | 105 | 151 | 200 |
| 4-point moving average (£) | | | 139.50 | 152.75 | 154.25 | 156.00 | 158.25 | |

And the graph we produced from the data.

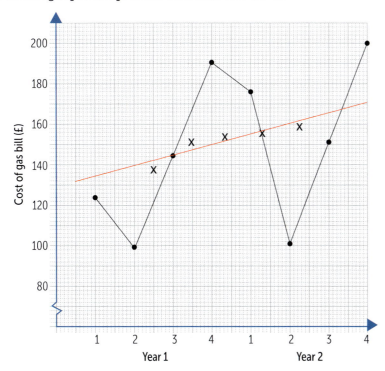

You can see that none of the data points lie exactly on the trend line, and there is a difference between each data point and the trend line. The difference between the trend line and the data point (just a subtraction calculation) is called the **seasonal effect**.

Seasonal effect = actual data point − trend line value.

For our gas bill data, the seasonal effect for Year 1 Quarter 1 is seen in this section of graph.

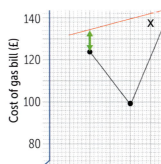

For Year 1 Quarter 1 seasonal effect, we calculate: 124 − 135.5 = −11.5.

For Quarter 1 in the second year, we calculate: 177 − 154 = 23.

**advice**

*Be careful to check whether your seasonal effect is a positive or negative value. Always start with the actual value. You will see some negative values but don't lose their negative sign along the way.*

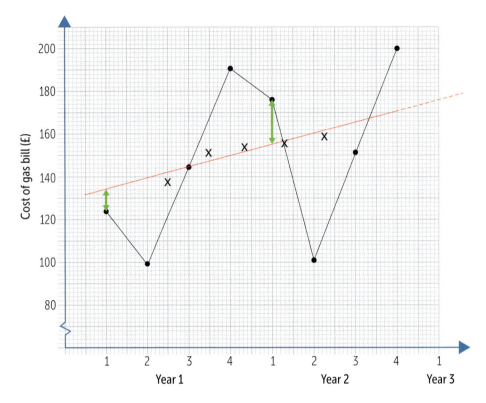

We can take this a stage further and calculate a **mean seasonal variation** by finding the means of all of the first quarters. Here there are only two, so we get $\frac{(-11.5 + 23)}{2}$ = £5.75

If we now extend the trend line, we could read off the trend line value for the first quarter of Year 3 and add on the mean seasonal value for Q1 to estimate the seasonally adjusted gas bill for the first quarter of Year 3.

From the trend line, Q1 of Year 3 has value 177, and then we add on 5.75 to give a seasonally adjusted forecast of £182.75 for that gas bill.

Be aware that these trends are often based on only a small number of previous values so they might not be very reliable.

## EXERCISE 1

**1.** Flamingo Heights, a new theme park, opened three years ago. The table shows the visitor figures for the first three years.

| MONTH | YEAR 1 Q1 | YEAR 1 Q2 | YEAR 1 Q3 | YEAR 1 Q4 | YEAR 2 Q1 | YEAR 2 Q2 |
|---|---|---|---|---|---|---|
| Number of visitors | 520000 | 560000 | 490000 | 400000 | 640000 | 656000 |

| MONTH | YEAR 2 Q3 | YEAR 2 Q4 | YEAR 3 Q1 | YEAR 3 Q2 | YEAR 3 Q3 | YEAR 3 Q4 |
|---|---|---|---|---|---|---|
| Number of visitors | 668000 | 608000 | 636000 | 632000 | 652000 | 622000 |

a. Plot the data as a time series graph.

b. Calculate and plot appropriate moving averages.

c. Draw on a trend line.

d. Use your trend line to calculate the mean seasonal effect for Q1.

**advice**

*Remember it's quite usual to have negative values in the mean seasonal effect.*

2. The table shows the data usage, in MB, on Josh's phone for three weeks.

| | WEEK 1 | WEEK 2 | WEEK 3 |
|---|---|---|---|
| Monday | 440 | 525 | 405 |
| Tuesday | 350 | 500 | 180 |
| Wednesday | 750 | 695 | 800 |
| Thursday | 900 | 920 | 840 |
| Friday | 5500 | 5700 | 5900 |
| Saturday | 4800 | 4700 | 4900 |
| Sunday | 1035 | 1215 | 1100 |

a. Plot the data as a time series graph.

b. Calculate and plot appropriate moving averages.

c. Draw on a trend line.

d. Use your trend line to calculate the mean seasonal effect for Fridays.

e. Use your answers to parts c and d to predict the visits to the site on Friday of Week 4.

3. A small charity, working with homeless people at weekends, has a new website. The website manager tracks how many visits are made to the site each day. He has recorded:

| | WEEK 1 | WEEK 2 | WEEK 3 | WEEK 4 |
|---|---|---|---|---|
| Monday | 1440 | 1425 | 1505 | 1550 |
| Tuesday | 951 | 850 | 987 | 1,001 |
| Wednesday | 304 | 244 | 298 | 316 |
| Thursday | 250 | 203 | 244 | 265 |
| Friday | 350 | 260 | 290 | 335 |
| Saturday | 1325 | 1247 | 1369 | 1401 |
| Sunday | 1500 | 1387 | 1499 | 1506 |

a. Plot the data as a time series graph.

b. Calculate and plot appropriate moving averages.

c. Draw on a trend line.

d. Use your trend line to calculate the mean seasonal effect for Mondays.

e. Use your answers to parts c and d to predict the visits to the site on Monday.

4. The village bakery needs to forecast future earnings to give a presentation to the bank. Fatima has been advertising recently and thinks she can show an upwards trend in the takings. Trading figures (in £) for the last month are:

| | WEEK 1 | WEEK 2 | WEEK 3 | WEEK 4 |
|---|---|---|---|---|
| Tuesday | 591 | 612 | 577 | 602 |
| Wednesday | 304 | 264 | 288 | 305 |
| Thursday | 780 | 760 | 790 | 810 |
| Friday | 760 | 755 | 864 | 877 |
| Saturday | 1325 | 1247 | 1369 | 1401 |

a. Plot the data as a time series graph.

b. Calculate and plot appropriate moving averages.

c. Draw on a trend line.

d. Does the trend line support Fatima's thought that there is an upward trend in takings?

e. Use your trend line to calculate the mean seasonal effect for Saturdays.

f. Use your answers to parts c and e to predict the takings on Saturday of Week 5.

5. Derek and Clive run a smoothie bar in a sports club. The smoothie bar is open each day from Thursday to Sunday. They record their takings each day for eight weeks, and then calculate seven-point moving averages to spot any trends in their takings. Explain why this is not the best method to use.

6. Calliope works for a cruise ship and has been asked to investigate whether or not passenger numbers are generally increasing or decreasing. She has this record of the passenger numbers for 10 weeks but has unfortunately splashed hot chocolate over two of the figures. Use the 3-point moving average figures she has calculated to work out the missing values.

| WEEK NUMBER | NUMBER OF PASSENGERS | 3-POINT MOVING AVERAGE |
|---|---|---|
| 1 | 2000 | |
| 2 | 2121 | 2033 |
| 3 | 1978 | 2038 |
| 4 | 2015 | 2075 |
| 5 | 2232 | 2185 |
| 6 | 2308 | 2177 |
| 7 | 1990 | 2148 |
| 8 | 2146 | 2152 |
| 9 | | 2156 |
| 10 | | |

**7.** Using the time series graph below, work out the average seasonal effect for Friday and use this to make a seasonally adjusted estimate for the sales on Friday of Week 4.

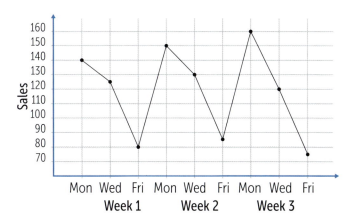

# Other types of mean

Sometimes, as we've seen, the arithmetic mean does not really suit our values. We have seen cases where the mode or the median would be more appropriate averages to use. There are other situations though where these averages are just as unsuitable. We need to consider different kinds of averages for those cases.

## Weighted mean

You've probably come across **weighted mean** without realising it. Have any of your exams been made up of more than one unit where one is worth more overall than another? This used to happen a lot when coursework was part of GCSE. The coursework was often worth 20% of the final grade, with the other 80% coming from a written exam. A weighted mean works in a very similar way to an

arithmetic mean, but instead of each data point contributing equally to the average value, they are given different "weights".
This means that there is greater emphasis on some values.

Consider the data set: 5, 7, 16, 22.

When we find the arithmetic mean, we give equal weight to all four values in the set, so they each have effectively a weight of $\frac{1}{4}$ (keeping the total weight to 1).

Arithmetic mean is: $\frac{(5 + 7 + 16 + 22)}{4}$ but we can think of this as being $\frac{1}{4} \times 5 + \frac{1}{4} \times 7 + \frac{1}{4} \times 16 + \frac{1}{4} \times 22$ (just by putting the $\frac{1}{4}$ in front of each number individually instead of dividing the whole thing by 4). Either way, we get an arithmetic mean of 12.5.

If we changed the individual weighting attached to each number in the data set, the weighted mean would be different to the arithmetic mean. Imagine, instead of having equal weighting, the 5 has a weight of 0.7 and the rest have a weight of 0.1 each. This changed the weighted mean calculation to: $0.7 \times 5 + 0.1 \times 7 + 0.1 \times 16 + 0.1 \times 22$, giving a weighted mean of 8 — quite a bit different from the arithmetic mean.

If you don't have weights that sum to 1, you simply divide the multiplied total by the sum of the weights.

## EXAMPLE

Chester has scored 32% in his coursework and 76% in his written exam. The coursework contributes 2 parts of his final mark, whilst the written exam contributes 5 parts. He needs an overall average of 65% to pass. Does Chester pass the course?

### SOLUTION

The weighted mean will be found by: $\frac{(2 \times 32 + 5 \times 76)}{7} = \frac{444}{7} = 63.42\%$

No, since 63.42 < 65, Chester does not pass the course. His good score on the exam wasn't enough to outweigh the poor coursework score.

The formal notation for calculating a weighted mean is written as $\frac{(\sum \text{value} \times \text{weight})}{(\sum \text{weights})}$

where $\sum$ stands for total or 'sum of' as we saw in Chapter 5.

## EXERCISE 2

1. Find the weighted mean of these values:

   **a.**

   | VALUE | 7 | 6 | 4 | 3 | 8 |
   |---|---|---|---|---|---|
   | WEIGHT | 0.1 | 0.2 | 0.3 | 0.15 | 0.25 |

   **b.**

   | VALUE | 16 | 74 | 21 | 89 | 32 | 45 | 63 | 50 |
   |---|---|---|---|---|---|---|---|---|
   | WEIGHT | 0.05 | 0.2 | 0.6 | 0.05 | 0.025 | 0.025 | 0.025 | 0.025 |

   **c.**

   | VALUE | 13 | 44 | 46 | 51 | 70 |
   |---|---|---|---|---|---|
   | WEIGHT | 0.2 | 0.2 | 0.4 | 0.15 | 0.05 |

   **d.**

   | VALUE | 124 | 99 | 76 | 201 | 44 | 36 | 101 | 87 |
   |---|---|---|---|---|---|---|---|---|
   | WEIGHT | 0.12 | 0.13 | 0.2 | 0.1 | 0.04 | 0.19 | 0.1 | 0.12 |

2. Minty's course is made up of 30% practical work, 20% project, and 50% written exam. She scores 27% for practical, 19 out of 20 for project, and 68 out of 80 for the written exam. Overall, she needs an average of 60% to pass the course. Does Minty pass her course or would you suggest that she re-takes any part of it?

3. Stainless steel comes in different grades. What you want to use it for determines what goes into it. Stainless steel 304 is made from 18% chromium, 8% nickel, and the rest is iron. Stainless steel 446 is made from 27% chromium, 0.25% nickel, and the rest is iron. Emeka has 100g of stainless steel 304 and 350g of stainless steel 446 that he melts together. What percentage of the new alloy will be chromium?

4. Sue makes a blanket from 84 crocheted squares. The 26 squares made of wool cost 76p each and the squares made from acrylic cost 45p each. Find the weighted mean cost of square.

5. Lily is buying a new tablet. She finds this table in a magazine that assigns a score out of 10 for each category.

   | | TABLET A | TABLET B | TABLET C |
   |---|---|---|---|
   | Battery life | 6 | 4 | 9 |
   | Mass | 3 | 6 | 2 |
   | Price | 7 | 5 | 7 |
   | Speed | 8 | 9 | 5 |
   | Storage | 5 | 10 | 6 |

**advice**

*Remember to divide by the sum of the weights when the weights don't sum to 100% (or 1).*

Lily applies her own rating system of:

| | |
|---|---|
| Battery life | 40% |
| Mass | 5% |
| Price | 30% |
| Speed | 15% |
| Storage | 10% |

**a.** Which tablet will she buy?

**b.** Colin also wants to buy a new tablet and has his own rating system of:

| | |
|---|---|
| Battery life | 15% |
| Mass | 15% |
| Price | 35% |
| Speed | 5% |
| Storage | 30% |

Which tablet will he buy?

**6.** There are 25 boys and 15 girls in a youth group who all take part in testing a *Guitar Hero* release. The average score for boys is 7.2 and the average score for girls is 8.6. What is the overall average score for the youth group?

**7.** Amanda sells aromatherapy blended oils. She uses a lot of lavender. Each blend is then diluted 10 ml of blend to 100 ml water to be sprayed around the room. The table shows how many drops of each oil are in the blends she has prepared.

| | LAVENDER | CHAMOMILE | ORANGE | LEMON | BERGAMOT | FRANKINCENSE | MARJORAM |
|---|---|---|---|---|---|---|---|
| Sleep | 9 | 1 | 2 | | 3 | | |
| Stress relief | 4 | | 4 | 3 | 5 | | |
| Pain relief | 10 | 2 | | | | 5 | 5 |

A customer asks for a personal blend, and Amanda decides to use these three blends in the ratio of sleep : stress relief : pain relief = 5 : 2 : 3.

What percentage of the custom blend is lavender?

## Geometric mean

The geometric mean is used when multiplied values need to be averaged. It is calculated in a similar way to the arithmetic mean, but the data set values are multiplied and rooted instead of being added and divided. The geometric mean is mostly used in questions involving interest rates, but you may see it in other situations. When interest rates are used, you will need to use the multiplier method.

Consider the data set

3, 5, 8, 14

the total of which, is 30.

When we find the arithmetic mean, we are searching for a value, $V$, such that

$V + V + V + V = 30$

I'm sure you've already calculated that the arithmetic mean of this set is 7.5. We have then found the value that we can replace each member of the data set with and leave the total unaltered:

$7.5 + 7.5 + 7.5 + 7.5 = 30$

With the geometric mean, we are searching for the value that we could replace each multiplier with and still finish up at the same end value.

Consider the data set

1.06, 1.09, 1.07

$1.06 \times 1.09 \times 1.07 = 1.236278$, so we are searching for the value, $V$, that would replace each of these in the equation $V \times V \times V$ or $V^3 = 1.236278$.

To get this value, we need to cube root 1.236278.

$\sqrt[3]{1.236278} = 1.073261079$, so $V = 1.073$ (to 3dp).

So, the geometric mean of $n$ numbers is $\sqrt[n]{\text{value}_1 \times \text{value}_2 \times \text{value}_n}$.

## EXAMPLE

The value of a house goes up by 8% in the first year, 12% in the second year, 10% in the third year, and 9.5% in the fourth year. What is the average percentage increase over the four years?

## SOLUTION

The only appropriate average to answer this question is the geometric mean as no other would give this average percentage.

Firstly, we need the multiplier for each of the increases.
These are: 1.08, 1.12, 1.1 and 1.095

Now we multiply those figures together.

$1.08 \times 1.12 \times 1.1 \times 1.095 = 1.4569632$

Then we take the fourth root (there are 4 values)
$\sqrt[4]{1.4569632} = 1.098657047$.

The average percentage increase is 9.9% (to 3dp).

### EXAMPLE

The value of Dot's investments go up by 27% in the first year but drop by 27% in the second year. Use the geometric mean to work out the overall increase or decrease for the two years.

### SOLUTION

The multipliers are 1.27 and 0.73 this time, as it was a 27% decrease.

$1.27 \times 0.73 = 0.9271$

$0.9271 = 0.96286$, so the investment has an overall decrease of 3.7%.

**advice**

*Remember to root the multiplied numbers, not divide.*

## EXERCISE 3

1. Find the geometric mean (to 2dp) of:

   a. 2 and 8

   b. 3, 5, and 9

   c. 14, 23, 30, and 45

2. Lucia buys an antique map which increases in value by 35% in the first year. In the second year, it decreases in value by 15%, but then increases in value by 20% in the third year. Use the geometric mean to work out the average percentage increase.

3. The geometric mean of two numbers is 10. One number is 20, what is the other number?

4. The geometric mean of three numbers is 8. Two of the numbers are 16 and 64. What is the third number?

5. The population of fish in a lake grew by 27% in the first year. Due to a disease, there was a 72% drop in population during the second year but once disease free, the third year saw an increase of 43% and the fourth year an increase of 31%. Overall, was there a percentage increase or decrease over the four years? Show working to support your answer.

6. The geometric mean of three numbers is 10. One number is 40 and the other two numbers are equal. What are the other two numbers?

## Index Numbers

An index number shows how a value (often a price) changes over time. This is measured by comparing it, to a base year. The base year is given the value of 100, and so if we see values below 100, it means that items have gone down in price, and if we see values above 100, items have gone up in price.

The formula to calculate index numbers is:

$$\text{Index number} = \frac{\text{current value of item}}{\text{value of item in base year}} \times 100$$

### EXAMPLE

The price of a pint of milk is given for each of 3 years in the table:

| Year | 1999 | 2000 | 2010 |
|---|---|---|---|
| Price (pence) | 17p | 31p | ??? |

a. Calculate the index number for 2000 using 1999 as base.

b. The index number for 2010 using 2000 as base is 175. Find, to the nearest penny, the price of a pint of milk in 2010.

### SOLUTION

a. $\frac{31}{17} \times 100 = 182.352941 = 182.35$ (2dp)

b. $175 = \frac{x}{31} \times 100$
Rearranging this gives $x = \frac{175 \times 31}{100}$
So $x = 54.25$p
$x = 54$p to the nearest penny

## Weighted index numbers

Where the price of an item is made up of different things, it's possible each of these things may have different rates of increase or decrease. If some of these things are more important than others, you need a weighted index number to take this into account.

This is very similar to finding the weighted mean we saw earlier in this chapter.

Here is the formula:

$$\text{Weighted index number} = \frac{(\text{index number} \times \text{weight})}{\text{weights}}$$

**EXAMPLE**

A shop advertises online and through the local newspaper.

In 2018 the online ads cost £3000 and the newspaper ads £2000.

In 2019 the online ads cost £5000 and the newspaper ads £1500.

The weighting of online ads to newspapers ads is 3:2.

Calculate a weighted index number for 2019 using 2018 as base.

**SOLUTION**

Firstly find the index numbers for online and newspaper ads separately.

Online: $\frac{5000}{3000} \times 100 = 166.666...$

Newspapers: $\frac{1500}{2000} \times 100 = 75$

Now the weighted index number is

$\frac{(166.666 \times 3) + (75 \times 2)}{(3 + 2)} = 130$.

### Birth and death rates

The way that numbers of important daily issues such as births, deaths, marriages, unemployment, etc., change are important to be able to track.

To calculate these rates we look at how many of the particular event occur per thousand of the population. These are called crude rates and you can use a formula for them.

For example, for births,

$$\text{Crude birth rate} = \left( \frac{\text{number of births}}{\text{total population}} \right) \times 1000$$

**EXAMPLE**

Hartley has a population of 4500.

In 2018 there were 58 registered births.

Calculate the crude birth rate for Hartley.

**SOLUTION**

$\frac{58}{4500} \times 1000 = 12.889$

This means that for every 1000 people, there are almost 13 births.

## EXERCISE 4

1. The numbers of customers at a cinema over four months is shown in the table:

| MONTH | Jan | Feb | Mar | Apr |
|---|---|---|---|---|
| NUMBER OF VISITORS | 1245 | 2055 | 997 | ??? |

   a. Using January as the base, work out the index numbers for February and March.

   b. The index number for April, using March as base, is 190. How many customers were there in April?

2. The prices of 100g of hand dyed yarn over five years are shown in the table:

| YEAR | 2014 | 2015 | 2016 | 2017 | 2018 |
|---|---|---|---|---|---|
| PRICE (£) | 12 | 12.75 | 13.50 | ??? | 16 |

   a. Using 2014 as the base year, work out the index numbers for 2015, 2016, and 2018.

   b. The index number for 2017, using 2015 as base, is 125. Calculate the price of 100g of hand dyed yarn in 2017.

3. The costs of a small shop are 65% for staffing, 30% for energy and services, and 5% on other items. The indices for these costs in 2019 using 2018 as base were:

   102 for staffing

   111 for energy and services

   108 for other items

   Calculate the weighted index for the shop's costs for 2019 using 2018 as a base.

4. The population of Bury is 180 000. In 2018, there were 360 deaths. Calculate the crude death rate for Bury in 2018.

5. The crude birth rate in Rye for 2018 was 11. The population of Rye in 2018 was 5000. How many births were there in Rye in 2018?

# Quality control

When we buy a product, we expect it to be just as described on the packaging and in perfect condition. Industry has to keep to the 500g of Rice Pops in the box and not drop down to 450g. The purchasing public would be very unhappy at losing 10% of the goods they had paid for, and the company could well be taken to court for mis-selling their product. It's often machines that are putting the contents into packets and they need to be checked regularly to make sure they aren't putting in too much or too little. Either situation would be bad for the industry! There will be someone in charge of the machine responsible for **quality control**.

The company may take a sample of Rice Pops each hour to monitor how much is going into each box. They will find the mean or median mass and plot these hourly averages on a **control chart**, which shows **action** and **warning lines**, to monitor the output of the machine. Each machine will have a quality control limit, that when the masses go beyond, the machine needs to be reset.

The quality control charts show the expected value as the x-axis with values either side as the y-axis. There will then be other horizontal lines (often shown as dashed lines) that are the action lines. When the sample means (or medians) start to cross these lines, the machine machine will need to be reset or adjusted in some way. There may also be warning lines drawn on the chart that indicate more frequent sampling is necessary as the data is headed towards the action lines.

This control chart shows the machine working beautifully within its limits.

**advice**

*These sample means could be sample medians, and you would create the chart in exactly the same way, plotting the sample medians instead of the sample means.*

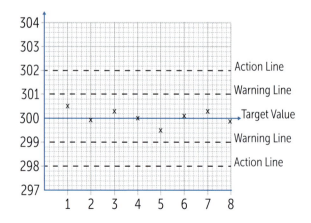

This control chart shows the machine working within its limits but all of the sample means lay below the expected line (the *x*-axis) and three have fallen below the warning line. It may be helpful to make a small adjustment to the machine so that a full reset isn't required later on.

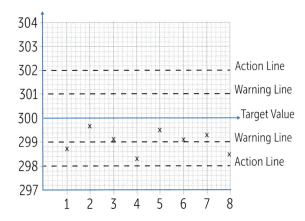

This control chart shows the machine working outside its limits. We can see erratic sample means which could indicate a machine fault. It's best to reset this machine.

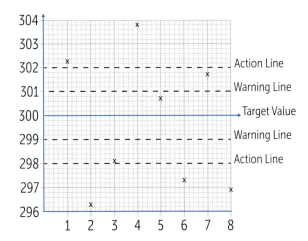

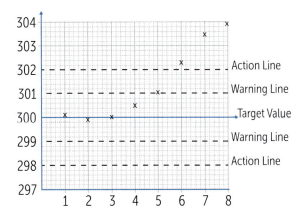

## EXAMPLE

There should be 500g of Rice Pops in each box. The action limit is 2g away from target and the warning limit is 1g away from target. The table shows the masses (in grams) in each of the sample boxes each hour. Draw a quality control chart for these hourly samples and determine whether any action needs to be taken.

| Hour 1 | 500 | 495.5 | 500.2 | 501.1 |
| Hour 2 | 499 | 498.5 | 500.4 | 501.2 |
| Hour 3 | 498 | 497.9 | 498.4 | 500.3 |
| Hour 4 | 505 | 498.4 | 498.9 | 500 |
| Hour 5 | 502 | 501.2 | 499.5 | 499 |
| Hour 6 | 502.5 | 501 | 500.9 | 503 |

## SOLUTION

The mean for each hour is:

Mean for Hour 1: $\frac{(500 + 495.5 + 500.2 + 501.1)}{4} = \frac{1996.8}{4} = 499.2$

Mean for Hour 2: $\frac{(499 + 498.5 + 500.4 + 501.2)}{4} = \frac{1999.1}{4} = 499.775$

Mean for Hour 3: $\frac{(498 + 497.9 + 498.4 + 500.3)}{4} = \frac{1994.6}{4} = 498.65$

Mean for Hour 4: $\frac{(505 + 498.4 + 498.9 + 500)}{4} = \frac{2002.3}{4} = 500.575$

Mean for Hour 5: $\frac{(502 + 501.2 + 499.5 + 499)}{4} = \frac{2001.7}{4} = 500.425$

Mean for Hour 6: $\frac{(502.5 + 501 + 500.9 + 503)}{4} = \frac{2007.4}{4} = 501.85$

We plot these on a control chart that has 500 g as the target value for the *x*-axis and draw on the two action lines at $500 \pm 2$ (so 498 and 502) and two warning lines at $500 \pm 1$ (so at 499 and 501).

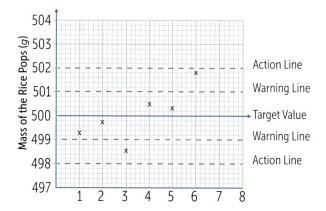

The machine needs no immediate action but it has gone past the warning line in Hours 3, 4, and 6, so extra sampling would be recommended to watch for further differences that would take the Rice Pops past the action limit.

A control chart for ranges is one way to keep track of the variation in each sample taken. It is possible for a machine to produce samples whose means lay safely within the bounds set but that have a large variation. For example, in the Rice Pops machine above, if a sample of 5 boxes is taken with masses 480g, 490g, 500g, 510g, and 520g, the overall sample mean and sample median would be 500g, and these would be plotted on the control chart, making it look as if the machine is working perfectly. When we plot the range for this sample however, we would be plotting a range of 40 g (when the action line would likely be around 10 g). The majority of these boxes of Rice Pops if plotted individually would fall out of the allowable area.

The sample ranges in this chart are very small and well away from the action line. No action needs to be taken with this machine.

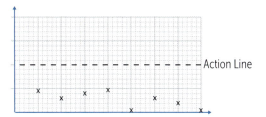

The range values on this chart do not go past the action line, but extra sampling would be advisable since there is a clear upward trend in the data, towards the action line.

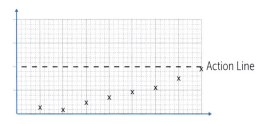

Many of the samples' ranges on this chart have gone beyond the action line. This machine needs immediate action taking to remedy the situation.

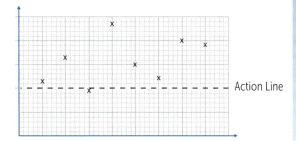

## EXERCISE 5

1. Emma works in a lab producing medication for dogs. Today, each bottle produced should contain 100 ml medicine ±1 ml. She takes a sample every two hours from each of the three machines producing the bottles. Emma then plots the sample means for each machine on a control chart. Examine the charts and see what action, if any, needs to be taken for any of the machines.

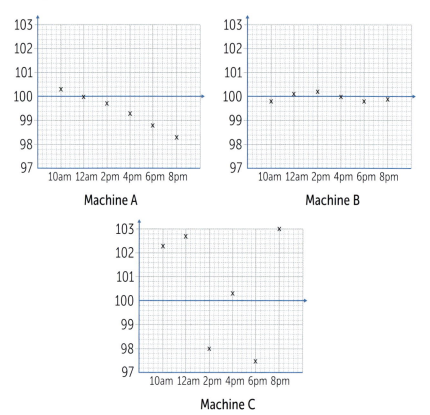

Machine A

Machine B

Machine C

2. Companies A, B and C are making medication for a heart condition. It's vital that the patient doesn't overdose on this medication. The control charts show the ranges of the first seven samples of the shift produced by each machine. For each machine, suggest if any action is necessary.

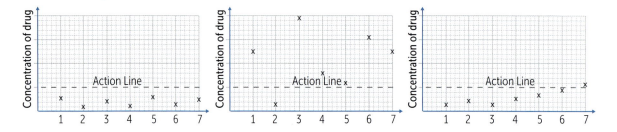

**3.** Alyson manages a group of dental practices. At each practice, they sell packs of flossing sticks. A customer has complained that instead of the 50 sticks that were supposed to be in the packet, her packet only contained 43. Alyson decides to investigate and asks each of the 6 practices to count how many sticks are in each pack that they have.

Here are the results:

| Practice 1 | Practice 2 | Practice 3 | Practice 4 | Practice 5 | Practice 6 |
|---|---|---|---|---|---|
| 48 | 50 | 49 | 48 | 48 | 50 |
| 49 | 49 | 50 | 50 | 49 | 50 |
| 50 | 49 | 50 | 51 | 49 | 49 |
| 50 | 49 | 50 | 49 | 50 | 50 |
| 50 | 50 | 50 | 50 | - | 50 |
| 47 | 49 | - | 50 | - | 49 |
| 48 | - | - | 51 | - | - |

**a.** Work out the mean number of flossing sticks for each practice.

**b.** Plot these means on a control chart.

**c.** Draw on action lines at 48 and 52.

**d.** Does your control chart suggest that Alyson needs to contact the manufacturer of the flossing sticks in any way?

**e.** Try the exercise again, using median instead of mean. Does this make a difference to your findings?

**4.** Jeff produces and sells artisan coffee blends. His coffee bags claim to contain 500 g of freshly roasted and ground organic coffee.

He samples the bags once they are filled to ensure he's not overfilling them. He has an action limit of 5 g. The last 10 samples contained mean masses of:

500 g  502 g  498 g  497 g  500 g
495 g  499 g  502 g  505 g  504 g

Draw a control graph and comment on the masses of the coffee bags.

# You should now be able to:

Calculate seasonal effect

Calculate mean seasonal variation

Calculate a weighted mean

Calculate a geometric mean

Understand a quality control situation

Plot and interpret a control chart

Plot and interpret action and warning lines

# Exam Practice Questions

**1.** A local firm makes cheese.

The table shows the sales of cheese, in tonnes per quarter, from Quarter 1 of 2011 to Quarter 2 of 2013.

The first four moving average values have been calculated and entered in the table.

| YEAR | QUARTER (Q) | SALES (TONNES) | MOVING AVERAGES |
|---|---|---|---|
| | 1 | 8.0 | |
| 2011 | 2 | 12.0 | 10.8 |
| | 3 | 14.2 | 11.4 |
| | 4 | 9.0 | 12.3 |
| | 1 | 10.4 | 13.5 |
| 2012 | 2 | 15.6 | ............... |
| | 3 | 19.0 | ............... |
| | 4 | 11.8 | ............... |
| 2013 | 1 | 15.2 | ............... |
| | 2 | 19.2 | |

**(a)** Calculate the missing moving average values.

**(b)** Plot the sales data, together with the first four moving averages, on a grid.

**(c)** Draw the trend line.

**(d)** The seasonal effects for Quarter 3 and Quarter 4 are

| Quarter 3 | Quarter 4 |
|---|---|
| + 3.65 | − 3.49 |

Use these and your trend line to predict the likely sales for Quarter 3 and Quarter 4 of 2013.

(e) The owners plan to close the business if they do not reach total sales of at least 85 tonnes during 2013.

Advise the owners whether they are likely to achieve this level of total sales. You **must** show your working.

© AQA 2013

2. Tins of tomatoes are produced on one of three machines A, B, or C.
Peter takes samples of tins at regular intervals from each machine.
He plots the mean mass for each sample on a control chart.

The results based on the first eight samples taken from each machine are shown.

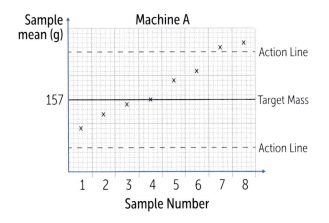

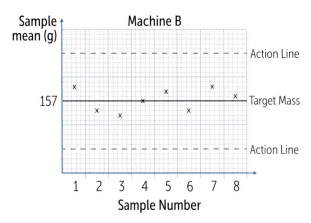

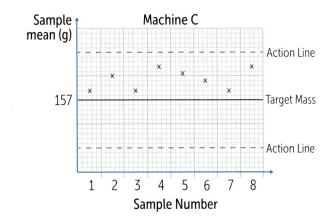

(a) For each machine, explain whether the chart shows it to be working satisfactorily or not.

(b) Why is a chart for sample ranges usually drawn in addition to the chart for sample means?

**3.** A machine in a factory puts custard into tins.

The target for the mass of custard in a tin is 410g.

The Quality Control Manager takes a sample of tins each hour and records the mean mass of custard in these tins.

**(a)** Give one reason why the manager does not measure the mass of custard in every tin.

The table shows the mean masses for the first eight samples taken one day.

| Sample number | 1 | 2 | 3 | 4 | 5 | 6 | 7 | 8 |
|---|---|---|---|---|---|---|---|---|
| Mean mass (g) | 409.6 | 412.6 | 410.4 | 410.2 | 409.6 | 409.0 | 408.8 | 408.4 |

The control chart shows some of the sample means.

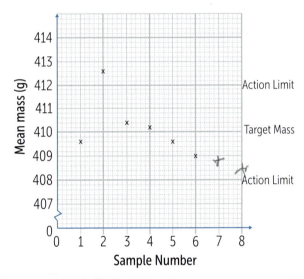

**(b)** Plot the missing sample means on a quality control chart.

**(c)** Give two reasons why the manager may think that the machine is not working satisfactorily.

**(d) (i)** Name a different **type** of statistical measure that the manager might want to plot on a control chart.

**(ii)** Explain in context what additional information this statistical measure would show.

© AQA 2017

**4.** The time series graph shows the value of online sales (£ billion) in Britain. (HIGHER TIER)

The data are shown every quarter from 2011 to 2013.

The four-point moving averages are also plotted.

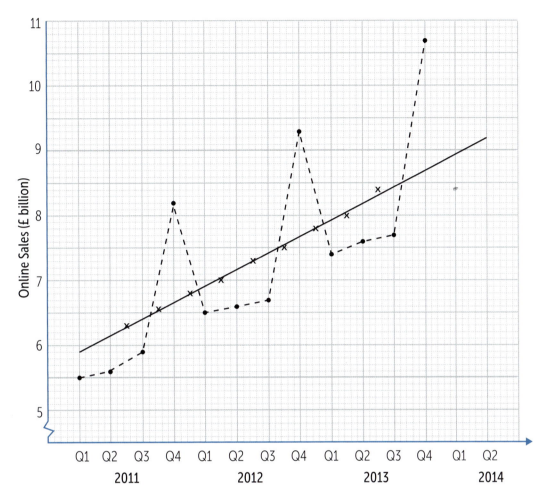

**(a)** Online sales are highest in Quarter 4.

Give a possible reason for this.

**(b)** Describe one other pattern in the data.

**(c)** Copy and complete the table to find the average seasonal effect for Quarter 1.

|  | ONLINE SALES (£ BILLION) | TREND LINE VALUE (£ BILLION) | SEASONAL EFFECT (£ BILLION) |
|---|---|---|---|
| 2011 Q1 | 5.5 | 5.9 | −0.4 |
| 2012 Q1 |  |  |  |
| 2013 Q1 |  |  |  |

Average seasonal effect =

**(d)** Use your answer to (c) to predict the value of online sales for Quarter 1 in 2014.

© AQA 2016

**5.** A firm produces tins of baked beans. For quality control purposes, a sample of five tins of baked beans is taken every hour and the mass of each tin is measured.

The mean mass and range of masses of each sample is calculated and plotted on separate graphs.

The graphs below show the mean mass and range of masses of the first seven samples.

The eighth sample has tins of baked beans of the following masses:

| 1.072 kg | 0.998 kg | 1.024 kg | 1.037 kg | 1.046 kg |

The mean mass of this sample is 1.0354 kg.

**(a)** Calculate the range of masses of this sample.

**(b)** Plot the values of the eighth sample on a copy of the appropriate graphs.

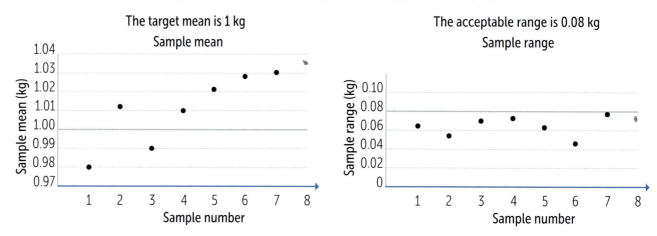

**(c)** Make one comment on each graph in relation to the production process.

**6.** The owner of a small cinema changed the film show every three weeks. He recorded the attendance at the cinema each week for ten weeks. His results are given in the table.

| WEEK NUMBER | ATTENDANCE | THREE-POINT MOVING AVERAGE |
|---|---|---|
| 1 | 382 | |
| 2 | 356 | 336 |
| 3 | 270 | ✗ 0 |
| 4 | 394 | 342 |
| 5 | 362 | 352 |
| 6 | 300 | 375 |
| 7 | 463 | 380 |
| 8 | 377 | 385 |
| 9 | 315 | 399 |
| 10 | 505 | |

Some of the three-point moving average values for the attendance figures have been calculated.

**(a)** Calculate the three missing values.

**(b)** Why is it appropriate to calculate three-point moving average values?

(c) Plot the data and moving average values on a time series graph.

(d) (i) Draw a trend line on the graph.

   (ii) Comment on what your trend line shows.

   (iii) Give a reason why this trend may not be expected to continue.

7. The number of weddings, in thousands, for 14 consecutive quarters are given in the table. Some of the four-point moving averages have been calculated.

| YEAR | QUARTER | NUMBER OF WEDDINGS (THOUSANDS) | FOUR-POINT MOVING AVERAGE (1dp) |
|------|---------|-------------------------------|-------------------------------|
| 1996 | 1 | 41.0 | |
| 1996 | 2 | 91.4 | |
| | | | 79.4 |
| 1996 | 3 | 129.4 | |
| | | | 79.0 |
| 1996 | 4 | 55.8 | |
| | | | 77.9 |
| 1997 | 1 | 39.3 | |
| | | | 77.8 |
| 1997 | 2 | 87.1 | |
| | | | 77.6 |
| 1997 | 3 | 128.9 | |
| | | | 77.2 |
| 1997 | 4 | 54.9 | |
| | | | 76.8 |
| 1997 | 1 | 37.7 | |
| | | | 75.9 |
| 1998 | 2 | 85.6 | |
| | | | 76.2 |
| 1998 | 3 | 125.5 | |
| 1998 | 4 | 56.0 | |
| 1999 | 1 | 36.9 | |
| 1999 | 2 | 83.2 | |

(a) Calculate the value of the next two four-point moving averages.

(b) The original data is plotted on the grid on the right. Copy and plot all the four-point moving averages on the same grid.

(c) The seasonal variations for Quarter 3 are 52 000, 52 000, and 49 000.

Use this information together with a trend line to obtain an estimate for the number of weddings in Quarter 3 of 1999.

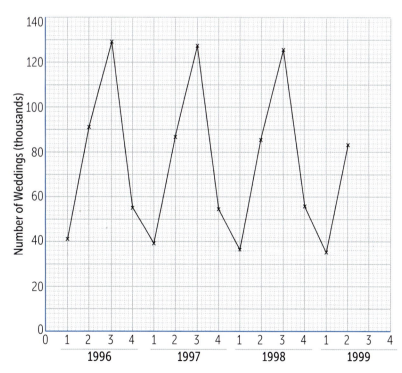

**8.** The number of sales made by a shop from 1999 to 2001 are given in the table below.

| PERIOD | SALES (1000s) | THREE-POINT MOVING AVERAGE |
|---|---|---|
| Jan—Apr 1999 | 30 | |
| May—Aug 1999 | 27 | 30 |
| Sept—Dec 1999 | 33 | 31 |
| Jan—Apr 2000 | 33 | 33 |
| May—Aug 2000 | 30 | 33.3 |
| Sept—Dec 2000 | 37 | 34.3 |
| Jan—Apr 2001 | 36 | |
| May—Aug 2001 | 32 | |
| Sept—Dec 2001 | 40 | |

**(a)** Give **one** reason why three-point moving averages are appropiate.

**(b)** Calculate the value of the next two moving averages.

**(c)** Calculate the average seasonal variation for the periods May-August.

**(d)** Draw the graph below and plot all the three-point moving averages.

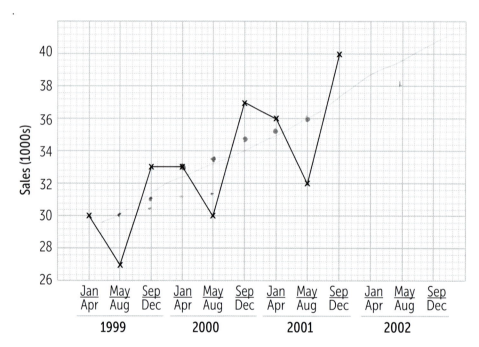

**(e)** Predict the sales for May to August 2002.

**9. (a)** Here are four numbers.

1.2    1.4    0.9    1.3

Work out how much larger the mean of these numbers is than the geometric mean.

You **must** show your working.

Give your answer to 3 decimal places.

**(b)** Zoe buys a painting.

The value of the painting:

increases by 20% in Year 1

increases by 40% in Year 2

**decreases** by 10% in Year 3

increases by 30% in Year 4

Use your working in **part (a)** to write down the average percentage increase in the value of the painting per year.

© AQA 2018

# 8 | Cumulative Frequency

## In this chapter you will learn to:

Draw and interpret cumulative frequency diagrams for continuous or discrete data

Calculate or estimate a median from a cumulative frequency table or diagram

Calculate or estimate a percentile

**HIGHER TIER** Calculate or estimate a percentile range

**HIGHER TIER** Calculate or estimate the interquartile range from a cumulative frequency table or diagram

**HIGHER TIER** Calculate or estimate an interpercentile range

## New Vocabulary

**Cumulative frequency**

**Cumulative frequency diagram**

**Cumulative frequency curve**

**Cumulative frequency polygon**

**Cumulative frequency step polygon**

**Percentile**

**Decile**

**Interdecile range**

**Interpercentile range**

When data are in a table, there is a frequency column that tells you how many times each value has occurred. Sometimes it is helpful for us to have a running total of how many values have occurred **so far**. This is called **cumulative frequency**. When we use cumulative frequency, we add on each new frequency to the one before and end up with the total number of values in the final row.

This table shows information about the maximum temperature for 30 days.

| TEMPERATURE, $t$ (°C) | FREQUENCY |
|---|---|
| $0 \leq t \leq 10$ | 4 |
| $10 < t \leq 14$ | 5 |
| $14 < t \leq 18$ | 11 |
| $18 < t \leq 22$ | 5 |
| $22 < t \leq 30$ | 3 |
| $30 < t \leq 35$ | 2 |

If we want to change this to a cumulative frequency table, as well as adding up the frequencies as we go down the table, we need to slightly alter the label for each group. The first group can remain the same (or alter in keeping with the rest of the table), but the next row will contain everything up to (and including) 14, and the row below that, everything up to 18, etc.

| TEMPERATURE, $t$ (°C) | FREQUENCY | CUMULATIVE FREQUENCY |
|---|---|---|
| $t \leq 10$ | 4 | 4 |
| $t \leq 14$ | 5 | (4 + 5 =) 9 |
| $t \leq 18$ | 11 | (9 + 11 =) 20 |
| $t \leq 22$ | 5 | (20 + 5 =) 25 |
| $t \leq 30$ | 3 | (25 + 3 =) 28 |
| $t \leq 35$ | 2 | (28 + 2 =) 30 |

**advice**

*It's a good idea to always check that the final value is equal to the total you are expecting (this might help you spot a potential error).*

**advice**

*You can see that the temperature column now has the upper class boundary in each row.*

# Cumulative frequency diagrams

A **cumulative frequency diagram** will not look like any other kind of graph you've drawn so far. There are two types of cumulative frequency diagrams for continuous data: a **cumulative frequency curve** (points joined by a smooth curve) and a **cumulative frequency polygon** (points joined by straight lines). If you are asked to draw a "cumulative frequency curve" or "cumulative frequency polygon" you should produce the diagram required, but usually you are simply asked for a "cumulative frequency diagram" so you may use either.

**advice**

*The cumulative frequency axis will always be the vertical axis.*

**advice**

*Whether you draw a cumulative frequency curve or a cumulative frequency polygon, each graph will be the shape of a stretched out S — always moving to the right and upwards (even if only a small amount). If your graph goes down or to the left, it has been drawn incorrectly.*

**advice**

*This is a different sort of polygon to those we see in maths. We are not wanting to see a closed shape here; there is no need to join the ends of your graph to anything else.*

## EXAMPLE

To draw a cumulative frequency curve for the temperature data, we have to plot the values from the cumulative frequency table at the upper bound values, i.e. at (10, 4), (14, 9), (18, 20), etc. Here, we also know from the original table that there are no values below zero, so we can join the curve back to (0, 0). This might not always be possible.

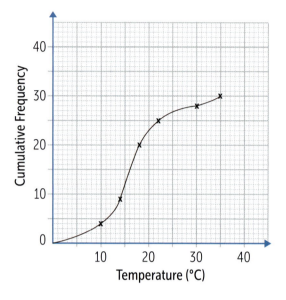

To draw a cumulative frequency polygon for the temperature data, we still have to plot the values from the cumulative frequency table, i.e., at (10, 4), (14, 9), (18, 20), but we will join these points with straight lines. As before, you can join this back to (0, 0) as we know there is no data below that.

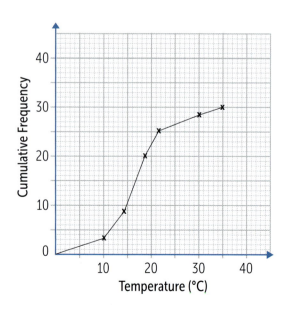

For *discrete* data, there is only one kind of cumulative frequency diagram that can be drawn: a **cumulative frequency step polygon**. As the name suggests, the graph will look like a series of steps (not necessarily each the same height) with the data points joined vertically and horizontally, rather than diagonally. This is because there are no intermediate values between those given, so a diagonal line or curve would have no meaning.

## EXAMPLE

The table shows the grades achieved by class 11P in a recent geography test.

| GRADE | 3 | 4 | 5 | 6 | 7 | 8 | 9 |
|---|---|---|---|---|---|---|---|
| FREQUENCY | 1 | 2 | 3 | 6 | 12 | 7 | 3 |

Draw a cumulative frequency step polygon to represent the data.

## SOLUTION

The table will look more familiar if we rewrite it in columns, rather than rows.

We can then include a cumulative frequency column.

| FREQUENCY | CUMULATIVE FREQUENCY |
|---|---|
| 1 | 1 |
| 2 | 3 |
| 3 | 6 |
| 6 | 12 |
| 12 | 24 |
| 7 | 31 |
| 3 | 34 |

Next we should plot the points. The points are then joined in "steps".

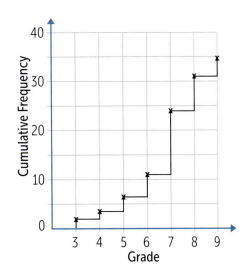

**advice**

*Note that the steps appear to end in mid-air. This is correct and they do not need joining back to an axis apart from the initial line (as we know that no one achieved less than grade 3).*

Choosing the correct type of graph is essential and you must think about whether the data are discrete or continuous.

Continuous data $\rightarrow$ cumulative frequency curve or cumulative frequency polygon

Discrete data $\rightarrow$ cumulative frequency step polygon

## EXERCISE 1

advice

*Each point is plotted at the upper end of each interval.*

1. The frequency table shows information about the cost of 20 holidays (to the nearest £).

| COST, C (£) | FREQUENCY |
|---|---|
| $0 \leq C \leq 200$ | 2 |
| $200 < C \leq 300$ | 3 |
| $300 < C \leq 400$ | 5 |
| $400 < C \leq 500$ | 6 |
| $500 < C \leq 600$ | 2 |
| $600 < C \leq 700$ | 1 |
| $700 < C \leq 800$ | 1 |

Create a cumulative frequency table for the data.

2. The frequency table shows information about the number of goals Sal has scored in 25 hockey matches.

Complete the cumulative frequency table.

| NUMBER OF GOALS | FREQUENCY |
|---|---|
| 0 | 5 |
| 1 | 4 |
| 2 | 2 |
| 3 | 1 |
| 4 | 6 |
| 5 | 3 |
| 6 | 4 |

| NUMBER OF GOALS | CUMULATIVE FREQUENCY |
|---|---|
| 0 | |
| $\leq 1$ | |
| $\leq 2$ | |
| $\leq 3$ | |
| $\leq 4$ | |
| $\leq 5$ | |
| $\leq 6$ | |

3. The frequency table shows information about the heights of some tomato plants (to the nearest cm).

| HEIGHT OF PLANT, h (CM) | FREQUENCY |
|---|---|
| $0 \leq h \leq 10$ | 6 |
| $10 < h \leq 15$ | 14 |
| $15 < h \leq 20$ | 16 |
| $20 < h \leq 25$ | 5 |
| $25 < h \leq 30$ | 1 |
| $30 < h \leq 40$ | 2 |
| $40 < h \leq 50$ | 1 |

**a.** Create a cumulative frequency table for the data.

**b.** Draw a cumulative frequency curve to show the data.

**4.** The table shows information about the times taken to complete a 5-km run.

| TIME TAKEN, $t$ (MINUTES) | FREQUENCY |
|---|---|
| $20 \leq t \leq 25$ | 5 |
| $25 < t \leq 28$ | 25 |
| $28 < t \leq 30$ | 45 |
| $30 < t \leq 32$ | 38 |
| $32 < t \leq 35$ | 64 |
| $35 < t \leq 40$ | 19 |
| $40 < t \leq 50$ | 4 |

**a.** Create a cumulative frequency table for the data.

**b.** Draw a cumulative frequency curve to show the data.

**c.** Runners who finished in under 29 minutes were awarded a certificate. Estimate the percentage of runners awarded a certificate.

**d.** Why is your answer to part c an estimate?

**5.** The table shows information about how many metres of ribbon are used on the costumes Torquil designs.

| NUMBER OF METRES OF RIBBON, $r$ | FREQUENCY |
|---|---|
| $0 \leq r \leq 10$ | 4 |
| $10 < r \leq 20$ | 10 |
| $20 < r \leq 30$ | 11 |
| $30 < r \leq 40$ | 18 |
| $40 < r \leq 50$ | 7 |

Draw a cumulative frequency polygon to show the data.

**6.** The table shows the number of goals in each game of a knockout tournament for football.

| NUMBER OF GOALS | FREQUENCY |
|---|---|
| 0 | 11 |
| 1 | 2 |
| 2 | 6 |
| 3 | 6 |
| 4 | 2 |
| 5 | 3 |

**a.** Explain why a cumulative frequency curve is **not** appropriate for these data.

**b.** Draw a cumulative frequency step polygon to show the data.

**7.** Lili-Mai is completing a word search puzzle. The table shows the number of letters in the words she has to find.

| NUMBER OF LETTERS | FREQUENCY |
|---|---|
| 4 | 16 |
| 5 | 12 |
| 6 | 6 |
| 7 | 8 |
| 8 | 2 |
| 9 | 15 |
| 10 | 3 |
| 11 | 1 |

Draw an appropriate cumulative frequency diagram to show the data.

**8.** This cumulative frequency diagram shows the lengths of time that some audio books last.

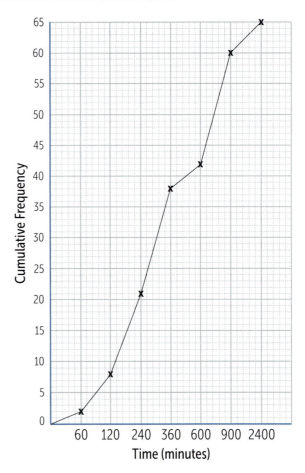

**a.** How many hours could the longest book last?

**b.** Explain why it is not appropriate to draw a frequency step polygon for this data.

**c.** How many audio books were represented on the cumulative frequency diagram?

**d.** Which group contained the fewest audio books?

**e.** Elias says that the largest number of books were in the $120 < t \leq 240$ group. Is he correct? Give a reason for your answer.

**9.** Humphrey has asked people on a bus how many cars are owned by people in their household.

| NUMBER OF CARS OWNED | FREQUENCY |
|---|---|
| 0 | 3 |
| 1 | 8 |
| 2 | 15 |
| 3 | 0 |
| 4 | 2 |
| 5 | 1 |
| 6 | 1 |

Humphrey drew this cumulative frequency graph for the data. Identify three errors in his work.

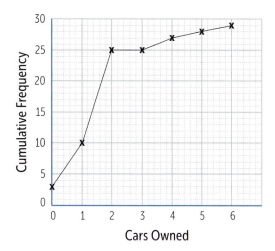

# Median and interquartile range from cumulative frequency diagrams

You've already seen how to calculate the median and interquartile range from frequency tables. If you are given a cumulative frequency diagram, it's very easy to read off the median and interquartile range. The median is the middle value of the ordered data. In a cumulative frequency graph, the data is already in order, so we just have to read off the half-way value. The interquartile range is the difference between the one-quarter value and the three-quarter value, and these can be read off one-quarter of the way up the graph and three-quarters of the way up the graph. Note that these values will all be estimates as we don't know the exact values in these graphs.

advice

*On cumulative frequency graphs, we are nearly always dealing with large numbers of values. We therefore don't need to worry about adding 1 before halving or quartering the number of values to get the position of the median or quartiles (they are estimates anyway).*

## EXAMPLE

Estimate the median and interquartile range for the temperature data used at the start of this chapter. Here is the data again.

| TEMPERATURE, $t$ (°C) | FREQUENCY |
|---|---|
| $0 \leq t \leq 10$ | 4 |
| $10 < t \leq 14$ | 5 |
| $14 < t \leq 18$ | 11 |
| $18 < t \leq 22$ | 5 |
| $22 < t \leq 30$ | 3 |
| $30 < t \leq 35$ | 2 |

Here is the cumulative frequency curve again.

We can see from the table or the graph that there are 30 temperatures represented. The median therefore will be at 15, so we go across from 15 on the vertical axis and when we hit the graph, we follow this down to read off the median value.

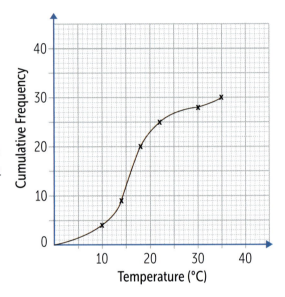

If you follow the pink line across at 15 and down to the temperature axis, you can see that the median temperature is estimated to be 15°C.

In the same way, we can work out an estimate for the interquartile range by finding the one-quarter and three-quarter values (also called the lower and upper quartiles). These will be at 7.5 and 22.5 and once found, we subtract the lower value from the upper value.

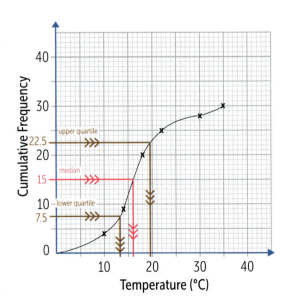

Following the brown lines this time, the upper quartile temperature is 20°C and the lower quartile temperature is 13°C, making the interquartile range: 20 − 13 = 7°C.

You can also read off a **percentile** from a cumulative frequency graph. Just as quartiles split the data into quarters, percentiles split the data into 100 equal parts. To read off the 88$^{th}$ percentile, you will need to read off 88% of the way up the vertical axis.

## EXAMPLE

For the cumulative frequency graph we have just been using, 88% of the 30 temperatures would be at $\frac{88}{100} \times 30 = 26.4$

We need to read off at 26.4 on the vertical axis and follow this down to the horizontal axis to get the answer.

Therefore an estimate for the 86$^{th}$ percentile is 26°C.

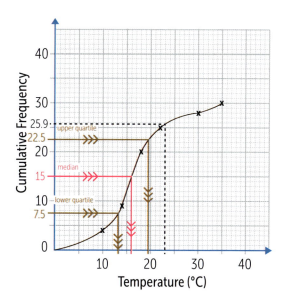

**advice**

*If you carry out these calculations on the cumulative frequency curve and on the cumulative frequency polygon for the same data set, you may end up with slightly different answers because of the different slopes between the points. Don't worry, this is perfectly normal and either answer is acceptable (whereas calculations from a step polygon are exact).*

## EXERCISE 2

1. **a.** Draw a cumulative frequency curve for the data in Question 1 of Exercise 1.

   **b.** Use your cumulative frequency curve to estimate the median cost.

2. **a.** Draw a cumulative frequency step polygon for the data in Question 2 of Exercise 1.

   **b.** Use your cumulative frequency step polygon to calculate the median number of goals.

3. **a.** Create a cumulative frequency diagram for the data in Question 4 of Exercise 1.

   **b.** Use your diagram to estimate the median time taken.

   **c.** Use your diagram to work out an estimate for the interquartile range.

**4.** The table shows information about how long it took the students from both of Miss Woods's maths classes to travel to school yesterday.

| TIME TAKEN, $t$ (MINUTES) | FREQUENCY |
|---|---|
| $0 \leq t \leq 5$ | 12 |
| $5 < t \leq 10$ | 3 |
| $10 < t \leq 15$ | 18 |
| $15 < t \leq 20$ | 5 |
| $20 < t \leq 25$ | 14 |
| $25 < t \leq 30$ | 3 |
| $30 < t \leq 60$ | 1 |

Pawel has drawn this cumulative frequency diagram to show the times.

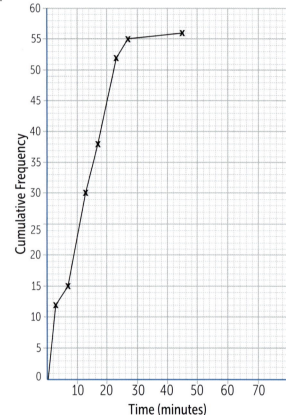

**a.** Explain the two things Pawel has done wrong when drawing the graph.

**b.** Draw a correct cumulative frequency diagram for these times.

**c.** Use your correct graph to estimate the median and interquartile range for these times.

**d.** Miss Woods says, "Half the classes' times were under 14 minutes." Use your graph to discuss her statement.

**5.** The table shows the numbers of dogs in a park on different days in April when Thaddius takes his dog for a walk.

| NUMBER OF DOGS | FREQUENCY |
|:---:|:---:|
| 0 | 3 |
| 1 | 7 |
| 2 | 12 |
| 3 | 4 |
| 4 | 3 |
| 5 | 1 |

   **a.** Draw an appropriate cumulative frequency diagram to show the data.

   **b.** Use your diagram to calculate the median number of dogs.

   **c.** Use your diagram to work out the interquartile range.

**6.** Use this cumulative frequency diagram to create a box plot for the same data. The range of temperatures was 35°C.

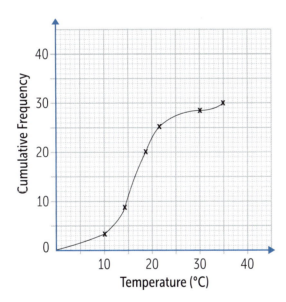

**7.** Here is the data for the results of the Class 10C chemistry test.

| SCORE, $s$ (cm) | FREQUENCY |
|:---:|:---:|
| $0 \leq s \leq 30$ | 14 |
| $30 < s \leq 40$ | 5 |
| $40 < s \leq 50$ | 3 |
| $50 < s \leq 55$ | 5 |
| $55 < s \leq 60$ | 1 |
| $60 < s \leq 70$ | 4 |

   **a.** Draw a cumulative frequency polygon to show the results.

**b.** Miss Muffet sets a pass mark of 52 for the test. Use your cumulative frequency polygon to estimate how many people passed the test.

**c.** The students with the bottom 15% of scores were given a detention. Estimate the 15th percentile from the graph.

**8.** The table shows information about the ages of people on the train departing Longfield at 8 a.m.

| AGE, $a$ (YEARS) | FREQUENCY |
|---|---|
| $0 \leq a \leq 10$ | 4 |
| $10 < a \leq 20$ | 21 |
| $20 < a \leq 40$ | 33 |
| $40 < a \leq 50$ | 10 |
| $50 < a \leq 70$ | 54 |
| $70 < a \leq 100$ | 3 |

**a.** Draw a cumulative frequency diagram to show the ages.

**b.** This box plot shows information about the ages of people on the train departing Retford at 8 a.m.

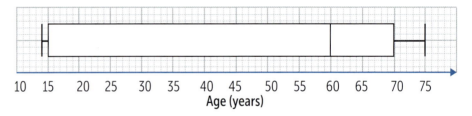

Age (years)

**c.** Compare the ages of the people on the two trains.

**d.** Bartholomew says that the oldest person on these two trains must be on the Longfield train. Is he correct? Explain your decision.

**9.** Viktor does a lot of shopping online during December. The table shows information about the numbers of parcels that arrive at his home each day from the 1st to the 24th December.

| NUMBER OF PARCELS, $p$ | FREQUENCY |
|---|---|
| 0 | 2 |
| 1 | 5 |
| 2 | 1 |
| 3 | 6 |
| 4 | 3 |
| 5 | 1 |
| 6 | 0 |
| 7 | 2 |
| 8 | 3 |
| 9 | 0 |
| 10 | 1 |

**a.** Draw a cumulative frequency diagram to show the data.

**b.** Use your diagram to work out the median number of parcels.

**c.** Stan has also been shopping online during December. Use this box plot, showing information about his parcel deliveries each day, to compare the numbers of parcels for the two shoppers.

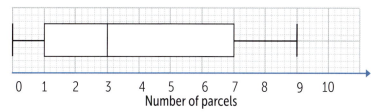

# Further calculations from cumulative frequency diagrams

In Higher Tier, as well as reading quartiles and percentiles from a cumulative frequency graph, you will also need to read **deciles**. Just as percentiles split the data into 100 equal groups, deciles split the data into 10 equal groups. The first decile will be at $\frac{1}{10}$ of the way through the data and will coincide with the $10^{\text{th}}$ percentile $\left(\frac{1}{10} = \frac{10}{100}\right)$. The median will coincide with the $5^{\text{th}}$ decile and the $50^{\text{th}}$ percentile. Just as with quartiles, you should go from the vertical axis, across to the graph, and down to read off the answer from the horizontal axis. As before, where these are continuous graphs, values are estimates.

The deciles can be shown with special notation to make them easier to write down, e.g. the $8^{\text{th}}$ decile can be written as $D_8$ and the $3^{\text{rd}}$ decile as $D_3$. You can use similar notation for percentiles, so the $64^{\text{th}}$ percentile would be written as $P_{64}$.

If you think about it, the interquartile range only uses the central 50% of the data, ignoring the rest.

We can still leave out the very extremes, but use far more of the data if we use interdecile or **interpercentile ranges**.

e.g.  $D_9 - D_1$ uses 80% of the data

$P_{95} - P_5$ uses 90% of the data

The advantage over range and standard deviation remain, but the sizes of a much wider part of the data are considered.

**advice**

*An* **interdecile range** *will require you to read off at each given decile and subtract. These may or may not be symmetrical about the median, e.g.* $D_9 - D_1$ *is symmetrical* $D_8 - D_1$ *is not symmetrical.*

**advice**

*You will learn about standard deviation in Chapter 12.*

## EXAMPLE

The table shows information about the distance travelled each day by a salesman.

**a.** Draw a cumulative frequency polygon for the data.

**b.** Use the diagram to work out an estimate of the interdecile range between the 1st and 7th deciles.

| DISTANCE, $m$ (MILES) | FREQUENCY |
|---|---|
| $0 \leq m \leq 10$ | 1 |
| $10 < m \leq 20$ | 6 |
| $20 < m \leq 40$ | 14 |
| $40 < m \leq 50$ | 10 |
| $50 < m \leq 70$ | 7 |
| $70 < m \leq 100$ | 22 |
| $100 < m \leq 150$ | 10 |

## SOLUTION

**a.**

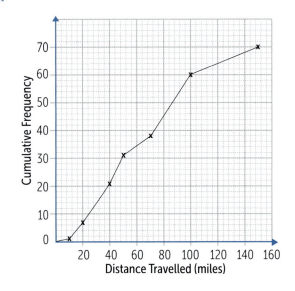

**b.**

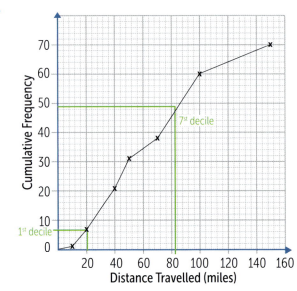

There are 70 distances given, so to find the 1st decile, we have to calculate $\frac{1}{10} \times 70 = 7$.

We read off the 1st decile at 7 to get an answer of 20.

To find the 7th decile, we have to calculate $\frac{7}{10} \times 70 = 49$.

We read off the 7th decile at 49 to get an answer of 84.

The estimate for the interdecile range is then $84 - 20 = 64$.

# Estimating quartiles and percentiles from frequency tables

Earlier in this chapter, we have used frequency tables and cumulative frequency graphs to estimate statistics, such as the median and the interquartile range. You need to be able to interpolate tables in order to estimate deciles, percentiles and their ranges.

### EXAMPLE

The grouped frequency table shows the time taken in hours for an artist, Mark, to produce each of 80 paintings.

| TIME TAKEN, $h$ (HOURS) | FREQUENCY |
|---|---|
| $0 \leq h \leq 20$ | 3 |
| $20 < h \leq 40$ | 17 |
| $40 < h \leq 50$ | 31 |
| $50 < h \leq 60$ | 21 |
| $60 < h \leq 90$ | 8 |

**a.** Use interpolation to calculate an estimate of the 35th percentile.

**b.** Amanda says to Mark that 90% of his paintings are done in less than 55 hours. Comment on her statement.

**c.** Use interpolation to estimate the interdecile range between the 2nd and 8th deciles.

### SOLUTION

**a.** 35% of 80 = 27

We need to find the 27th value in the table.

The first 20 items are in the first two groups, and the 27th item is $\frac{7}{31}$ of the way through the third group.

183

We calculate the lower bound of that group, added on to the estimate of the 7th value in that group:

$40 + 731 \times 10 = 42.26$

**b.** Here we need the 90th percentile (or 9th decile):

90% of 80 = 72, so we need to find the 72nd value in the table. If we use cumulative frequencies, we can see that this is at the upper bound of the penultimate group.

| TIME TAKEN, $h$ (HOURS) | CUMULATIVE FREQUENCY |
|:---:|:---:|
| $h \leq 20$ | 3 |
| $h \leq 40$ | 20 |
| $h \leq 50$ | 51 |
| $h \leq 60$ | 72 |
| $h \leq 90$ | 90 |

Amanda's statement is incorrect, 90% of Mark's paintings are completed in less than 60 hours.

**c.** Here we need to find the values of the 2nd and 8th deciles and then find their difference.

2nd decile: $20 + 1317 \times 20 = 35.2941$

8th decile: $50 + 1321 \times 10 = 56.1905$

Difference between: $56.1905 - 35.2941 = 20.896$

**HIGHER TIER**

## EXERCISE 3

**1.** Which of the following statements are true?

    **a.** The 7th decile is equal to the upper quartile.

    **b.** The lower quartile is equal to the 2nd decile.

    **c.** The interquartile range can also be found from the 75th and 25th percentile.

    **d.** The 5th decile is equal to the interquartile range.

    **e.** The interquartile range will contain as much data as the difference between the 80th percentile and the 3rd decile.

**2.** The table shows information about the times taken to complete a 5-km run.

| TIME TAKEN, $t$ (MINUTES) | FREQUENCY |
|---|---|
| $20 \leq t \leq 25$ | 8 |
| $25 < t \leq 28$ | 22 |
| $28 < t \leq 30$ | 40 |
| $30 < t \leq 32$ | 43 |
| $32 < t \leq 35$ | 50 |
| $35 < t \leq 40$ | 33 |
| $40 < t \leq 50$ | 4 |

**a.** Create a cumulative frequency diagram for the data.

**b.** Use your diagram to calculate an estimate of the interpercentile range between the 15th and 65th percentiles.

**c.** Use your diagram to calculate an estimate of the interdecile range between the 4th and 6th deciles.

**3.** Avtar catches a train to work. She often encounters delays on the journey and can claim compensation, depending on how long the delay is. She keeps a note of how long each delay is during June.

| DELAY, $t$ (MINUTES) | FREQUENCY |
|---|---|
| $0 \leq t \leq 5$ | 11 |
| $5 < t \leq 10$ | 4 |
| $10 < t \leq 15$ | 4 |
| $15 < t \leq 20$ | 3 |
| $20 < t \leq 40$ | 7 |
| $40 < t \leq 60$ | 1 |

**a.** Draw an appropriate cumulative frequency diagram for the data.

**b.** Avtar can claim compensation if her journey is delayed for more than 30 minutes. Use your diagram to estimate the number of journeys that will qualify for compensation.

**c.** Work out an estimate of the interdecile range between the 3rd and 9th deciles.

**d.** Avtar says that her train was late by more than 35 minutes on 3 days. Use your graph to decide whether she is likely to be correct. Give a reason for your answer.

**4.** Here are four cumulative frequency diagrams on the same scale.

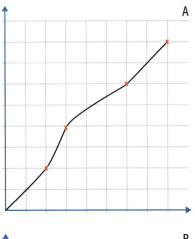

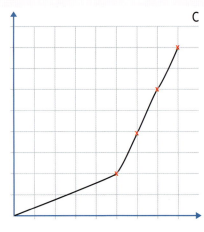

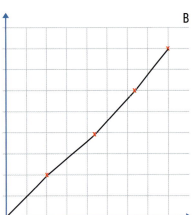

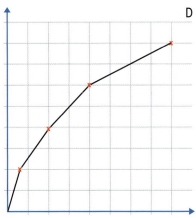

Here are four box plots.

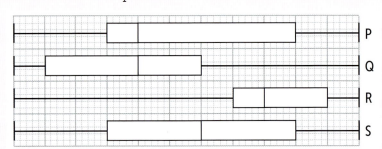

Match each cumulative frequency curve to the corresponding box plot.

**5.** Stefani has 90 apples from her garden. She has weighed each one. The table shows her results.

| MASS, $m$ (GRAMS) | FREQUENCY |
|---|---|
| $0 \leq m \leq 5$ | 5 |
| $5 < m \leq 10$ | 11 |
| $10 < m \leq 15$ | 27 |
| $15 < m \leq 20$ | 24 |
| $20 < m \leq 40$ | 10 |
| $40 < m \leq 60$ | 13 |

**a.** Draw a cumulative frequency diagram to show the data.

**b.** Use your diagram to estimate the median mass of an apple.

**c.** Use your diagram to find an estimate of the interpercentile range between the 25th and 80th percentiles.

**6.** Ricardo enjoys going to the cinema. The table shows the lengths of films he has seen recently.

| LENGTH OF FILM, $f$ (MINUTES) | FREQUENCY |
|---|---|
| $60 \le f \le 70$ | 4 |
| $70 < f \le 90$ | 6 |
| $90 < f \le 100$ | 25 |
| $100 < f \le 110$ | 7 |
| $110 < f \le 120$ | 5 |
| $120 < f \le 140$ | 1 |
| $140 < f \le 160$ | 2 |

**a.** Draw a cumulative frequency diagram to show the film times.

**b.** Use your diagram to work out an estimate of the interdecile range $D_7 - D_2$.

**c.** Use your graph to draw a box plot. The minimum length film was 63 minutes and the maximum length film was 155 minutes.

**7.** Lou loves jelly babies, especially the red ones.

She opens some packets and counts (and eats!) all the red ones.

The table shows the number of packets with certain numbers of red jelly babies.

| NUMBER OF RED JELLY BABIES | FREQUENCY |
|---|---|
| 1 | 1 |
| 5 | 1 |
| 6 | 3 |
| 7 | 8 |
| 8 | 15 |
| 9 | 8 |
| 10 | 9 |
| 11 | 4 |
| 12 | 3 |
| 15 | 2 |

**a.** Draw an appropriate cumulative frequency diagram

for these data.

**b.** From your diagram, work out the median and interquartile range.

**c.** Are the values of 1 and 15 outliers? Justify your decision.

**d.** Work out an appropriate symmetrical interpercentile range as wide as possible but which will not include any outliers.

**8.** Sarah-Jane sells scented wax to be used in warmers. As part of her market research, she asks her customers to record how long they use their warmers for (in minutes) one day. The results are shown in the grouped frequency table:

| TIME, $m$ (MINUTES) | FREQUENCY |
|---|---|
| $0 \le m \le 20$ | 3 |
| $20 < m \le 40$ | 17 |
| $40 < m \le 50$ | 31 |
| $50 < m \le 60$ | 21 |
| $60 < m \le 90$ | 8 |

**a.** Use interpolation to calculate an estimate of the 3rd decile.

**b.** Use interpolation to calculate an estimate of the 69th percentile.

**9.** Mr Moore sets a piece of maths homework and asks his students to record how long, in minutes, the homework takes to complete. The grouped frequency table shows the results.

| TIME, $m$ (MINUTES) | FREQUENCY |
|---|---|
| $0 \le m \le 10$ | 2 |
| $10 < m \le 20$ | 3 |
| $20 < m \le 30$ | 6 |
| $30 < m \le 40$ | 9 |
| $40 < m \le 50$ | 7 |
| $50 < m \le 60$ | 2 |
| $60 < m \le 120$ | 1 |

**a.** Use interpolation to calculate an estimate of the 73rd percentile.

**b.** Mr. Moore says that 85% of the class had completed the homework in less than 45 minutes. Comment on Mr. Moore's statement.

**c.** Use interpolation to calculate an estimate of the inter-percentile range between the 35th and 65th percentiles.

# You should now be able to:

Draw and interpret cumulative frequency diagrams for continuous or discrete data

Calculate or estimate a median from a cumulative frequency table or diagram

Calculate or estimate a percentile

(HIGHER TIER) **Calculate or estimate a percentile range**

(HIGHER TIER) **Calculate or estimate the interquartile range from a cumulative frequency table or diagram**

(HIGHER TIER) **Calculate or estimate an interpercentile range**

# Exam Practice Questions

**1.** Heights of 50 trees in a wood are recorded in the frequency distribution:

| HEIGHT, $h$ (m) | FREQUENCY |
|---|---|
| $0 < x \leq 2$ | 3 |
| $2 < x \leq 4$ | 9 |
| $4 < x \leq 6$ | 15 |
| $6 < x \leq 8$ | 12 |
| $8 < x \leq 10$ | 7 |
| $10 < x \leq 12$ | 4 |

Use a **graphical** method to estimate the median of the distribution.

**2.** The graph shows the diameters (mm) of 60 bolts manufactured in a factory.

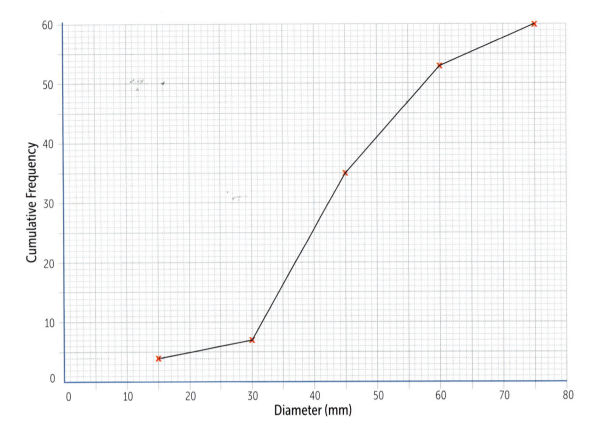

(a) Estimate the median diameter of one of the bolts.

(b) Write down the number of bolts with a diameter of 55 mm or less.

(c) Write down the probability that a bolt chosen at random has a diameter of 45 mm or less.

**3.** A doctor asked 100 patients how much time they had waited in the waiting room for their appointment.

The table shows the results.

| WAIT TIME, $t$ (MINUTES) | FREQUENCY | CUMULATIVE FREQUENCY |
|---|---|---|
| $0 \leq t < 10$ | 23 | 23 |
| $10 \leq t < 20$ | 31 | 54 |
| $20 \leq t < 30$ | 36 | 90 |
| $30 \leq t < 40$ | 6 | 96 |
| $40 \leq t < 50$ | 4 | 100 |

(a) Write down the modal class.

(b) Copy and complete the cumulative frequency column in the table above.

(c) Draw a cumulative frequency graph to show the data.

(d) Use the graph to estimate the median wait time.

(e) Estimate the number of patients waiting more than 25 minutes.

© AQA 2017

**4.** Pat and Nisha are investigating the distance that people live from their nearest postbox.

Pat designs the data collection sheet below to record data for a sample of 100 people living in **towns**.

| DISTANCE FROM NEAREST POSTBOX, $d$ (METRES) | TALLY | FREQUENCY |
|---|---|---|
| $0 < d \leq 100$ | | |
| $100 < d \leq 200$ | | |
| $200 < d \leq 300$ | | |
| $300 < d \leq 400$ | | |
| $400 < d \leq 500$ | | |
| $d > 500$ | | |

Pat found that in towns nobody lived further than 500 metres from a postbox. His results are shown in the frequency polygon.

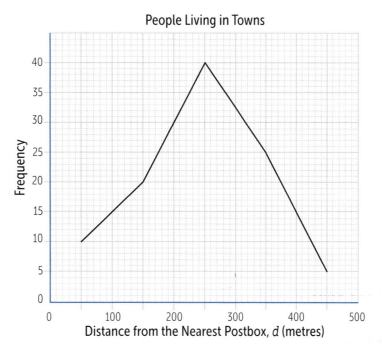

(a) Draw a cumulative frequency graph to show the information for the 100 people living in towns.

(b) Estimate the median and the interquartile range for the distance from the nearest postbox.

(c) Nisha collects data from people living in the **countryside**.

She finds that for people living in the countryside:

The median distance from the nearest postbox is 340 metres.

The interquartile range for the distance is 410 metres.

Use this information and part (c) to compare the distance from the nearest postbox for people living in towns with the distance for people living in the countryside.

© AQA 2017

**5.** Matt owns a lorry company.

He regularly sends lorries from his depot to Dover.

He records the amount of fuel used (litres) for a sample of 120 of these journeys.

His results are shown in the table.

**(a)** Copy and complete the cumulative frequency column below.

| AMOUNT OF FUEL USED x (LITRES) | FREQUENCY | CUMULATIVE FREQUENCY |
|---|---|---|
| $40 < x \leq 50$ | 8 | 8 |
| $50 < x \leq 60$ | 22 | 30 |
| $60 < x \leq 70$ | 50 | |
| $70 < x \leq 80$ | 26 | |
| $80 < x \leq 90$ | 10 | |
| $90 < x \leq 100$ | 4 | |

**(b)** Draw a cumulative frequency graph to show the data.

**(c)** The company has a target that at least three-quarters of the trips to Dover should use 75 litres of fuel or less.

Do the data suggest that the company's target is being met?

Show how you worked out your answer.

HIGHER TIER

**(d)** Work out the interpercentile range between the 10th and 90th percentiles.

**(e)** Write down **one** advantage of using the interpercentile range as a measure of spread rather than the range.

© AQA 2015

**6.** The table shows the number of times a sample of Year 11 students checked their e-mails last Tuesday.

| NUMBER OF TIMES CHECKED E-MAILS | NUMBER OF STUDENTS |
|---|---|
| 0 | 20 |
| 1 | 23 |
| 2 | 16 |
| 3 | 11 |
| 4 | 9 |
| 5 | 0 |
| 6 | 5 |
| 7 | 4 |
| 8 | 2 |
| Total | 90 |

(a) Draw a cumulative frequency step polygon for the data.

(b) (i) Work out the median.

HIGHER TIER     (ii) Work out the range between the 3rd and 8th decile.

7. A dry cleaning company records the number of items of clothing customers bring in to its shop for cleaning.

The company had 90 customers last week.

| NUMBER OF ITEMS OF CLOTHING | FREQUENCY |
|:---:|:---:|
| 1 | 14 |
| 2 | 20 |
| 3 | 16 |
| 4 | 14 |
| 5 | 6 |
| 6 | 8 |
| 7 | 10 |
| 8 | 2 |

(a) Draw a cumulative frequency step polygon to show the number of items of clothing.

**HIGHER TIER**

(b) Every week the shop has to send a summary report to Head Office. Copy and complete the report form for last week.

---
**Head Office Report Form**

**Week** 20th to 26th June 2016

**Number of items of clothing**

Median ............................

2nd decile = ............................          8th decile = ............................

Range between 2nd and 8th deciles = ............................

---

© AQA 2016

8. Heather has been offered a job at Willows and also a job at Borodars. She decides to compare the wages of the two companies before choosing which job to accept. Both companies have 120 employees.

The wages for each company are represented by the cumulative frequency graphs.

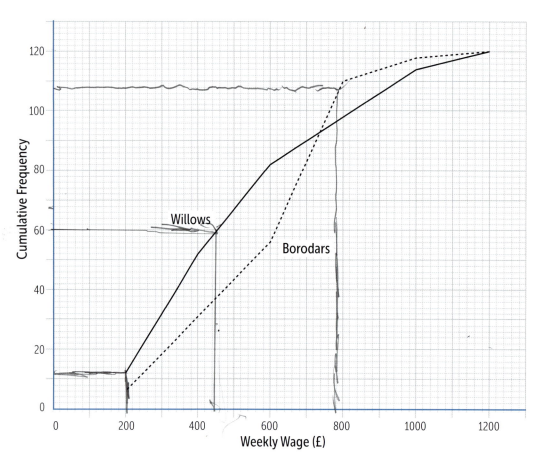

(a) Write down the median wage at Willows.

(b) Estimate the range between the 1st and 9th deciles for the wages at Borodars.

(c) Find the **total** number of employees at both firms who have a weekly wage over £500.

(d) Heather wants to earn at least £400 a week. Which job offer should she accept and why?

**THIS PAGE IS INTENTIONALLY LEFT BLANK**

# 9 | Probability 2

## In this chapter you will learn to:

Calculate an expected frequency

Calculate a relative frequency

Calculate probabilities from tables

Set up and use Venn diagrams

Determine and interpret relative risks

Use formal notation for conditional probability

HIGHER TIER Understand when a binomial distribution can be used

HIGHER TIER Calculate binomial probabilities

HIGHER TIER Calculate in capture-recapture situations

## New Vocabulary

Expectation

Theoretical probability

Experimental probability (relative frequency)

Trial

Venn diagram

Risk

Relative risk

Conditional probability

Binomial distribution

Capture-recapture

# Expectation

If you are using probability to predict future events, you are looking at how many times you **expect** an outcome to occur. To be able to do this, you need to have some theoretical probabilities to work with. When you work out an expected frequency, you multiply the probability of that outcome occurring by the number of trials that will be happening.

When we roll a fair, 6-sided dice, the probability of it landing on any of 1, 2, 3, 4, 5, or 6 is $\frac{1}{6}$.

If we wanted to know how many 5s to expect when we roll the dice 90 times, we calculate:

$\frac{1}{6} \times 90 = 15$

so we can expect to see approximately 15 5s when we roll the dice 90 times.

Of course, we probably won't see exactly 15 5s, due to natural variation, and this doesn't necessarily mean the dice is biased, but there should be *approximately* 15 5s overall. The more trials that are done, the more reliable the results will be. You are much more likely to see the balance of numbers you would expect to see if you have thrown the dice 120 times than if you had thrown it 12 times, and even more likely to see the balance when you've thrown 1200 times!

### EXAMPLE

In an online game, Jak is in a team with 5 of his friends. The game matches them in pairs. The probability that Jak is paired with Suki is $\frac{7}{20}$. Over the next 100 games, how many times should Jak expect to be paired with Suki?

### SOLUTION

$\frac{7}{20} \times 100 = 35$

Over the next 100 games, Jak should expect to be paired with Suki 35 times.

Earlier we talked about results not necessarily matching the expected outcomes often not being a problem. Sometimes however, comparing experimental data with the theoretical expectation *can* identify that the data collection methods may have been biased. For example, the probability of asking a male or a female in a random sample of the UK population should be fairly close to $\frac{1}{2}$, but if you are collecting a sample and you get 85% of one gender, you may well be introducing bias, perhaps in where you are collecting your

advice

*You will not always have a whole number as your answer for an expected number, so be prepared to round up or down as appropriate. This is only an estimate after all!*

data from. For example, if you sampled from only primary school teachers for a hypothesis about the teaching profession, this would be biased, and a higher than expected proportion of females in the sample should raise awareness of this bias.

## EXERCISE 1

1. If you flip a fair coin 500 times, how many heads should you expect?

2. When you roll a fair, 6-sided dice 780 times, how many times should you expect to get a 4?

3. Sienna has 1000 tracks on her Spotify playlist. 240 of these are tracks from the 1960s. She has her playlist on random shuffle. Out of the next 30 tracks that play, how many do you expect will be from the 1960s?

4. When Lucas plays snooker against Miguel, the probability that Lucas wins is 34%. They play four games every week. How many of these games can Lucas expect to win?

5. When Kieron goes to the vending machine at the swimming pool, the probability that they have run out of his favourite drink is 0.26. Kieron goes to the pool and gets a drink from the machine twice every week. Over the whole year, how many times can he expect to get his favourite drink?

6. There are 4 blue and 5 red beads in a box. One is taken out at random, its colour is written down, and then it is put back into the box. Jolene does this 540 times. How many times will she expect:

   a. a red bead

   b. a blue bead

7. Bertie and Sylvie think they have a biased coin. They are flipping the coin and noting down the number of heads and tails.

Bertie goes first and he gets:

| HEADS | TAILS |
|---|---|
| 13 | 17 |

When Sylvie throws, she gets:

| HEADS | TAILS |
|---|---|
| 100 | 200 |

Do you think their coin is biased? Give a reason for your answer.

8. Try this experiment for yourself. Roll a dice 24 times, making a note of each number that appears. Now roll the dice until you have rolled a total of 150 times. How many of each number should you expect to have? How do your results compare? How far away from the expected numbers do you think means it is biased?

9. Keiva is researching the use of social media in adults. She asked a group of retired office workers whether they had a Facebook account. The proportion who did was much lower than previous research showed. Comment on whether you feel the experimental design has led to a bias.

## Experimental probability

All of the probabilities that we have looked at so far have been **theoretical probabilities**; that is to say that "in theory" those things will happen with the calculated probabilities. The calculated probabilities are not guaranteed to happen though. As discussed before, if you play a board game where you need to roll a 6 to start, it can take 20 or 30 rolls sometimes to get that 6; it's not guaranteed to happen within six rolls!

Sometimes it is not possible to use theoretical probability. On these occasions we need to carry out experiments and then calculate **relative frequencies** (often called **experimental probabilities**) from the results. Each time the experiment is repeated is called a **trial** and more trials mean more reliable relative frequencies that can be used to estimate the probabilities.

advice

*These work in the same way as expectation in the previous section. We are now just using "real" data.*

### EXAMPLE

Toby has to drive through the Blackwall Tunnel each day that he works. He records the number of trips and the number of times he gets stuck in traffic.

| Number of trips | 1 | 5 | 10 | 20 | 30 |
|---|---|---|---|---|---|
| Number of times stuck in traffic | 1 | 3 | 7 | 16 | 21 |

What is the estimated probability of Toby getting stuck in traffic the next time he goes through the Blackwall Tunnel?

## SOLUTION

We can work out the relative frequency for each of the recorded number of trips.

| Number of trips | 1 | 5 | 10 | 20 | 30 |
|---|---|---|---|---|---|
| Number of times stuck in traffic | 1 | 3 | 7 | 16 | 21 |
| Relative frequency | $1 \div 1 = 1$ | $3 \div 5 = 0.6$ | $7 \div 10 = 0.7$ | $16 \div 20 = 0.8$ | $21 \div 30 = 0.7$ |

We can see that the relative frequency changes each time it has been calculated, but we need to remember that it is the relative frequency attached to the greatest number of trials that is the most reliable as an estimate of the probability, so the answer to give is 0.7.

## EXERCISE 2

1. Gaston loses money if he is late for work. He has recorded how many times he is late recently. Work out the relative frequency for each column, and use your results to estimate the probability that he will be late for work tomorrow.

| Number of days worked | 5 | 10 | 25 | 50 |
|---|---|---|---|---|
| Number of days late | 3 | 4 | 12 | 15 |

2. Sarra works in a factory that makes Raspberry Pi computers. Her boss thinks that there is a fault on the production line and asks her to sample some computers each day.

   Here are her results:

| | DAY | | | | | |
|---|---|---|---|---|---|---|
| | 1 | 2 | 3 | 4 | 5 | 6 |
| Number tested | 50 | 75 | 40 | 65 | 80 | 100 |
| Number faulty | 3 | 2 | 2 | 1 | 3 | 3 |

   a. What is the relative frequency of a computer that was tested on Day 3 being faulty?

   b. Over the six days, what is the relative frequency of a computer being faulty?

   c. Estimate how many of next week's 500 000 computers are likely to be faulty.

   d. What assumption did you have to make in answering part (c)?

**3.** Jemima is given a bag containing 200 identically sized buttons. She does not know how many of each colour there are, so she performs an experiment to find out. Each time she takes a button out of the bag at random, she records the colour and replaces the button. Here are her results:

| Colour | Blue | Red | Green | Black |
|---|---|---|---|---|
| Frequency | 9 | 21 | 7 | 13 |

How many of each colour do you expect to be in the bag?

**4.** 200 people were asked if they own a dog. 120 people answered "yes". What is the relative frequency that a person from that group does not own a dog?

**5.** This spinner is spun.

The spinner is spun 20 times and lands on these colours:

| B | W | W | W | P | G | P | B | B | P |
|---|---|---|---|---|---|---|---|---|---|
| P | W | B | G | B | W | W | P | W | B |

**a.** Work out the relative frequency of the spinner landing on each colour.

**b.** Here are the relative frequencies of a different set of trials with the same spinner:

| Colour | Black | White | Pink | Green |
|---|---|---|---|---|
| Relative frequency | $\frac{51}{200}$ | $\frac{48}{200}$ | $\frac{40}{200}$ | $\frac{61}{200}$ |

Is the set of relative frequencies from part (a) or is this new set of relative frequencies likely to be the more reliable outcome? Give a reason for your answer.

**6.** Noelle has estimated that there will be 15 seeds which will not germinate from the 500 she has planted. How many of the 100 seeds in her first experiment did not germinate?

**7.** Reuben sells tick repellent for horses; he earns £5 for each bottle he sells. At a horse show, 4 of the first 15 horses he inspects have ticks, so he can sell the repellent to the owner.

**a.** How many horses do you estimate Reuben needs to inspect before he has earned £100 from selling the tick repellent to owners?

**b.** What assumption have you made in part (a)?

# Probabilities from tables

It is easy enough to calculate probabilities from information presented in a table, you just need to be careful to take the data from the appropriate row or column.

### EXAMPLE

The table shows the lunch choices made by children in a primary school.

| | PACKED LUNCH | | SCHOOL DINNER | |
|---|---|---|---|---|
| | Boy | Girl | Boy | Girl |
| Starfish class | 5 | 11 | 9 | 4 |
| Dolphin class | 14 | 8 | 3 | 1 |
| Turtle class | 2 | 5 | 16 | 8 |
| Seahorse class | 9 | 8 | 3 | 14 |

**a.** How many children are in the Turtle class?

**b.** Work out the probability that a child chosen at random is a boy from the Starfish class who has a school dinner.

**c.** Work out the probability that a girl chosen at random is from the Seahorse class.

These questions can easily go wrong if you don't select the correct information. Take the time to select carefully and these questions should be straightforward for you.

### SOLUTION

**a.** 2 + 5 + 16 + 8 = 31

**b.** There are 9 boys in the Starfish class that have a school dinner.

There are 5 + 11 + 9 + 4 + 14 + 8 + 3 + 1 + 2 + 5 + 16 + 8 + 9 + 8 + 3 + 14 = 120 children altogether.

So, P(boy from the Starfish class having school dinner) $= \frac{9}{120}$

**c.** There are 8 + 14 = 22 girls in the Seahorse class.

There are 11 + 4 + 8 + 1 + 5 + 8 + 8 + 14 = 59 girls in total P (girl...) chosen at random is from the Seahorse class) $= \frac{22}{59}$

## EXERCISE 3

1. Mehdi is the supervisor on a Bronze Duke of Edinburgh expedition. He asks the group at the end of the expedition who will be taking their Silver Duke of Edinburgh award. The results are:

| | YES | NO | TOTAL |
|---|---|---|---|
| Female | 48 | 11 | |
| Male | 25 | 16 | |
| Total | | | |

Use the table to estimate the probability that a person chosen at random from the group is:

    **a.** male and wanting to do Silver award

    **b.** female and not wanting to do Silver award

    **c.** wanting to do Silver award

2. A dog training teacher asks each member of her group if they would like to take part in an agility competition. The results are in this two-way table and separated for dog size:

| | YES | NO |
|---|---|---|
| Small dog | 12 | 5 |
| Medium dog | 3 | 18 |
| Large dog | 14 | 23 |

A person is chosen at random. Use the table to estimate the probability that the member:

    **a.** said yes

    **b.** said no for large dog agility

    **c.** answered for a medium dog

3. Claudia has tagged each track on her phone by genre and length of track. The two-way table shows the different categories she used.

| | | LENGTH OF TRACK | | |
|---|---|---|---|---|
| | | < 3 mins | 3 to 5 mins | > 5 mins |
| | Rock | 29 | 84 | 17 |
| | Pop | 42 | 206 | 8 |
| GENRE | Classical | 67 | 108 | 519 |
| | Rap | 5 | 2 | 0 |
| | Metal | 103 | 143 | 29 |

Use the table to estimate the probability that the next track to be played when on "shuffle" is a:

    **a.** classical track that lasts less than three minutes

    **b.** metal track that lasts between three and five minutes

    **c.** rock track

    **d.** track that lasts longer than five minutes

**4.** This table shows some information about the seating for the audience at a concert.

| | | SEATING | | | |
|---|---|---|---|---|---|
| | | Stalls | Circle | Upper circle | Box |
| **TYPE OF TICKET** | Child | 46 | 20 | 11 | 1 |
| | Member | 103 | 65 | 87 | 18 |
| | Adult | 204 | 99 | 41 | 36 |
| | Senior citizen | 40 | 67 | 55 | 11 |

    **a.** How many people attended the concert?

    **b.** How many children sat in the upper circle?

    **c.** What is the probability that a person chosen at random from the audience is seated in a box?

    **d.** What is the probability that a person chosen at random from the audience is a Member seated in the stalls?

    **e.** A member of the audience is sitting in the upper circle. What is the probability that they are a senior citizen?

    **f.** A member of the audience is an adult. What is the probability they are not in the circle?

**advice**

*You do not need great artistic ability, you just need the "circles" to be clear and to have a large enough overlap for you to be able to write in.*

# Venn diagrams

A **Venn diagram** is an alternative, more visual, way to show the information that could appear in a two-way table. It contains all the same information but is laid out quite differently. Instead of cells in a table for each different category, we use circles, so we need to interpret their overlaps and the outside area.

Here is an ordinary two-way table with information about the numbers of people who were immunised (or not) against TB as a child and then went on to suffer (or not) with TB.

| | SUFFERED WITH TB | DID NOT SUFFER WITH TB |
|---|---|---|
| Immunised against TB | 6 | 54 |
| Not immunised against TB | 48 | 32 |

To set this up as a Venn diagram we need two overlapping circles; one for "Suffered with TB" and one for "Immunised". We then put a box around both circles to create an area outside the circles.

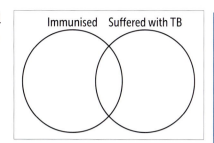

From here, we can start to slot in the numbers from the two-way table. The first one to place is the number of people who were immunised AND who suffered from TB. These 6 people will go into the overlap of the two circles.

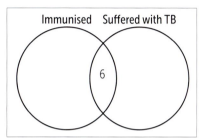

The 54 people who were immunised but did not suffer with TB need to go into the "Immunised" circle but not into the overlap area.

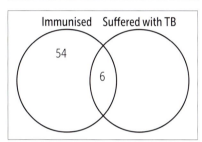

The 48 people who were not immunised but suffered with TB need to go into the "Suffered with TB" circle but not into the overlap area.

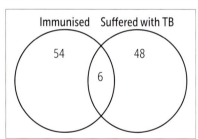

Finally, the 32 people who were not immunised and did not suffer with TB cannot go into either circle. They go anywhere outside the circles but still within the rectangle (there must always be a rectangle surrounding the circles).

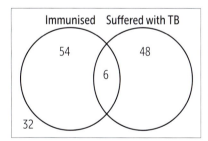

Let's look at how the table matches precisely the information now in the Venn diagram.

|  | SUFFERED WITH TB | DID NOT SUFFER WITH TB |
|---|---|---|
| Immunised against TB | 6 | 54 |
| Not immunised against TB | 48 | 32 |

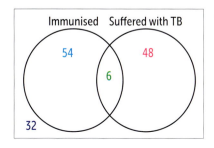

In the same way that probability questions were asked from information in two-way tables, they will be asked from information in Venn diagrams. Just make sure, as before, that you find the appropriate piece of information.

We can also use the two-way table or the Venn diagram to assess the **risk** of something happening. We talk about risk in the real world as being associated with accidents or health ("If I have the operation, what's the risk it won't work"...). We use **relative risk** to compare the chances of something happening between two groups, in other words, how many times more likely the event is for one group compared to the other.

## EXAMPLE

Compare the risk of suffering with TB having been immunised against TB against the risk of suffering TB not having been immunised against TB.

## SOLUTION

60 people were immunised against TB and 6 of them suffered TB, so 10%.

80 were not immunised against TB and 48 of them suffered TB, so 60%.

It's clear to see there is a much larger risk of suffering TB if you have not been immunised against it!

These results could now be expressed in terms of relative frequencies of the groups in the two-way table. You might have thousands of people who are immunised and you could now calculate 10% of that figure to get an idea of the numbers who might still get TB. Similarly you could find 60% of the number of a group of people who were not immunised. These expected frequencies could then be added to give estimates for the total numbers likely to catch TB.

These types of calculations are used widely to estimate numbers who will "experience" particular outcomes. Another example is the insurance industry who calculate risk of accidents occurring in order to charge people appropriately for the insurance.

## EXAMPLE

This Venn diagram shows the lunch club choices of the Year 9 students in a school. They can choose to go to any, all, or none of Carnegie Shadowing, Debating, and Chess as the clubs are on different days.

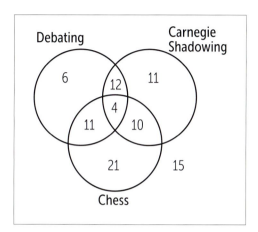

**a.** How many students go to Chess club?

**b.** How many students go to both Debating and Carnegie Shadowing?

**c.** What is the probability that a Year 9 student chosen at random goes to the Debating club?

**d.** What is the probability that a Year 9 student chosen at random attends Chess or Debating clubs?

## SOLUTION

**a.** In the circle for Chess, there are
21 + 11 + 4 + 10 = 46 students.

**b.** In the overlap of Debating and Chess, there are
11 + 4 = 15 students.

**c.** In the circle for Debating, there are
6 + 11 + 4 + 12 = 33 students.

Altogether, there are
6 + 12 + 11 + 11 + 4 + 10 + 21 + 15 = 90 students, so
P(Debating) = $\frac{33}{90}$.

**d.** In the Chess and Debating circles, there are
6 + 12 + 4 + 11 + 21 + 10 = 64 students so
P(Debating or Chess) = $\frac{64}{90}$.

## EXERCISE 4

1. 80 members at a gym were asked which classes they had attended last month. The Venn diagram shows their responses.

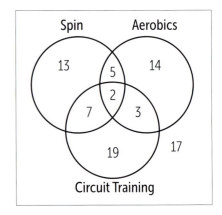

a. How many members attended Aerobics?

b. How many members attended Circuit Training and Spin?

c. What is the probability that a member chosen at random attended Spin?

d. What is the probability that a member chosen at random did not attend Aerobics?

e. What is the probability that a member chosen at random attended Spin or Circuit Training?

2. 700 people at Euston station were asked about the pets they own. The two-way table is a summary of their responses. Represent this information in the form of a Venn diagram.

| | OWNS A CAT | DOES NOT OWN A CAT |
|---|---|---|
| Owns a dog | 158 | 237 |
| Does not own a dog | 204 | 101 |

3. Ibrahim was chatting to his friends at swimming club whilst waiting for his next race. They were discussing which subscription they each had to listen to music. Of the 15 people in the discussion, 10 of them used Spotify, and of these 10, 4 also used Amazon Music. 2 of the group used neither Spotify nor Amazon Music.

a. Represent this information in a Venn diagram.

b. What is the probability that a person, chosen at random, from the group has a Spotify subscription but not one from Amazon Music?

c. How many of the group have a subscription to Amazon Music?

d. What is the probability that a person from the group, chosen at random, does not have a subscription to Amazon Music?

**4.** Jackson asked 100 people which drinks they like.

77 said cola, and, of these, 53 also liked ginger beer.

71 people liked ginger beer.

49 said they liked cola, ginger beer, and lemonade, but 3 people liked none of them.

2 people liked ginger beer and lemonade, but not cola.

6 people liked lemonade and cola, but not ginger beer.

   **a.** How many people like lemonade?

   **b.** How many people like ginger beer, but not cola?

   **c.** How many people do not like ginger beer?

   **d.** What is the probability that someone chosen at random likes cola and lemonade?

   **e.** What is the probability that a person chosen at random likes only cola?

**5.** The table shows the number of people in a sample who had a car accident in 2018 according to whether they had taken an advanced driving test or not.

|  | HAS TAKEN AN ADVANCED TEST | NOT TAKEN AN ADVANCED TEST |
|---|---|---|
| Had an accident | 4 | 42 |
| Did not have an accident | 76 | 630 |

   **a.** Convert the information in the table to a Venn diagram.

   **b.** Compare the risk of an accident for those who have taken an advanced driving test to those who haven't.

   **c.** For the next 20 000 drivers who take an advanced test, estimate the number who will have an accident in the next year.

**6.** Fred travels to work either by car or train. In the last year, when he travelled to work by train, he was late 8 out of 112 occasions. When he travelled to work by car, he was late on 35 out of 92 occasions.

Compare the relative risk of Fred being late for work when travelling by train and by car.

# Conditional probability

We learned about independent events in Probability 1. These were events where the outcome of one event did not affect the outcome of another event. We also saw that when we did not replace the counters in a bag, the second draw outcomes *were* affected by the result of the first draw. This can happen more clearly in real life. For example, it could be that your performance in one race affects your performance in the next race; a win could significantly boost your own morale and impact upon your next race. When this situation occurs and the outcome of one event affects the outcome of another, we call it **conditional probability**.

**advice**

*It's easier to see what's going on if we draw a tree diagram. It's not essential but can be very helpful to put the appropriate probabilities together before multiplying.*

## EXAMPLE

If Marty has pizza for dinner, the probability of him choosing cola to drink is 0.8. If he does not have pizza for dinner, the probability of him choosing cola to drink is 0.45. The probability that he has pizza for dinner is 0.03. Calculate the probability that Marty drinks cola with his dinner.

## SOLUTION

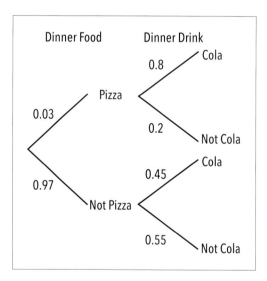

It's now much clearer to see we need to do:

P(pizza and cola) + P(not pizza and cola) = 0.03 × 0.8 + 0.97 × 0.45

= 0.024 + 0.4365

= 0.4605

## EXAMPLE

Let's look again at the Venn diagram we used earlier.

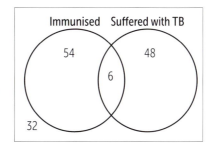

We may like to work out the probability that someone suffered TB when we know they had been immunised. This means we only need to look at the "Immunised" circle, because we have been given the fact that they were immunised.

Our total number of people being considered is now only 54 + 6 = 60.

Therefore, P(suffered TB given that they were immunised) = $\frac{6}{60}$.

When we had independent events, we had the multiplication rule: P(A and B) = P(A) × P(B).

For conditional probability, when we are "given" additional information we use:

P(B | A) = $\frac{P(A \text{ and } B)}{P(A)}$ .

For the vertical line between the B and the A, we read this as "The probability of B given A...".

This tells us that if we are looking at a Venn diagram, we only need to look within the circle for event A. You will need to learn this formula and how to use it unless you can work through these problems logically!

**advice**

*This only works if we are using probabilities, so for the TB example, we would need to change over to probabilities, not numbers of people.*

## EXAMPLE

Look again at the Venn diagram with the information about lunchtime clubs on it. What is the probability that a student goes to Chess, given that they go to Debating?

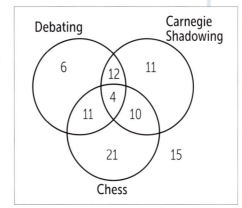

## SOLUTION

"Given that they go to Debating" means that we only need to look within the Debating circle.

Within the Debating circle, there are 6 + 12 + 4 + 11 = 33 people.

In the Chess/Debating overlap, there are 11 + 4 = 15 people.

P(Chess | Debating) = $\frac{15}{33}$

## EXAMPLE

Events M and T are exhaustive and mutually exclusive.

P(M) = 0.7          P(M and T) = 0.25

**a.** Work out P(T | M).

**b.** Work out P(M | T).

## SOLUTION

**a.** $P(T \mid M) = \frac{P(M \text{ and } T)}{P(M)} = \frac{0.25}{0.7} = 0.357$ (to 3dp)

**b.** We need P(T) in order to work this out.

Since T and M are exhaustive and mutually exclusive, P(T) = 1 − P(M)

P(T) = 1 − 0.7 = 0.3

$P(M \mid T) = \frac{P(M \text{ and } T)}{P(T)} = \frac{0.25}{0.3} = 0.833$ (to 3dp)

## EXERCISE 5

1. 700 people at Euston station were asked about the pets they own. The two-way table is a summary of their responses.

|  | OWNS A CAT | DOES NOT OWN A CAT |
|---|---|---|
| Owns a dog | 158 | 237 |
| Does not own a dog | 204 | 101 |

**a.** Re-write each entry in the table as a probability.

**b.** Calculate the probability that a person chosen at random owns a cat.

**c.** Calculate the probability that a person chosen at random owns a cat, given that they do not own a dog.

**d.** Calculate the probability that a person chosen at random owns a dog, given that they own a cat.

2. Here again, is the two-way table about TB and immunisations.

|  | SUFFERED WITH TB | DID NOT SUFFER WITH TB |
|---|---|---|
| Immunised against TB | 6 | 54 |
| Not immunised against TB | 48 | 32 |

**a.** What is the probability that a person chosen at random was immunised against TB?

**b.** What is the probability that a person chosen at random suffered with TB?

**c.** What is the probability that a person chosen at random suffered with TB, given that they were not immunised against TB?

**d.** What is the probability that a person chosen at random was immunised against TB, given that they suffered TB?

**3.** Here is the Venn diagram once more, about the classes members of a gym took last month.

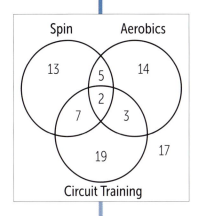

**a.** Calculate P(Spin).

**b.** Calculate P(Aerobics given Spin).

**c.** Calculate P(Circuit Training given Aerobics).

**4.** Two events, D and E are exhaustive and mutually exclusive.

P(D') = 0.8      P(D and E) = 0.42

**a.** Write down P(E).

**b.** Write down P(D).

**c.** Work out P(D | E).

**5.** The probability that Montgomery is late for work when he takes the bus is 0.4. The probability that Montgomery is late for work when he does not take the bus is 0.45. Are the two events "late for work" and "catch the bus" independent? Give a reason for your answer.

**advice**

*You may see this new notation used elsewhere: P(F') means "the probability of not F", so it's the same as 1 − P(F).*

**6.** The tree diagram shows some information about the choices Jude makes for breakfast. She has either porridge or toast and then either orange juice or milk. The probability that she has orange juice as her breakfast drink is 0.355. Complete the tree diagram and probabilities.

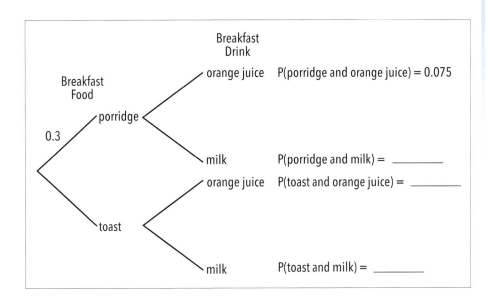

7. At night, Elsie reads a book or listens to a radio play. The probability that she reads a book is 0.62. If she reads a book, the probability that she has a hot chocolate is 0.7. If Elsie listens to a radio play, the probability that she has a coffee is 0.55.

   Are you able to calculate the probability that Elsie reads a book and has a coffee? Show your calculations or give a reason for your answer.

8. Events M and T are exhaustive and mutually exclusive.
   P(M) = 0.35 P(M and T) = 0.17

   a. Work out P(T | M).

   b. Work out P(M | T).

9. Events F and Q are exhaustive.

   P(F) = 0.4    P(F | Q) = 0.5

   Work out P(Q | F).

10. If Barney has sandwiches for lunch, the probability that he also has a hot drink is 0.7.

    If Barney has soup for lunch, the probability that he also has a hot drink is 0.1.

    The probability that he has sandwiches for lunch is 0.4.

    a. Calculate the probability that Barney has a cold drink with his lunch.

    b. Describe an assumption you made when answering part a.

( HIGHER TIER ————————————————

# Binomial distributions

In statistics, you will find that certain situations occur quite regularly.

One such situation is where there are just two possible outcomes to each trial that can take place. If the probability (P) of one of these outcomes is always the same (i.e. fixed) then for a fixed number of trials (n), we have something called a **binomial distribution**. One of the outcomes is often called a 'success'.

The most common binomial distribution is generated when a coin is flipped a number of times.

**advice**

*At this level, the maximum number of trials you will have to deal with is 5.*

## EXAMPLE

A fair coin is flipped three times.

Explain why the number of "heads" obtained follows a binomial distribution.

## SOLUTION

Two conditions for a binomial distribution have been met here.

**1.** the number of trials is fixed at 3 (we would use the notation $n = 3$)

**2.** the probability of a "head" each time is fixed at 0.5 (we would use the notation $p = 0.5$)

It is also true that trials in a binomial situation are independent, so we can use our knowledge of working with independent events to calculate binomial probabilities. We also sometimes use sample space diagrams or careful listing of possible outcomes.

## EXAMPLE

When a fair coin is flipped three times, what is the probability of exactly 2 heads being obtained?

## SOLUTION

Carefully list all the possible outcomes when three coins are flipped:

HHH   HHT   HTH   THH   HTT   THT   TTH   TTT

advice

*Notice the attempt to be systematic in the listing to ensure no options are missed.*

We have two ways to proceed now but only because the probability of a success (a head) is $\frac{1}{2}$ so the probability of a failure (a tail) is also $\frac{1}{2}$.

There are 8 possible outcomes for the three flips.

3 of these outcomes have exactly 2 heads, therefore,

P(exactly 2 heads) is $\frac{3}{8}$ (but this method only works when $p = \frac{1}{2}$ because probabilities are symmetrical in this case).

Alternatively we need to list the successful outcomes and calculate their probability.

HHT $= \frac{1}{2} \times \frac{1}{2} \times \frac{1}{2} = \frac{1}{8}$
HTH $= \frac{1}{2} \times \frac{1}{2} \times \frac{1}{2} = \frac{1}{8}$
THH $= \frac{1}{2} \times \frac{1}{2} \times \frac{1}{2} = \frac{1}{8}$

So the chances of two heads is HHT or HTH or THH. These individual outcomes are mutually exclusive and so can be added.

$\frac{1}{8} + \frac{1}{8} + \frac{1}{8} = \frac{3}{8}$.

## EXAMPLE

Over a long period of time a vet has found the following probabilities of different animals needing treatment.

| ANIMAL | PROBABILITY |
|---|---|
| Dog | 0.40 |
| Cat | 0.35 |
| Rabbit | 0.15 |
| Other | 0.10 |

a. What is the probability that, of the next four animals, exactly three are rabbits?

b. What assumption did you have to make to use the binomial?

c. Comment on the validity of your assumption.

## SOLUTION

You may be thinking that this isn't binomial as there are at least four different outcomes.

However you can consider (as rabbits are of interest here) that the next animal arriving is either a rabbit or not a rabbit, giving you the two options for each trial.

a. $n = 4$ and $p = 0.15$ each time from the data collected by the surgery.

The possible outcomes that would match the question are (R = rabbit, R' = not a rabbit)

RRRR'    RRR'R    RR'RR    R'RRR

giving probabilities of

$(0.15 \times 0.15 \times 0.15 \times 0.85) + (0.15 \times 0.15 \times 0.85 \times 0.15) + (0.15 \times 0.85 \times 0.15 \times 0.15) + (0.85 \times 0.15 \times 0.15 \times 0.15)$

= 0.00286875 + 0.00286875 + 0.00286875 + 0.00286875
= 0.011475 (or $\frac{459}{40000}$ as a fraction)

b. You had to assume that each animal that appeared was independent of the one before or after.

c. Though usually valid, there is a chance that occasionally one person may bring more than one animal in at once and this is more likely to be two of the same animal.

A shorthand notation for writing a situation is a binomial with a certain probability ($p$) and a certain number of experiments ($n$) is $X : B(n, p)$.

**advice**

*You may have noticed that to obtain the final probability you can simply multiply the probability of one outcome by the number of ways the required outcome can occur (in this example that would be 0.00286875 × 4). This is a perfectly valid approach.*

**advice**

*You do NOT need to know this notation for the exam, but it can help you write things down more quickly. It will be used if you study maths or statistics at a higher level than GCSE.*

Example X: B (4, 0.34) find P(X=1).

P(X = 1) means the probability of one "success" and three that were not "successes", let's call them "failures". These could happen in these orders:

SSSF     SSFS     SFSS     FSSS

Using the idea that the final probability is achievable by multiplying the probability of one outcome by the number of ways the required outcome can occur,

$P(X = 1) = 4 \times 0.34 \times 0.66 \times 0.66 \times 0.66$

$\qquad\qquad = 0.39099456$

$\qquad\qquad = 0.391 \text{ (3dp)}$

# Capture and recapture

A good example of using probability in the real world is the **capture-recapture** method for estimating the size of a population.

There are some important features that you must comply with for this estimate to be reliable.

1. When you return the first sample to the population, you must give sufficient time for that sample to have mixed completely with the population.

2. The process of catching and marking the first sample must not affect their behaviour and make them more or less likely to be captured again in the second sample.

3. You must not carry this out on a population liable to short term significant changes in population size.

### EXAMPLE

Olivia is estimating the number of fish in a lake.

She captures 50 fish and marks them with a harmless dye before releasing them back into the lake.

Two weeks later, she returns and captures a second sample of 40 of the fish.

She finds that 8 of them are marked with the dye.

Estimate the population of fish in the lake.

**advice**

*This equation is using the assumption that the proportion of marked fish in the lake is the same as the proportion of marked fish in the second sample.*

## SOLUTION

Let $n$ be the number of fish in the lake.

Then $\frac{50}{n} = \frac{8}{40}$.

Rearranging this equation gives $n = 50 \times \frac{40}{8}$.

So, the estimate for the number of fish in the lake, $n$, is 250.

## EXERCISE 6

1. A fair coin is flipped 5 times.

   What is the probability of obtaining exactly 4 heads?

2. A fair dice is rolled three times. The number of times a 3 appears is noted.

   a. Explain why this is a binomial situation.

   b. Calculate the probability of exactly one 3 being obtained.

   c. Sam says "the probability of getting exactly one 3 and exactly two 3s is the same".

   Is Sam correct? Justify your answer with calculations.

3. Here is the vet data again.

   | ANIMAL | PROBABILITY |
   |--------|-------------|
   | Dog | 0.40 |
   | Cat | 0.35 |
   | Rabbit | 0.15 |
   | Other | 0.10 |

   a. For the next three animals, calculate the probability they are all rabbits.

   b. For the next four animals, calculate the probability none of them is a cat.

   c. For the next five animals, calculate the probability there's exactly one animal that is neither a cat, a dog, nor a rabbit.

4. A road sometimes has a mobile speed camera on it.

   When the speed camera is there, the probability a car is breaking the speed limit is 0.03.

   When the speed camera is not there, the probability is nine times greater.

   Assume the binomial is an appropriate distribution to use in this question.

**a.** On a day where the camera is there, what is the probability that out of the next five cars:

    **i.** exactly one breaks the speed limit

    **ii.** all of them break the speed limit

**b.** On a day where the camera isn't there, what is the probability that out of the next five cars:

    **i.** exactly one breaks the speed limit

    **ii.** all of them break the speed limit

**c.** Use your answers to parts (a) and (b) to write a short comparison of cars speeding or not when the camera is there or not.

**d.** Give one reason why the binomial *might not* be appropriate for this situation.

**5.** Work out the following probabilities:

    **a.** $X : B (3, 0.8)$ find $P(X = 2)$

    **b.** $X : B (4, 0.76)$ find $P(X = 3)$

    **c.** $X : B (4, 0.08)$ find $P(X = 2)$

    **d.** $X : B (5, 0.61)$ find

      **i.** $P(X = 1)$   **ii.** $P(X < 2)$   **iii.** $P(X$ is at least $2)$   **iv.** $P(X \neq 4)$

**6.** $X : B (4, 0.375)$

What is the most likely value of X?

**7.** The table shows the probabilities of Bob's train being late and by how many minutes, on a given day.

| LATE OR NOT | EARLY OR ON TIME | LATE, BUT LESS THAN 30 MINUTES LATE | LATE, BY BETWEEN 30 AND 59 MINUTES | LATE, BY AN HOUR OR MORE |
|---|---|---|---|---|
| Probability | 0.56 | 0.29 | 0.11 | 0.04 |
| Compensation | none | none | 50% of the fare | 100% of the fare |

One week Bob travels to work 4 times, so has 4 journeys out and 4 journeys back.

**a.** For the journeys out, what is the probability that:

    **i.** he is always early or on time

    **ii.** he is late by more than an hour once

    **iii.** every time he is late by between 30 and 59 minutes

advice

*Consider whether there is more than one way he could end up getting £7.50 back*

**b.** For the journeys back, Bob pays a fare of £7.50 per journey.

What is the probability that he:

  **i.** receives £3.75 back in compensation that week

  **ii.** receives £7.50 back in compensation that week

**8.** Norris is playing archery.

The probability he misses the target every time out of 5 attempts is exactly 0.32768.

Assuming this is a binomial distribution, work out the values of n and p, where p is the probability he hits the target.

advice

*Remember n is the number of trials p is the success of probability*

**9.** At the beginning of a game of chess, there are three options.

A – move a pawn two squares

B – move a pawn one square

C – move a knight

Kirstie plays many games and realises that she has the following probabilities of making each move.

P(A) = 0.98    P(B) = 0.015    P(C) = 0.005

  **a.** Emma wants to work out the chances of Kirstie making move A five times in a row. She says this isn't a binomial probability situation as there are three possible options. Explain why Emma is wrong.

  **b.** Complete Emma's calculation (assuming it is a binomial situation).

  **c.** In 800 games of chess played by Kirstie, how many times would you expect her to move a knight first?

**10.** A large metal jar contains an unknown number of marbles.

Madi takes a sample of 20 marbles out of the jar without replacement and marks each one with a black permanent marker.

She returns the marbles to the jar and shakes the jar vigorously for 5 minutes.

A sample of 32 of the marbles is then seen to have 9 marked ones in it.

  **a.** Why is the sampling without replacement?

  **b.** Why does Madi shake the jar for so long?

  **c.** Estimate the number of marbles in the jar.

11. Rod and Anita go fishing in two different lakes.

    Rod catches 60 fish and marks them with a harmless dye before replacing them.

    Anita catches 45 fish and marks them with a harmless dye before replacing them.

    One month later, Rod samples 40 fish and finds that 12 have the dye marks on them.

    Also one month later, Anita samples 50 fish and finds that 15 have the dye marks on them.

    Whose lake would be estimated to have more fish in?

    Show your working.

12. A butterfly farm owner doesn't know how many butterflies live in the main enclosed area of the farm. Suggest a method for the owner to estimate the number of butterflies that live there.

# You should now be able to:

| Calculate an expected frequency |
| --- |
| Calculate a relative frequency |
| Calculate probabilities from tables |
| Set up and use Venn diagrams |
| Determine and interpret relative risks |
| Use formal notation for conditional probability |
| HIGHER TIER **Understand when a binomial distribution can be used** |
| HIGHER TIER **Calculate binomial probabilities** |
| HIGHER TIER **Calculate in capture–recapture situations** |

# Exam Practice Questions

**1.** A garage sells cars with a petrol engine, a diesel engine or a hybrid engine.

The garage sold 4000 cars in 2015.

The table shows the type of engine in these cars and the gender of the buyers.

| | MALE | FEMALE | TOTAL |
|---|---|---|---|
| Petrol engine | 1180 | 908 | 2088 |
| Diesel engine | 702 | 296 | 998 |
| Hybrid engine | 468 | 446 | 914 |
| Total | 2350 | 1650 | 4000 |

One of the 4000 buyers is chosen at random.

**(a)** Write down the probability that the person chosen:

    **(i)** bought a car with a petrol engine

    **(ii)** is male **and** bought a car with a diesel engine.

**(b)** A sales person says:

    "Male buyers are more likely than female buyers to buy a hybrid car".
    Is the sales person correct? Show how you worked out your answer.

© AQA 2017

**2.** A survey of the times taken by bus and by train of journeys from Oxford to London is taken.

Information about the times of 80 of these journeys is shown in the Venn diagram.

**(a)** Explain what the 8 represents.

**(b)** How many of the bus and train journeys take 100 minutes or less?

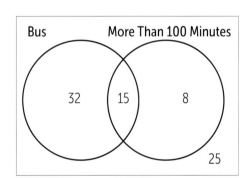

**(c)** A **bus** journey is chosen at random.

    What is the probability it took longer than 100 minutes?

© AQA 2015

**3.** Usman has a bag with 40 counters.

The probability of picking a black counter at random from his bag is $\frac{1}{5}$.

How many black counters are there in Usman's bag?

**4. (a)** Kiran has three different breeds of cow.

    He has 280 cows altogether.

    One-quarter of his cows are Angus breed, 125 are Hereford, and the rest are Ayrshire.

    Kiran needs to test all his cows for a disease but has so far only been able to test 40% of each breed.

Copy and complete the table to show this information.

| | ANGUS | HEREFORD | AYRSHIRE | TOTAL |
|---|---|---|---|---|
| Tested | 28 | 50 | | 112 |
| Not tested | 42 | 75 | | 168 |
| Total | 70 | 125 | 85 | 280 |

**(b)** One of the cows is selected at random.

Work out the probability that the cow chosen is

**(i)** a "Hereford" and "not tested"

**(ii) not** an "Ayrshire"

© AQA 2014

**5.** One hundred and fifty students were asked which daily newspaper(s) they read.

The result are shown in the diagram.

**(a)** Find the probability that a student chosen at random reads:

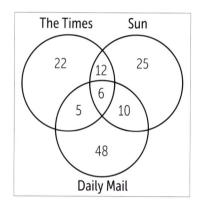

    **(i)** *The Times*     **(ii)** only one of the papers

    **(iii)** none of the three papers     **(iv)** the *Sun* or *The Times* or both but not the *Daily Mail*

**(b)** One of the students, Jean, reads the *Daily Mail*. Find the probability that she also reads *The Times*.

**6.** Records for a local library show for each book whether it is in the fiction, non-fiction, or classics category and whether it is a hardback or softback version.

When the library is closed on Wednesday last week, 2700 books were out on loan.

Of the books on loan, 72% were in the fiction category.

Of the 620 hardback books on loan, 55% were in the non-fiction category and 25% in the classics category.

In total, 176 classics were on loan.

**(a)** Copy and complete the table, entering the number of books on loan in each case.

| CATEGORY / VERSION | HARDBACK | SOFTBACK | TOTAL |
|---|---|---|---|
| Fiction | 124 | | 1944 |
| Non-fiction | 341 | | 580 |
| Classics | 155 | | 176 |
| TOTALS | 620 | | 2700 |

**(b)** A library record for a book on loan is chosen at random. Use the table to calculate the probability that the book is:

(i) non-fiction and softback version

(ii) non-fiction or a hardback version

(iii) fiction, given that it is a softback version

**(c)** How many of the first 200 books taken out on loan on the following day would you expect to be hardback classics?

7. A survey of 24 students was carried out about the number of students who wear glasses and wear earrings. The Venn diagram shows the data.

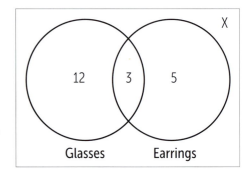

**(a)** Work out the number that should be in the section labelled X.

**(b)** What can you say about the students in the section labelled X?

**(c)** One student is chosen at random. What is the probability that the student:

(i) wears earrings, but does not wear glasses

(ii) wears earrings and wears glasses

**(d)** A student chosen at random wears earrings. What is the probability that this student also wears glasses?

8. A department store manager surveys 120 people who visit the store.

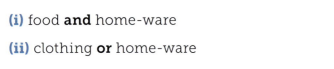

- 9 buy clothing, food and home-ware
- 5 buy food and home-ware, but **not** clothing
- 13 buy clothing and home-ware, but **not** food
- 89 buy clothing, 55 buy food, and 31 buy home-ware
- 40 buy clothing and food

**(a)** Use the data to help you complete the Venn diagram.

**(b)** How many people did **not** buy clothing or food or home-ware?

**(c)** One of these 120 people is chosen at random.

Find the probability that the person bought

(i) food **and** home-ware

(ii) clothing **or** home-ware

(iii) home-ware **given** that they bought clothing

© AQA 2015

9. A clothing store stocks coats in three different sizes (small, medium, and large) and three different colours (black, grey, and brown).

At the start of last week, there were 100 coats in stock as shown in the table.

| SIZE | COLOUR | | |
|---|---|---|---|
| | Black | Grey | Brown |
| Small | 11 | 25 | 10 |
| Medium | 9 | 12 | 8 |
| Large | 0 | 7 | 18 |

(a) As part of a quality check, an assistant selects at random one of the 100 coats.

Calculate the probability that the coat chosen is large, given that it is grey.

(b) Later, 3 of these 100 coats are found to have faults in the material.

Calculate the probability that none of them is a small, grey coat.

© AQA 2013

10. The table gives the number of pairs of shoes sold by size and width fitting by a local shop.

| | WIDTH FITTING | | | | |
|---|---|---|---|---|---|
| | C | D | E | F | Total |
| 5 | 3 | 5 | 3 | 2 | 13 |
| 6 | 4 | 7 | 8 | 3 | 22 |
| SHOE SIZE 7 | 2 | 4 | 5 | 3 | 14 |
| 8 | 1 | 2 | 3 | 1 | 7 |
| Total | 10 | 18 | 19 | 9 | 56 |

(a) What is the probability that a person selected at random buys a pair of shoes of size 5 width D?

(b) What is the probability that a person selected at random buys a pair of size 5 shoes?

(c) What is the probability that a person selected at random buys shoes of width D, given that they bought shoes of size 5?

(d) Two people are selected at random. What is the probability that that both bought shoes size 5?

11. Jakob is a warden at a nature reserve.
He wants to estimate the number of lions in the reserve.

He captures and marks 180 lions.
These lions are released.
One month later, he captures 330 lions and finds that 24 are already marked.

(a) Calculate an estimate of the number of lions in the reserve.

(b) State two conditions that must be met so that the estimate of the number of lions is valid.

© AQA 2018

# 10 | Charts and Diagrams 3 (HIGHER TIER)

## In this chapter you will learn to:

HIGHER TIER **Create and interpret proportional pie charts**

HIGHER TIER **Create and interpret histograms of unequal class width**

HIGHER TIER **Create and interpret 2D and 3D comparative diagrams**

Everything in this chapter is tested on the Higher tier only.

We have already looked at creating basic pie charts and histograms in Charts and Diagrams 1. In this chapter, we will see how to work with pie charts to take account of the total figures being represented and how to deal with histograms that have unequal class widths.

## New Vocabulary

**Proportional (comparative) pie chart**

**Frequency density**

# Proportional pie charts

In Chapter 3, we saw this question asked:

These pie charts show the items borrowed at two libraries yesterday.

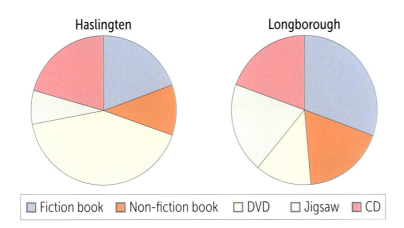

Mabel thinks that more people borrowed fiction books from Longborough library than from Haslingten library. Explain why she may be wrong.

The problem with this question is that we do not know how many items were borrowed from each library. If the two libraries had exactly the same number of items borrowed, then, of course, Longborough library, with the larger sector, had more fiction books borrowed than Haslingten library. But what if we were given different totals for each library?

Imagine that we are told that Haslingten had a total of 540 items borrowed yesterday and Longborough had 396 items borrowed yesterday. How will this affect our answer? It's not obvious which had more fiction books borrowed yet.

Haslingten had 70° for fiction books, which gives us $\frac{70}{360} \times 540 = 105$ fiction books.

Longborough had 110° for fiction books, which gives us $\frac{11}{360} \times 396$ = 121 fiction books, so Longborough library still had more fiction books borrowed.

If the figures instead were 360 items borrowed from Longborough and 720 from Haslingten, then we see:

Haslingten had 70° for fiction books, which gives us $\frac{70}{360} \times 720 = 140$ fiction books.

Longborough had 110° for fiction books, which gives us $\frac{11}{360} \times 360 =$ 110 fiction books.

So now, even though Longborough's pie chart has the larger angle for fiction, Haslingten had more fiction books borrowed.

When looking at two ordinary pie charts, we are unable to tell which represents the larger amount. In a **proportional pie chart**, the area of each sector represents the frequency, so it would be easier to tell which sector represents the larger amount at a glance. In order to account for different totals being represented, we vary the radius of the pie chart.

## EXAMPLE

Haslingten library had a total of 400 items borrowed and Longborough library, a total of 300. We need to start with a size for one of them, so we can give (for example) Haslingten a 5 cm radius.

The area of the pie chart for Haslingten represents 400 items.

The area of the pie chart will be $\pi \times 5^2 = 25\pi$, so $25\pi$ represents 400 items.

For the two pie charts, the ratio of the areas must be equal to the ratio of the total frequencies. If we call the radius of the Longborough pie chart, $R$ then we can see that its area will be $\pi \times R^2$ which represents 300 items.

Dividing both areas and both totals, we get $\frac{25\pi}{\pi \times R^2} = \frac{400}{300}$.

On the left hand side, both top and bottom will divide by $\pi$, leaving $\frac{25}{R^2} = \frac{4}{3}$ (after cancelling the right hand side).

We can rearrange this to have $R^2 = \frac{25 \times 3}{4}$ or $R^2 = 18.75$, meaning $R = 4.3$ cm (to 1dp).

**advice**

*Rearrange these carefully and remember to take the square root to get the new radius.*

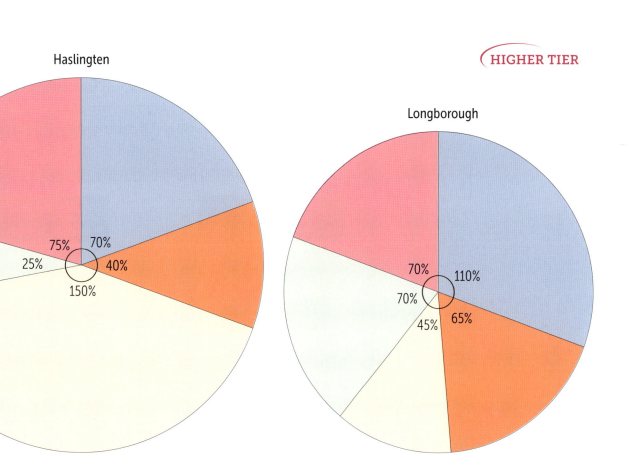

Haslingten

Longborough

Fiction book  Non-fiction book  DVD  Jigsaw  CD

# Alternative method

Haslingten represents 400 items and has an area of $\pi \times 5^2$.

Therefore one item is represented by $\frac{\pi \times 5^2}{400} = 0.19634954$ cm$^2$.

Longborough represents 300 items so should have a total area of $300 \times 0.19634954 = 58.9048622$ cm$^2$.

Again using R to stand for the radius of the Longborough pie chart, we get $\pi \times R^2 = 58.9048622$, which leads to $R = 4.3$ cm to one decimal place again.

## EXERCISE 1

1.  A pie chart, of radius 4 cm, is drawn to represent the 200 orders at a coffee shop between 6 a.m and 7 a.m. A second pie chart is to be drawn to represent the 350 orders taken between 7 a.m and 8 a.m. What will be the radius of the second pie chart?

2.  A pie chart, of radius 7 cm is drawn to represent the 2000 fish caught on a fishing boat on Monday. A second pie chart is to be drawn to represent the 1650 fish caught on Tuesday. What will be the radius of the second pie chart?

3. A pie chart of radius 6 cm is drawn to represent 500 people visiting a museum on Friday morning. How many people will the pie chart of radius 9.3 cm represent for Saturday morning?

4. Tim manages two farms. The farms have these animals:

| APPLE TREE FARM | |
|---|---|
| ANIMAL | FREQUENCY |
| Pig | 188 |
| Cow | 358 |
| Sheep | 379 |
| Goat | 75 |

| SUNNYBROOK FARM | |
|---|---|
| ANIMAL | FREQUENCY |
| Pig | 322 |
| Cow | 651 |
| Sheep | 381 |
| Goat | 146 |

Draw comparative pie charts to represent the animals at the two farms. Use a radius of 5 cm for Apple Tree Farm.

5. Year 7 and Year 8 are raising money for charity. They each hold fundraising events. The table shows the amounts raised by each year for each event.

| YEAR 7 | |
|---|---|
| EVENT | TOTAL RAISED (£) |
| Quiz | 251 |
| Cake sale | 67 |
| Sponsored silence | 124 |
| Book sale | 58 |

| YEAR 8 | |
|---|---|
| EVENT | TOTAL RAISED (£) |
| Quiz | 301 |
| Cake sale | 42 |
| Sponsored silence | 238 |
| Book sale | 69 |

Draw comparative pie charts to represent the amounts raised by each year. Use a radius of 7 cm for Year 7.

6. The tables show the different houses on two roads.

| NORTHFIELD ROAD | |
|---|---|
| NUMBER OF BEDROOMS | FREQUENCY |
| 1 | 10 |
| 2 | 23 |
| 3 | 47 |
| 4 | 56 |
| 5+ | 24 |

| SOUTHWOOD ROAD | |
|---|---|
| NUMBER OF BEDROOMS | FREQUENCY |
| 1 | 15 |
| 2 | 31 |
| 3 | 72 |
| 4 | 32 |
| 5+ | 45 |

Draw comparative pie charts to represent the different houses on each road. Use a radius of 4 cm for Northfield Road.

**7.** These two comparative pie charts represent the masses of fish caught in Looe and Padstow yesterday.

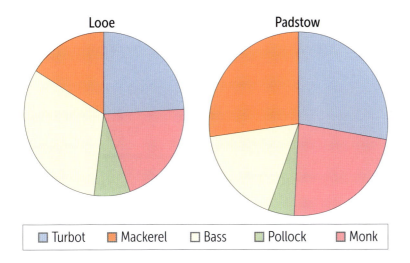

Looe    Padstow

| ▢ Turbot | ▩ Mackerel | ☐ Bass | ▩ Pollock | ▩ Monk |

Make a comparison between the mass of fish caught in Looe and the mass of fish caught in Padstow yesterday.

**advice**

*Remember, it's not enough to compare the size of the angles.*

**8.** These two comparative pie charts represent the favourite games of people in years 10 and 11.

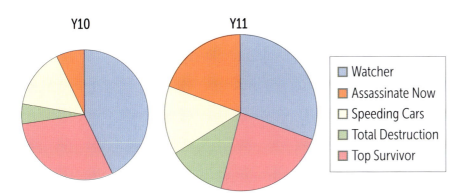

Y10    Y11

| ▩ Watcher |
| ▩ Assassinate Now |
| ☐ Speeding Cars |
| ▩ Total Destruction |
| ▩ Top Survivor |

Make two comparisons between the two Years and their favourite games.

# Histograms of unequal class widths

We encountered histograms in Charts and Diagrams 1. There, every histogram came from data with equal class widths. This will not always be the case; often data is best presented in classes of unequal widths.

## EXAMPLE

The table shows the journey times to school of 60 students.

| JOURNEY TIME, $t$ (MINUTES) | FREQUENCY |
|---|---|
| $0 \le t < 10$ | 32 |
| $10 \le t < 20$ | 14 |
| $20 \le t < 30$ | 6 |
| $30 \le t < 40$ | 4 |
| $40 \le t < 50$ | 3 |
| $50 \le t < 60$ | 1 |

If we were to draw the histograms with these classes, the bars for $30 \le t < 40$, $40 \le t < 50$ and $50 \le t < 60$ would each be very small. It would make a better looking diagram if we combined the last three classes.

| JOURNEY TIME, $t$ (MINUTES) | FREQUENCY |
|---|---|
| $0 \le t < 10$ | 32 |
| $10 \le t < 20$ | 14 |
| $20 \le t < 30$ | 6 |
| $30 \le t < 60$ | 8 |

This now, however, means that we cannot draw bars of equal width. Since the area of each bar represents the frequency of that class, heights will need to be adjusted accordingly. We need heights such that:

height of bar × width of bar = frequency for each class

This can be rearranged to calculate each height:

height of bar = frequency ÷ width

The height of the bar, for unequal class widths, is called the **frequency density**.

We can extend the table to work out the width of each class and the corresponding frequency density. The class width is found by subtracting the lower bound from the upper bound.

**advice**

*If you set out the extended table in this way, you divide across the page in the order the numbers appear.*

| TIME OF JOURNEY, $t$ (MINUTES) | FREQUENCY | CLASS WIDTH | FREQUENCY DENSITY |
|---|---|---|---|
| $0 \le t < 10$ | 32 | $(10 - 0 =) 10$ | $32 \div 10 = 3.2$ |
| $10 \le t < 20$ | 14 | $(20 - 10 =) 10$ | $14 \div 10 = 1.4$ |
| $20 \le t < 30$ | 6 | $(30 - 20 =) 10$ | $6 \div 10 = 0.6$ |
| $30 \le t < 60$ | 9 | $(60 - 30 =) 30$ | $9 \div 30 = 0.3$ |

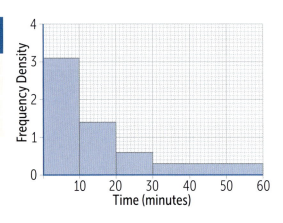

## EXERCISE 2

**1.** The table shows some information about the speeds of 60 vehicles on a motorway.

| SPEED, $s$ (MPH) | FREQUENCY |
|---|---|
| $45 \leq s < 55$ | 5 |
| $55 \leq s < 60$ | 11 |
| $60 \leq s < 65$ | 7 |
| $65 \leq s < 70$ | 16 |
| $70 \leq s \leq 85$ | 21 |

Draw a histogram to represent the speeds of these cars.

**2.** The histogram shows some information about the masses (in grams) of cakes on sale at a school fair.

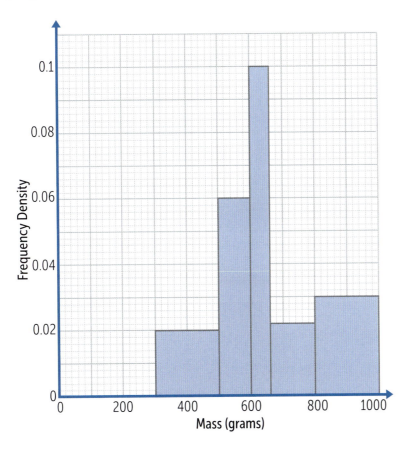

**a.** What is the smallest possible mass of cake on sale?

**b.** How many cakes had a mass of between 800 g and 1 kg?

**c.** How many cakes were on sale?

**advice**

*Remember, the horizontal axis should be a continuous scale, not set out in the groups that the table shows.*

**3.** The histogram shows some information about how long people in Year 11 spent playing online games over the weekend.

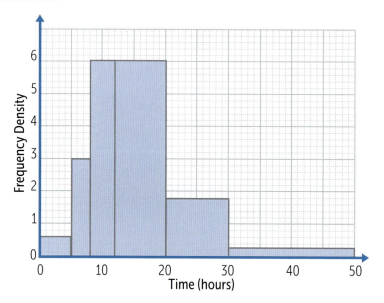

**a.** How many people played for between 8 and 12 hours?

**b.** How people played over 20 hours?

**c.** What percentage of people played for under 8 hours?

**4.** The table and the histogram show some information about the ages of people on an aeroplane.

Complete the histogram and the table.

**advice**

*There is one group that is shown in both the table and the histogram. Use this group to work out the frequency density scale.*

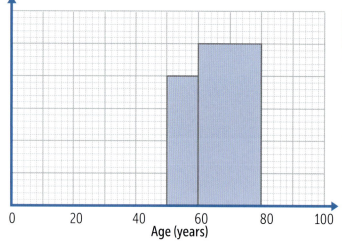

| AGE, *a* (YEARS) | FREQUENCY |
|---|---|
| $0 \le a < 10$ | 30 |
| $10 \le a < 25$ | 165 |
| $25 \le a < 40$ | 135 |
| $40 \le a < 50$ | 60 |
| $50 \le a < 60$ | |
| $60 \le a < 80$ | 100 |

**5.** Julian catches the train to work. He has noticed that the trains are often late and has recorded how late each train is (in minutes). The table and histogram show some of that information.

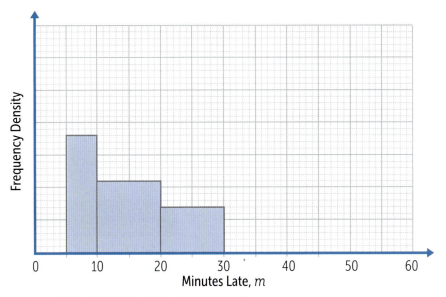

| MINUTES LATE, $m$ | FREQUENCY |
|---|---|
| $0 < m \leq 5$ | 18 |
| $5 < m \leq 10$ | |
| $10 < m \leq 20$ | 11 |
| $20 < m \leq 30$ | |
| $30 < m \leq 60$ | 6 |

**a.** Complete the histogram and complete the table.

**b.** How many trains were less than 10 minutes late?

**c.** Julian can claim some money back if his train is over 30 minutes late. What percentage of the trains were over 30 minutes late?

**6.** Jemima runs a business from home and regularly has to go the post office. She records the masses of the parcels she takes each time. The table shows this information.

| MASS $m$, (GRAMS) | FREQUENCY |
|---|---|
| $0 < m < 100$ | 60 |
| $100 \leq m < 150$ | 90 |
| $150 \leq m < 200$ | 80 |
| $200 \leq m < 350$ | 120 |
| $350 \leq m < 400$ | 75 |
| $400 \leq m < 500$ | 30 |
| $500 \leq m < 1000$ | 50 |

Jemima is making a histogram to show the distributions of the masses of the parcels. She creates this table:

| MASS $m$, (GRAMS) | FREQUENCY | CLASS WIDTH | FREQUENCY DENSITY |
|---|---|---|---|
| $0 < m < 100$ | 60 | 100 | 0.6 |
| $100 \leq m < 150$ | 90 | 150 | 0.6 |
| $150 \leq m < 200$ | 80 | 50 | 1.6 |
| $200 \leq m < 350$ | 120 | 150 | 0.8 |
| $350 \leq m < 400$ | 75 | 50 | 1.5 |
| $400 \leq m < 500$ | 30 | 100 | 3 |
| $500 \leq m < 1000$ | 50 | 50 | 1 |

Jermaine spots three mistakes Jemima has made. Identify the mistakes and correct her table.

7. Lula has lots of music on her phone. Some tracks are long and some are short. The table shows the distribution of the lengths of the tracks (to the nearest minute).

| LENGTH $m$, (MINUTES) | FREQUENCY |
|---|---|
| $0 < m < 1$ | 10 |
| $1 \leq m < 2$ | 20 |
| $2 \leq m < 4$ | 110 |
| $4 \leq m < 5$ | 55 |
| $5 \leq m < 7$ | 70 |
| $7 \leq m < 10$ | 12 |
| $10 \leq m < 20$ | 15 |

Lula then creates this histogram to show the data in a visual way.

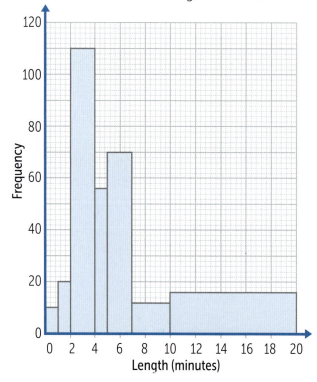

Explain why this is not a histogram and draw the correct histogram.

**8.** Armaan is working on creating a histogram from the information in this table.

| MASS $w$, (GRAMS) | FREQUENCY |
|---|---|
| $0 < w < 10$ | 8 |
| $10 \leq w < 15$ | 11 |
| $15 \leq w < 20$ | 19 |
| $20 \leq w < 40$ | 15 |
| $40 \leq w < 80$ | 20 |
| $80 \leq w < 100$ | 9 |

He calculates the frequency densities to be:

| MASS $w$, (GRAMS) | FREQUENCY | FREQUENCY DENSITY |
|---|---|---|
| $0 < w < 10$ | 8 | 1.25 |
| $10 \leq w < 15$ | 11 | 0.45 |
| $15 \leq w < 20$ | 19 | 0.26 |
| $20 \leq w < 40$ | 15 | 1.3 |
| $40 \leq w < 80$ | 20 | 2 |
| $80 \leq w < 100$ | 9 | 2.2 |

    **a.** Explain the mistake Armaan has made when finding the frequency densities.

    **b.** Calculate the correct frequency densities.

    **c.** Draw the histogram for Armaan, using the correct frequency densities.

**9.** The table shows some information about the heights of sunflowers Jeff has grown on his allotment.

| HEIGHT (NEAREST METRE) | FREQUENCY |
|---|---|
| 6 | 4 |
| 7 | 17 |
| 8 | 35 |
| 9–10 | 23 |
| 11–15 | 11 |

Draw a histogram to represent this data.

# Comparative 2D and 3D diagrams

We see what are meant to be comparative diagrams quite often in newspapers and magazines, but they are often badly constructed (or even deliberately mis-constructed) and end up being misleading. We need to be very careful to accurately represent data in order to give an unbiased view to the reader.

You will need to call on maths skills to find areas or volumes and to find the appropriate scale factors. If it is a more difficult shape like a sphere, you would be given any formulae you need. You just need to have in mind, for example, that doubling each length of a cuboid, does not double the volume, so be careful when you draw!

### EXAMPLE

To compare the sales of two salesmen, two cuboids are drawn. Arthur has sold 50 items, and Bertam has sold 65 items. The cuboid for Arthur is 10 cm × 2 cm × 5 cm; calculate dimensions for the cuboid for Bertram.

### SOLUTION

The cuboid for Arthur has volume $10 \times 2 \times 5 = 100$ cm³ and represents 50 items.

The volume for the cuboid for Bertram needs to have volume $\frac{65}{50} \times 100 = 130$ cm³, so we need dimensions that multiply to get to 130 cm³. You can choose any figures that will achieve this, such as 13 cm × 5 cm × 2 cm.

### EXAMPLE

This graphic was seen in a newspaper, to show that the cost of a house in a particular village had doubled in 10 years.

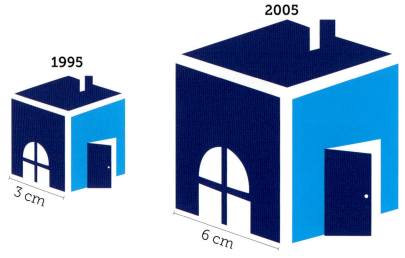

Explain why the graphic does not show a doubling of the house price.

## SOLUTION

If we said the volume of the original house represented the original price, then the volume of the second house should represent the doubled price. The 1995 house is drawn as a cube with side 3 cm, giving it a volume of 27 cm³. The 2005 house therefore should have a volume of 54 cm³.

We can see by measuring that each side of the 2005 house is 6 cm, therefore the volume is 216 cm³. This is in fact **8 times** larger than the original volume, not double the original volume!

If we double each length we get:

length × 2 × width × 2 × height × 2 which gives us the new volume.

You can see that we do not have just one lot of × 2, but three lots, which ends up giving us × 8, which is the reason the new volume is 8 times larger than the original. This is the reason the graphic is misleading; it's not showing an image with double the volume, but with 8 times the volume!

In fact the second house should have dimensions that are $\sqrt[3]{2}$ times bigger, not 2 times bigger, if all lengths are to be scaled equally.

## EXERCISE 3

1. To compare the price of perfume in Spain and in Denmark, two rectangles are drawn to represent the perfume boxes. The perfume costs €28 and €40 in Denmark. The rectangle for the price in Spain has dimensions 7 cm × 2 cm. The rectangle for Denmark will also have one side that measures 2 cm; calculate the length of the other side.

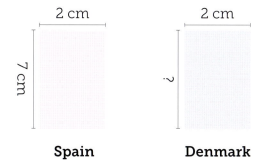

Spain          Denmark

**2.** A supermarket has a special offer on peas. Liesl has to create a poster to advertise the offer. The poster needs to show a 300 g tin for which Liesl uses a 5 cm diameter and a 7 cm height. The poster also needs to show a 600 g tin. Explain **two** different ways that Lisel could alter the smaller diagram to show that the larger tin is exactly double the mass.

**3.** Bella has groomed 25 dogs this week, whilst Basil has groomed 16. To illustrate how many dogs they have each groomed, Bella draws a square for each of them. Bella's has a side length of 5 cm. What length will the square for Basil have?

**4.** Dorota is delivering parcels. She delivers 450 on Monday, 600 on Tuesday, and 550 on Wednesday. She has this picture of a parcel to represent the Monday parcels. If the base of the image stays the same, calculate the heights of the two parcels she will draw to represent Tuesday's and Wednesday's parcels.

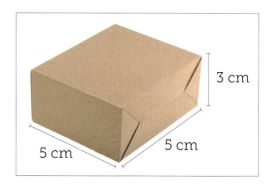

**5.** Alyson wants to create square-based pyramids to represent the amounts of data available on different phone packages.

Explain, with calculations, whether her models will be correct representations or whether they will be misleading.

| AMOUNT OF DATA | LENGTH OF SQUARE | HEIGHT OF PYRAMID |
|---|---|---|
| 2 GB | 2 cm | 3 cm |
| 5 GB | 3 cm | 5 cm |
| 11 GB | 3 cm | 11 cm |

You may need to use the formula:

volume of pyramid = $\frac{1}{3}$ × base area × height

**6.** The chart shows the recycling rates for some countries.

Give two criticisms of the chart.

# You should now be able to:

| | |
|---|---|
| HIGHER TIER | **Create and interpret proportional pie charts** |
| HIGHER TIER | **Create and interpret histograms of unequal class width** |
| HIGHER TIER | **Create and interpret 2D and 3D comparative diagrams** |

# Exam Practice Questions

**1.** The graph was used to show how much more rubbish has been produced since 1960.

Give **two** different criticisms of the graph.

© AQA 2014

**2.** The table shows information about the distance travelled (in kilometres) by a sample of 132 visitors to a theme park.

| DISTANCE TRAVELLED, $x$ (KM) | $0 < x \leq 5$ | $5 < x \leq 10$ | $10 < x \leq 20$ | $20 < x \leq 35$ | $35 < x \leq 60$ |
|---|---|---|---|---|---|
| FREQUENCY | 18 | 30 | 48 | 21 | 15 |

**(a)** Estimate how many of these visitors travelled 7 km or more.

**(b)** Complete a histogram for these data.

**(c)** Later the data were regrouped using the following classes:

$$0 < x \leq 20$$
$$20 < x \leq 60$$

Give **one** disadvantage of grouping the data using these classes.

© AQA 2014

**3.** Supermarket A sells loaves of white bread in-store and online.

The comparative pie charts show the sales of white bread in 2005 and 2015.

The supermarket sold 2.175 million loaves of white bread **online** in 2005.

Calculate the number of loaves of white bread the supermarket sold online in 2015.

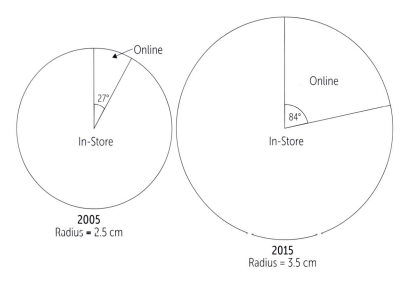

© AQA 2017

**4.** The table shows the time (minutes) that 200 primary school pupils spent reading one Monday.

| TIME, $t$ (MINUTES) | FREQUENCY |
|---|---|
| $10 \leq t < 15$ | 65 |
| $15 \leq t < 20$ | 52 |
| $20 \leq t < 30$ | 62 |
| $30 \leq t < 40$ | 13 |
| $40 \leq t < 60$ | 8 |

The incomplete histogram shows some of the information.

Copy and complete the histogram.

© AQA 2017

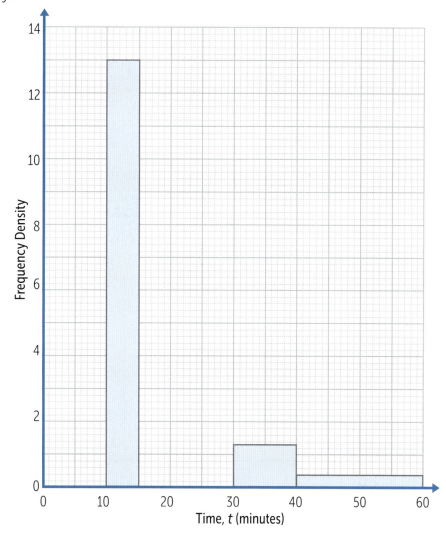

**5.** The comparative pie charts show information about the number of visitors to attractions on the Isle of Skye during April and August.

In April the total number of visitors was 56,250.

**(a)** How many people visited the Fairy Pools in April?

**(b)** The radii for April and August are 1.5 cm and 2 cm respectively. Calculate how many visitors there were in August.

**(c)** Write down 2 differences between the pattern of visitors in April and August.

**APRIL**

72° 54° 198°

**AUGUST**

108° 90° 18° 144°

- Castle
- Fairy Pools
- Dinosaur Museum
- Old Man of Storr

- Castle
- Fairy Pools
- Dinosaur Museum
- Old Man of Storr

6. James is in charge of the 100 penguins at his local zoo. He has to weigh them and record the results in a table.

| MASS OF PENGUINS, $x$ (KG) | NUMBER OF PENGUINS |
|---|---|
| $0 \leq x < 5$ | 4 |
| $5 \leq x < 10$ | 12 |
| $10 \leq x < 20$ | 22 |
| $20 \leq x < 30$ | 33 |
| $30 \leq x < 35$ | 18 |
| $35 \leq x < 45$ | 11 |

James drew a histogram to illustrate the mass but he made a mistake.

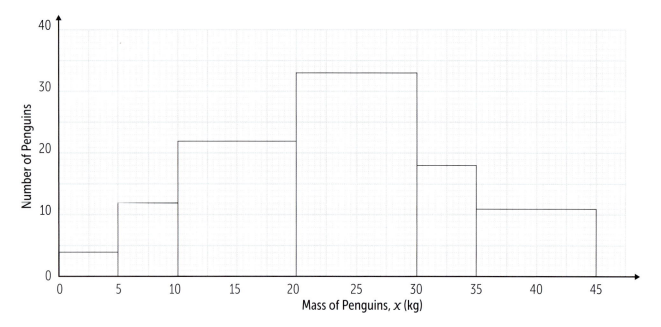

(a) What has James done wrong?

(b) Draw a correct histogram to represent the masses of penguins.

**7.** An egg producer says that over the last three years the amount of eggs produced has doubled every year. He draws a diagram to show this information.

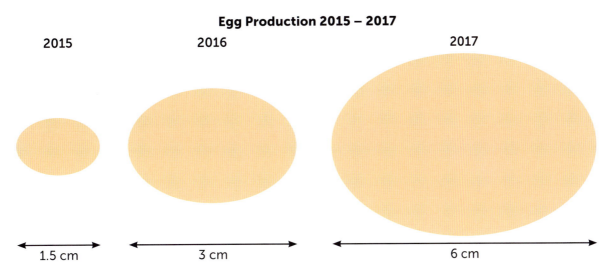

**Egg Production 2015 – 2017**

2015          2016                    2017

1.5 cm          3 cm                    6 cm

Explain how the above diagram may be misleading.

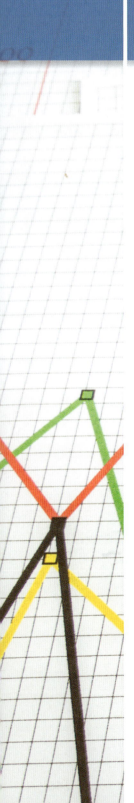

# 11 | Scatter Diagrams, Correlation and Regression

## In this chapter you will learn to:

Recognise types and strength of correlation

Plot and interpret scatter diagrams

Use double mean points to draw lines of best fit

HIGHER TIER Use the regression equation to draw lines of best fit

Know that correlation might not mean causation

Interpret Spearman's rank correlation coefficient

Understand the differences between interpolation and extrapolation and the dangers of the latter.

HIGHER TIER Calculate Spearman's rank correlation coefficient

HIGHER TIER Interpret product moment correlation coefficient

HIGHER TIER Understand the difference between the two measures of correlation

## New Vocabulary

Scatter diagram

Correlation (association)

Positive correlation

Negative correlation

No correlation

Strong correlation

Weak correlation

Line of best fit

Interpolation

Extrapolation

Double mean point

Causality

Spearman's rank correlation coefficient

Pearson's product moment correlation coefficient

# Scatter diagrams

**Scatter diagrams** are used to plot bivariate data. We will then be able to see if the two variables in the data are linked in any way. We can use the connection to estimate values for missing data.

Any connection between the two data sets is known as **correlation** (may also be referred to as the two variables having an **association**). We can tell that there is a correlation if the data points plotted appear to form a line or close to a line. We may see **positive correlation**, **negative correlation**, or **no correlation**. We also refer to them as a **strong correlation** or a **weak correlation**.

**advice**

*Scatter diagrams come under many names: scatter chart, scatter plot, scattergram, and scatter graph. They all refer to the same type of diagram, but you need to be aware that they can be called slightly different things.*

**Positive correlation** — The data is such that as one variable increases, so does the other.

| | | |
|---|---|---|
| **Weak positive** | 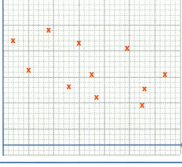 | It's only just an upward trend of data points here. If you were to draw a bubble around the data points, you would see that it does show the trend of bottom left to upper right, giving us a positive correlation. |
| **Strong positive** | | There is a very clear, nearly straight line of data points formed, showing an upward trend. |

**Negative correlation** — The data is such that as one variable increases, the other decreases.

| | | |
|---|---|---|
| **Weak negative** | | It's only just a downward trend of data points here. If you were to draw a bubble around the data points, you would see that it does show the trend of bottom right to upper left, giving us a negative correlation. |

247

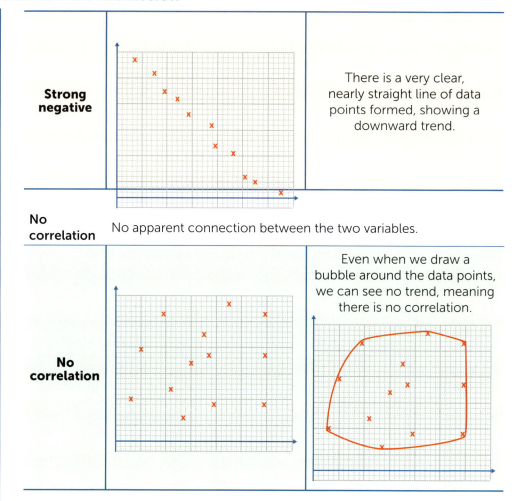

| Strong negative | | There is a very clear, nearly straight line of data points formed, showing a downward trend. |
|---|---|---|
| No correlation | No apparent connection between the two variables. | |
| No correlation | | Even when we draw a bubble around the data points, we can see no trend, meaning there is no correlation. |

Let's look at plotting a scatter diagram.

## EXAMPLE

The table shows the marks of eight students who have taken a maths test and a science test.

| STUDENT | JIM | FRED | SALLY | NAZ | WING | TAL | CLARA | HILDA |
|---|---|---|---|---|---|---|---|---|
| Maths mark | 46 | 63 | 41 | 52 | 25 | 84 | 57 | 14 |
| Science mark | 52 | 58 | 35 | 58 | 22 | 78 | 63 | 25 |

a. Plot the data points on a scatter diagram.

b. Describe the correlation shown in the scatter diagram and explain what this means.

## SOLUTION

a. It's generally the rule that the top line of data in the table will be the horizontal axis.

So we need a horizontal axis that goes up to 84 and a vertical axis that goes up to 78. It's good to draw your diagram as large as possible on the page, but it's not necessary to use the same scale on both axes.

**advice**

*Remember to:*
- *give each axis a title*
- *plot each data point clearly as a cross*
- *use the top line of the table as the horizontal axis*

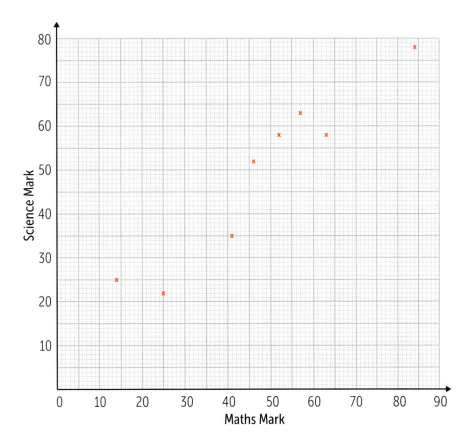

**b.** The data is forming a general pattern from bottom left to upper right, so is showing quite a strong positive correlation. This means that a student who gets a high mark in the maths test usually gets a high mark in the science test.

If we were to draw a line roughly through the middle of the data points, we would be able to estimate the marks of a student who sat one test but missed the other. This line is called a **line of best fit**. You should try to get roughly equal numbers of data points on either side of the line of best fit. For the example above, we should aim for 4 points on either side of the line. We can then use this line to estimate missing data values. When an estimate is made within the data range, it is called **interpolation**, and when the estimate is made outside the data range, it is called **extrapolation**. Estimates made using extrapolation are less likely to be reliable, as we have no evidence that the relationship we see between the data will actually continue beyond the given data.

**advice**

*Estimates made from a strong correlation are likely to be more reliable than those made from a weak correlation.*

Lines of best fit must also always

- be straight and ruled

- reach the full extent of the data

- not normally go beyond the plotted points

## EXAMPLE

**a.** For the data in the previous table, draw a line of best fit on your scatter diagram and use it to estimate the mark on the science test for a student who scored 70 on the maths test.

**b.** Did your estimate use interpolation or extrapolation? Give a reason for your answer.

## SOLUTION

**a.**

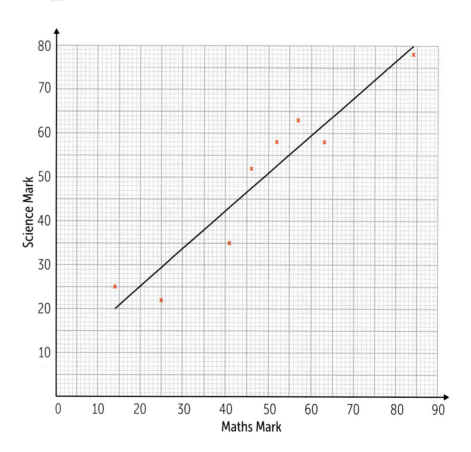

If we read up at 70 from the horizontal axis and then read across when this line meets the line of best fit, we can see that the estimated score would be 68 for the science test.

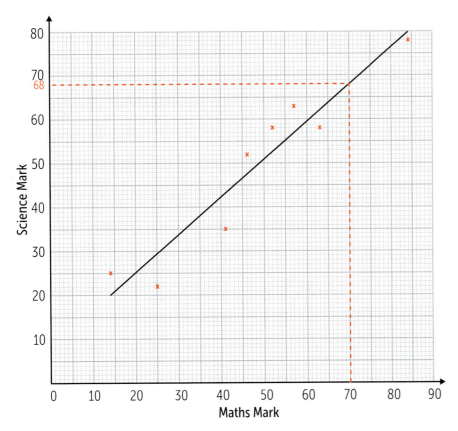

**b.** The estimate was made using interpolation because the maths mark of 68 was within the original data set.

## EXERCISE 1

**1.** Describe the type and strength of the correlation shown in the scatter diagram.

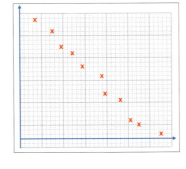

**2.** The table shows the ages of some cars and the distance they need in which to stop when travelling at 40 mph.

| AGE OF CAR (MONTHS) | 5 | 10 | 15 | 20 | 25 | 30 | 45 | 65 | 60 | 80 | 90 |
|---|---|---|---|---|---|---|---|---|---|---|---|
| STOPPING DISTANCE (METRES) | 35.2 | 35.7 | 35.9 | 38.1 | 39.2 | 40.5 | 41.0 | 42.6 | 43.7 | 44.6 | 44.9 |

**a.** Draw a scatter diagram of these results.

**b.** Describe the correlation shown in your scatter diagram and explain what this means.

3. Explain the difference between estimating using interpolation and estimating using extrapolation.

4. Charlie and Hamish have joined a chocolate tasting club. Each month they are sent the same 10 chocolates. They both score each chocolate as a score out of 10. The table shows their scores.

| CHOCOLATE | A | B | C | D | E | F | G | H | I | J |
|---|---|---|---|---|---|---|---|---|---|---|
| CHARLIE'S SCORE | 7 | 3 | 9 | 6 | 7 | 2 | 4 | 7 | 6 | 9 |
| HAMISH'S SCORE | 5 | 5 | 4 | 8 | 3 | 4 | 6 | 6 | 7 | 7 |

a. Draw a scatter diagram of the scores.

b. Explain whether the data shows any correlation.

5. Dani runs a coffee bar outside a railway station. The table shows the temperature at 7 a.m. for the last 10 days and the numbers of coffees he sold during the period 6:30 a.m. – 8:30 a.m.

| TEMPERATURE (°C) | 0 | 5 | 7 | 2 | 1 | 1 | 3 | 0 | 4 | 2 | 4 |
|---|---|---|---|---|---|---|---|---|---|---|---|
| NUMBER OF COFFEES SOLD | 7 | 33 | 27 | 44 | 47 | 49 | 42 | 52 | 38 | 45 | 41 |

a. Draw a scatter diagram of the scores.

b. Identify the outlier on your graph, and ignoring the outlier, draw a line of best fit on your diagram.

c. Use your line of best fit to estimate the number of coffees sold when the temperature at 7 a.m. is 6°C.

d. Use your line of best fit to estimate the number of coffees sold when the temperature at 7 a.m. is 10°C.

e. Is your answer to (c) or (d) likely to be more reliable? Give a reason for your answer.

6. Give a real-life example of bivariate data sets that have:

a. a positive correlation

b. a negative correlation

c. no correlation

7. Use the Internet to gather data about the average maximum temperature and the number of hours of sunshine in 15 capital cities around the world. Draw a scatter diagram to show the data you have gathered and use it to investigate the relationship between the average maximum temperature and the number of hours of sunshine. Check your findings against data for other capital cities not in your original data set.

# Double mean point

A more accurate way to draw a line of best fit onto a scatter diagram is to first plot the **double mean point** and then to have the line of best fit go through this point. The double mean point is found by finding the mean of each set of data and plotting them as the first point on the scatter diagram.

In the example used in the previous section, the mean of the maths mark is:

$(46 + 63 + 41 + 52 + 25 + 84 + 57 + 14) \div 8 = 46$

The mean of the science marks is:

$(52 + 58 + 35 + 58 + 22 + 78 + 63 + 25) \div 8 = 48.875$

Therefore the point (46, 48.875) should be plotted on the diagram, before the line of best fit is drawn.

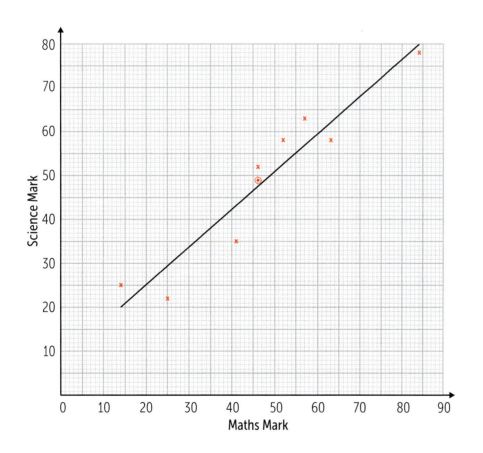

**advice**

You should use a double mean point in all lines of best fit from now on.

**advice**

Use a different symbol for the double mean point such as ● to make it appear different to the plotted data points.

# Using the equation of the line of best fit

Even when you use the double mean point as a centre point for your line of best fit, there is still an element of judgement in where you draw your line.

It is possible to use the equation of the line of best fit, the regression equation. This is properly called the "least squares regression line" as it minimises the vertical distances between the points and the drawn line.

You can use your knowledge from GCSE Maths of how to find $m$ and $c$ in $y = mx + c$ if you need to find the equation of a line that has been drawn already, but for GCSE Statistics you only need to be able to plot the line given its equation.

## EXAMPLE

The time taken by Quinn to solve a puzzle is measured over 14 attempts.

The results are shown in the table, but the time for the 7th attempt is missing.

| ATTEMPT NUMBER ($X$) | 1 | 2 | 3 | 4 | 5 | 6 | 7 |
|---|---|---|---|---|---|---|---|
| TIME (SECONDS) ($Y$) | 93 | 88 | 82 | 68 | 72 | 58 | |

| ATTEMPT NUMBER ($X$) | 8 | 9 | 10 | 11 | 12 | 13 | 14 |
|---|---|---|---|---|---|---|---|
| TIME (SECONDS) ($Y$) | 44 | 35 | 32 | 29 | 21 | 15 | 13 |

**a.** Plot a scatter diagram for these data.

**b.** Describe the type and strength of correlation observed.

**c.** Interpret your answer to part (b) in the context of the question.

**d.** You are given that the equation of the line of best fit (regression line) for these data is $y = 98.8 - 6.45x$.

Plot this on your scatter diagram.

**e.** Use your line of best fit on the graph to estimate the time taken in the 7th attempt.

**f.** How reliable do you think this answer is?

**g.** Explain why you cannot use this line of best fit to estimate the time taken on the 16th attempt.

## SOLUTION

**a.**

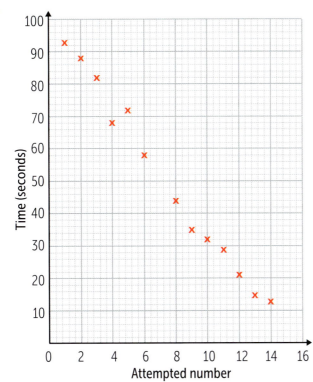

**advice**

*You can use any x values, so choose easy ones to work out.*

**b.** The graph shows strong negative correlation.

**c.** Every time Quinn attempts the puzzle he usually solves it quicker than the previous time.

**d.** To plot a straight line you need at least two points.

Use $x = 0$ in the regression equation and you know that (0, 98.8) is a point on this line.

Use $x = 10$ in the regression equation and you know that (10, 34.3) is a point on this line.

Now plot these points and join them up.

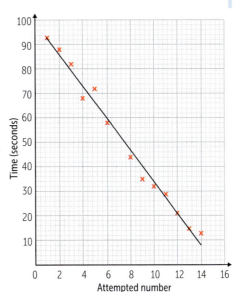

**e.** Draw a line up from 7 on the *x* axis up to the line of best fit and read across (it is also possible to sub *x* = 7 into the equation for the line but the question said use the graph).

Reading this off the graph = 53 seconds.

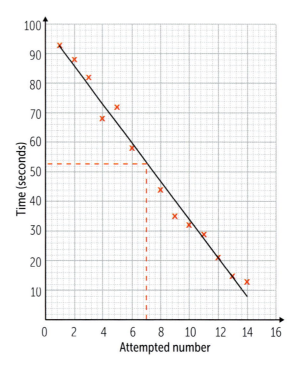

**f.** As there is a strong correlation, this should make the estimate reliable.

**g.** If you assume the pattern continued after 14 attempts, the time would eventually be negative, which is impossible!

## EXERCISE 2

**1.** Here again is the table showing the ages of some cars and the distance they need in which to stop when travelling at 40 mph.

| AGE OF CAR (MONTHS) | 5 | 10 | 15 | 20 | 25 | 30 | 45 | 65 | 60 | 80 | 90 |
|---|---|---|---|---|---|---|---|---|---|---|---|
| STOPPING DISTANCE (METRES) | 35.2 | 35.7 | 35.9 | 38.1 | 39.2 | 40.5 | 41.0 | 42.6 | 43.7 | 44.6 | 44.9 |

**a.** Calculate the mean age of the cars.

**b.** Calculate the mean stopping distance.

**c.** Plot the double mean point as you draw a scatter diagram to show the data.

**d.** Draw the line of best fit on your diagram.

2. Here are the scores for a different chocolate tasting club that Charlie and Hamish attended.

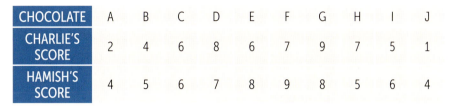

| CHOCOLATE | A | B | C | D | E | F | G | H | I | J |
|---|---|---|---|---|---|---|---|---|---|---|
| CHARLIE'S SCORE | 2 | 4 | 6 | 8 | 6 | 7 | 9 | 7 | 5 | 1 |
| HAMISH'S SCORE | 4 | 5 | 6 | 7 | 8 | 9 | 8 | 5 | 6 | 4 |

   a. Calculate the mean score for Charlie.

   b. Calculate the mean score for Hamish.

   c. Draw a scatter diagram to show the data and plot a line of best fit, using the double mean point.

   d. Use your line of best fit to estimate the score that Hamish would give to a chocolate that Charlie had scored as a 3.

3. Here is the data for Dani's coffee bar again.

| TEMPERATURE (°C) | 5 | 7 | 2 | 1 | 1 | 3 | 0 | 4 | 2 | 4 |
|---|---|---|---|---|---|---|---|---|---|---|
| NUMBER OF COFFEES SOLD | 33 | 27 | 44 | 47 | 49 | 42 | 52 | 38 | 45 | 41 |

   a. Calculate the double mean point for the data.

   b. Draw a line of best fit on your diagram.

   c. Use your line of best fit to estimate the number of coffees sold when the temperature at 7 a.m. is 6°C.

   d. Compare this estimate to the one from the previous exercise when you drew the line of best fit by eye.

4. Luigi walks past the village duck pond every day at noon. The bank displays a clock with the temperature also showing. Luigi makes a note of the temperature each day along with the number of ducks in the duck pond. The table shows some of his results.

| TEMPERATURE (°C) | 7 | 15 | 11 | 18 | 12 | 20 | 16 | 10 |
|---|---|---|---|---|---|---|---|---|
| NUMBER OF DUCKS | 25 | 8 | 15 | 6 | 14 | 3 | 10 | 19 |

   a. Plot a scatter diagram to show the data.

   b. Plot a line of best fit on the graph.

   c. Describe the type and strength of the correlation.

   d. Use your graph to estimate the number of ducks in the duck pond on a day where the temperature at noon is 13°C.

e. Explain why it would be unreliable to extend your line of best fit to estimate the number of ducks in the duck pond on a day where the temperature at noon is 23°C.

5. Howard works fixing gas boilers. He keeps a record of the minimum temperature overnight and the number of callouts he has each day. The table shows his results.

| TEMPERATURE (°C) | 5 | 7 | 2 | −1 | 1 | −3 | 0 | 4 | 2 | 4 |
|---|---|---|---|---|---|---|---|---|---|---|
| NUMBER OF CALLOUTS | 4 | 3 | 9 | 12 | 11 | 15 | 11 | 8 | 10 | 7 |

a. Plot a scatter diagram to show the data.

b. Draw a line of best fit on the scatter diagram.

c. Describe the type and strength of the correlation.

d. Use your graph to estimate the number of callouts Howard will get if the minimum temperature overnight is 1°C.

e. Marina wants to use her line of best fit to estimate the number of callouts Howard will get when the minimum temperature overnight is −8°C. Explain why her estimate is likely to be unreliable.

**HIGHER TIER** ————————————————

6. Clive is digging out a large area of earth for a patio. The table shows the length of time he works for each of 8 days and how many wheelbarrows of soil he removes each day.

| NUMBER OF HOURS ($X$) | 8 | 6 | 7 | 2 | 6 | 5.5 | 8 | 7 |
|---|---|---|---|---|---|---|---|---|
| NUMBER OF WHEELBARROWS OF SOIL ($Y$) | 32 | 25 | 30 | 6 | 21 | 22 | 35 | 26 |

a. What type of correlation are you expecting in this situation? Justify your answer.

b. One of these days had a thunderstorm. Which day do you think it was? Give a reason for your answer.

c. Plot a scatter diagram for these bivariate data.

d. The equation of the line of best fit for these data is $y = 4.55x − 3.5$. Plot this on your diagram and interpret the value of the gradient in the context of the question.

e. Estimate the number of wheelbarrows of soil he will dig out when he works for

   i. 6.5 hours   ii. 9 hours

f. Which estimate in part (d) is more reliable? Justify your choice.

**7.** The equation of the line of best fit for some bivariate data is $y = 20000 - 3000x$.

Give a possible context for bivariate data having a line of best fit with this equation.

# Causation

When two data sets show an association, it may look as though one event is causing the other to happen. This may or may not be the case, and we have to be very careful not to jump to any assumptions about **causality**. Causality is said to exist between two data sets when the effect of one variable increasing/decreasing *causes* the other variable to change accordingly. For example, in a simplified view, it may be said that spending too much time at the computer causes poorer eyesight. There is no doubt that these two events are linked, but there will be more factors to take into account, such as lighting levels, age, definition of screen being used, etc.

**advice**

*For causation to exist, there must be a correlation, BUT it doesn't mean that for every correlation there will be causation.*

## EXAMPLE

Nita has noticed that when it's raining, more people take a taxi home from the station. She says that the rain is causing people to take a taxi rather than walk. Huw agrees with her, but investigates further and discovers that when it rains heavily, the trains have to slow down on that particular bit of track which causes them to be late into the station. People who would then usually continue their journey by bus, will have missed the bus (due to the late arrival of the train), and have to take a taxi or wait an hour for the next bus. So we can see that there are factors (other than the rain itself) that cause more people to take a taxi.

Even when we have a causal relationship, it doesn't mean that each event can cause the other (both ways around). In the example above, whilst it is the case that the rain causes more people to take a taxi, it is most certainly not the case that if everyone getting off the train were to take a taxi, it would suddenly start pouring down!

## EXERCISE 3 ──────

Think about each of these pairs of variables and decide which will show:

    **a.** positive correlation (strong or weak)

    **b.** no correlation

    **c.** negative correlation (strong or weak)

    **d.** causality

Determine any other factors which aren't mentioned but may have an effect on causality.

| | | |
|---|---|---|
| 1 | Shoe size | Length of arm |
| 2 | Outdoor temperature | Number of ice-creams sold in beach kiosk |
| 3 | Height of a father | Height of his daughter |
| 4 | Number of miles driven | Number of minutes spent in the car |
| 5 | Number of trips to the dentist in 2 years | Number of fillings patient has |
| 6 | Number of accidents on a stretch of road | Presence of a new speed camera |
| 7 | Number of people stung by jellyfish | Sales of buckets and spades |
| 8 | Price of a ticket to a football match | Number of spectators at a football match |
| 9 | The cost to rent a 2-bedroom house | Distance of the house from the city centre |

# Spearman's rank correlation coefficient

As you have seen from some of the scatter diagrams earlier in this chapter, it's not always easy to decide whether there is a correlation or not just by looking at the pattern of data plots.

For this reason, we can use special calculations that indicate whether positive or negative correlation is present in bivariate data and how strong it is.

At Foundation Tier, you need to be able to interpret **Spearman's rank correlation coefficient**.

This is a scale between −1 and +1 where

- −1 represents perfect negative correlation
- +1 represents perfect positive correlation
- 0 represents no correlation

Here is the scale in full.

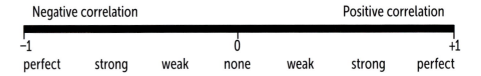

How do we know when to call correlation weak or strong?

As a general rule we will use these guidelines:

- strong negative correlation is < −0.6
- weak negative correlation is between −0.6 and −0.2 inclusive
- no correlation exists between −0.2 and + 0.2 inclusive
- weak positive correlation is between + 0.2 and + 0.6 inclusive
- strong positive correlation is > + 0.6

As indicated above, perfect correlation is indicated by +1 or 1.

Spearman's rank correlation uses the rank order of the values for the $x$ and $y$ coordinates, and so any graph where each value is above and to the right of the previous one would indicate a value of +1.

The graph below has a value of +1 for that reason, even though the values do not form a perfect straight line.

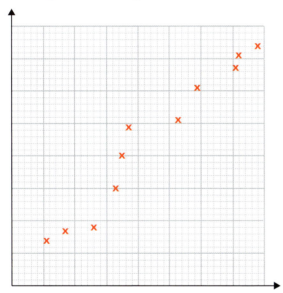

**advice**

*The sign tells you whether it is positive or negative correlation and the value of the number tells you whether it is strong or weak (or there is none).*

**HIGHER TIER**

If you are doing Higher Tier, we will talk about the differences between this and another measure of correlation shortly.

## EXAMPLE

Nicola has been working out values for Spearman's rank correlation coefficient between different pairs of variables.

The six values she came up with were.

$$+0.65 \quad −0.43 \quad +1.28 \quad +0.77 \quad −0.83 \quad +0.05$$

**a.** Identify the value for which she has definitely made a mistake. Give a reason for your answer.

**advice**

*Here you are not ordering the numbers from −1 to +1, you are looking at the size of the numbers − the sign of the number does not matter when looking at the strength of the correlation.*

**b.** Put the remaining five values in order from most correlation to least correlation.

## SOLUTION

**a.** +1.28 has to be wrong as values for Spearman's rank correlation coefficient have to be between −1 and + 1.

**B.** −0.83      +0.77      +0.65      −0.43      +0.05

**HIGHER TIER**

# Calculating Spearman's rank correlation coefficient

**advice**

*The formula which is used looks complicated but is easy to use and you do **not** have to learn it.*

At Higher Tier, you need to be able to calculate values for Spearman's from the ranked data or more likely from a summary of the ranked data.

Spearman's rank correlation coefficient (given the symbol $r_s$) is given by:

$$r_s = 1 - \frac{6\sum d^2}{n\,(n^2-1)}$$

where $d$ is the difference in the ranks of the two variables and $n$ is the number of pairs of data.

You are often given the value of $\sum d^2$, but this example shows how to obtain it if you are not.

## EXAMPLE

Six friends, who took the same college course, compared their final exam score (in %) with their salary 3 years later.

The results are shown in the table.

| PERSON | ANN | BETH | CAZ | DINA | ERNIE | FOO |
|---|---|---|---|---|---|---|
| FINAL EXAM % | 65 | 82 | 77 | 51 | 48 | 77 |
| SALARY (£) | 18 000 | 21 000 | 32 000 | 23 000 | 19 000 | 34 500 |

**a.** Calculate the value of Spearman's rank correlation coefficient for these data.

**b.** Interpret your answer in the context of the question.

**c.** Foo says,"The better you do in the final exam, the higher salary you get".

Give two reasons why Foo might not be correct.

## SOLUTION

**a.** It is vital that the calculation for Spearman's rank correlation coefficient is done with **ranked** data not the original values.

For that reason, it is wise to add extra rows (or columns as appropriate) to the original table.

You rank from either lowest to highest OR highest to lowest but you must use the same for both variables.

In the table below we have used highest as a rank of 1.

| PERSON | ANN | BETH | CAZ | DINA | ERNIE | FOO |
|---|---|---|---|---|---|---|
| FINAL EXAM % | 65 | 82 | 77 | 51 | 48 | 77 |
| SALARY (£) | 18 000 | 21 000 | 32 000 | 23 000 | 19 000 | 34 500 |
| RANK OF EXAM % | 4 | 1 | 2.5 | 5 | 6 | 2.5 |
| RANK OF SALARY | 6 | 4 | 2 | 3 | 5 | 1 |
| $d$ | −2 | −3 | 0.5 | 2 | 1 | 1.5 |
| $d^2$ | 4 | 9 | 0.25 | 4 | 1 | 2.25 |

$$\sum d^2 = 4 + 9 + 0.25 + 4 + 1 + 2.25 = 20.5$$

**advice**

To rank the data *just means to put it in order,* giving it a number in the list. You should order each variable separately.

Notice the use of ranking of 2.5 for Caz and Foo in exam % as they had a tied value of 77% for their final exam. These two values were for rankings of 2 and 3, so we use the mean of these and give them both a rank of 2.5.

$d$ is the difference in the ranks. Technically you should include the − sign if this is negative although all these values will be squared to get $d^2$.

$n$ is the number of pairs of data, so in this case, this is 6

(if you were given $\sum d^2$ the answer would begin at this point).

Using the formula $r_s = 1 - \dfrac{6\sum d^2}{n\,(n^2 - 1)}$ (which will be given in the

exam) we get $r_s = 1 - \dfrac{6 \times 20.5}{6\,(6^2 - 1)} = 1 - 0.5857... = \underline{0.414}$.

**b.** The result is 0.414, so there is weak positive correlation between the final % in the exam and the earnings of the people three years later. Therefore, a higher final % can come with a higher salary but not always.

**c.** Foo may not be right for two reasons:

    **i.** The correlation is only weak so the positive association between final score and salary is by no means certain.

    **ii.** The size of the sample used is small at only six; much more data is needed to be sure of making a statement like the one Foo made.

# Pearson's product moment correlation coefficient

Spearman's measure is not the only measure of correlation that exists. It is fairly basic, and as we saw, a scatter diagram where the points were not really anywhere near a straight line can get a value of +1 (if each point is above and to the right of the last).

**Pearson's product moment correlation coefficient** (sometimes just called the product moment correlation coefficient or PMCC) doesn't use the ranks of the data, it uses the actual data values, and so it is a much more refined method.

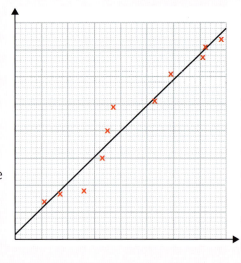

We do not cover how to calculate it at GCSE, only how to interpret it, but it is worth knowing that it is based around calculating the vertical distances of each point in the scatter diagram from the line of best fit.

Look at that earlier scatter diagram again, this time with the line of best fit on.

Remember this has a Spearman's value of +1.

However, because the points do not all lie on the line this cannot have a PMCC of +1. In fact it is +0.79.

The only way to get a PMCC of +1 would be a scatter diagram such as this one. Every point is exactly on the line of best fit.

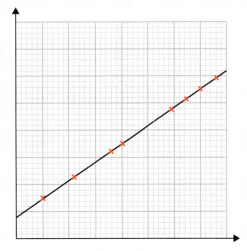

To interpret PMCC we use the same scale and values as for Spearman's.

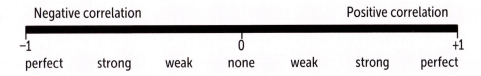

### EXAMPLE

Niles has a sandwich shop.

He collects data for three variables over 40 days:

A – the number of sandwiches he sells each day

B – the maximum temperature each day

C – the amount of rainfall in mm each day

The table shows the value of the PMCC for each pair of variables.

| PAIR OF VARIABLES | VALUE OF PMCC |
|---|---|
| A and B | +0.45 |
| A and C | −0.71 |
| B and C | −0.23 |

Interpret each value of PMCC in the context of the question.

### SOLUTION

A and B – this shows a weak positive correlation, the warmer it is the more sandwiches he sells.

A and C – this shows a strong negative correlation, the more it rains, the fewer sandwiches he sells.

B and C – this shows a (very) weak negative correlation, the more it rains, the cooler it is.

## EXERCISE 4

1. The table shows values of Spearman's rank correlation coefficient for some sets of bivariate data.

| PART | FIRST VARIABLE | SECOND VARIABLE | VALUE OF SPEARMAN'S |
|------|----------------|-----------------|---------------------|
| a | Age of car | Price of car | −0.49 |
| b | Length of song | Chart position | 0.12 |
| c | Score in test | Number of hours' revision | 0.77 |
| d | Sales of sunglasses | Amount of rain | −0.94 |
| e | Cost of house | Cost of home insurance | 0.38 |

For each part, interpret the value of Spearman's in the context of the variables.

2. Draw a scatter diagram with a value of Spearman's rank correlation coefficient between -0.2 and +0.2.

3. Draw a scatter diagram with a value of Spearman's rank correlation coefficient of −1.

4. Write down an estimate of the value of Spearman's rank correlation for each of these scatter diagrams.

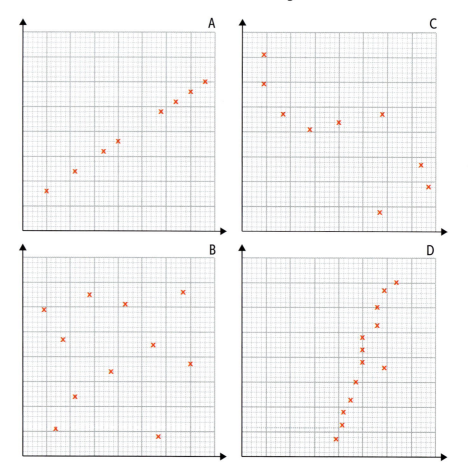

**HIGHER TIER**

**5.** Calculate and interpret the value of Spearman's rank correlation coefficient for each of these sets of data.

**a.** time to finish the London Marathon compared to the age of the runner

| AGE | 34 | 27 | 19 | 46 | 23 | 25 | 33 |
|---|---|---|---|---|---|---|---|
| TIME TO FINISH MARATHON (HRS) | 3.5 | 2.9 | 2.6 | 3.3 | 3.4 | 2.8 | 3.2 |

**b.** number of dogs owned and number of cats owned by people who own at least one of each

| NUMBER OF DOGS | 3 | 1 | 2 | 1 | 4 |
|---|---|---|---|---|---|
| NUMBER OF CATS | 3 | 5 | 1 | 8 | 2 |

**c.** height and mass of 8 guinea pigs

| NAME | Keith | Piggy | Straw | Patch | Charlie | DJ pig | GP | Hunter |
|---|---|---|---|---|---|---|---|---|
| HEIGHT (CM) | 13.2 | 14.2 | 10.5 | 11.5 | 13.2 | 16.3 | 13.2 | 10.3 |
| MASS (G) | 765 | 1032 | 808 | 689 | 914 | 1101 | 800 | 777 |

**6.** Here is a scatter diagram for the number of texts received and the number of app notifications for 8 different students' phones in 1 hour.

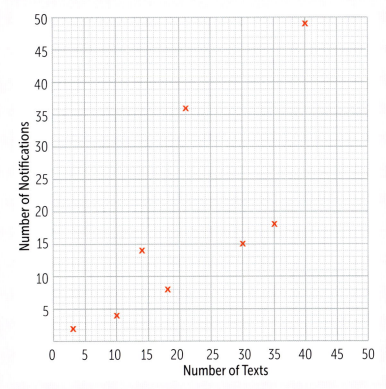

    **a.** Estimate, from the graph, the value of Spearman's rank correlation coefficient.

    **b.** Calculate the actual value of Spearman's rank correlation coefficient.

    **c.** Comment on the accuracy of your estimate.

**7.** Draw a scatter diagram so that the points have a Pearson's product moment correlation coefficient of –1.

**8.** What are the main differences between Spearman's Rank Correlation Coefficient and Product Moment Correlation Coefficient?

# You should now be able to:

**Recognise types and strength of correlation**

**Plot and interpret scatter diagrams**

**Use double mean points to draw lines of best fit**

(HIGHER TIER) **Use the regression equation to draw lines of best fit**

**Know that correlation might not mean causation**

**Interpret Spearman's rank correlation coefficient**

**Understand the differences between interpolation and extrapolation and the dangers of the latter.**

(HIGHER TIER) **Calculate Spearman's rank correlation coefficient**

(HIGHER TIER) **Interpret product moment correlation coefficient**

(HIGHER TIER) **Understand the difference between the two measures of correlation**

# Exam Practice Questions

**1.** The table shows the number of miles travelled (thousands) and depth of tread (mm) on eight tyres of the same type.

| NUMBER OF MILES (THOUSANDS) | 5 | 10 | 15 | 25 | 31 | 36 | 40 | 46 |
|---|---|---|---|---|---|---|---|---|
| DEPTH OF TREAD (MM) | 7.2 | 6.6 | 6.2 | 4.9 | 4.8 | 3.8 | 3.3 | 2.4 |

**(a)** Draw a scatter diagram for the data.

**(b)** For the data, the mean number of miles is 26 thousand. Work out the mean depth of tread. Use these mean values to help you draw a line of best fit on your scatter diagram.

**(c)** Use your line of best fit to estimate the depth of tread for a tyre which has travelled 20 thousand miles.

**(d)** It is illegal to have less than 1.6 mm of tread on a tyre.

Use your line to estimate the number of miles travelled before a tyre becomes illegal.

**(e)** Which of your answers, (c) or (d), do you think is **more** reliable? Give a reason for your choice.

**(f)** Is there likely to be a **causal** relationship between the number of miles travelled and the depth of tread? Give a reason for your answer.

© AQA 2013

**2.** Jane measures the heart rate, in beats per minute, of athletes whilst they are running at different speeds in a gym.

**(a)** Write down one reason why Jane may want to do her experiment in a gym rather than on an athletics track.

Graham is one of the athletes.

Graham's measurements are shown in the scatter diagram.

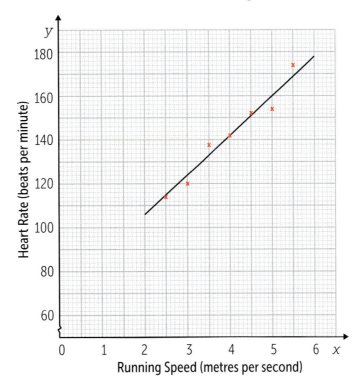

**(b)** What type of correlation does the scatter diagram show?

**(c)** Use the line of best fit to estimate Graham's heart rate when he is running at 3.9 metres per second.

© AQA 2017

**3.** Mary and Paul are bakers.

They each rank the quality of white bread sold in eight supermarkets.

|  | RANKS FOR MARY | RANKS FOR PAUL |
|---|---|---|
| Supermarket A | 5 | 7 |
| Supermarket B | 3 | 2 |
| Supermarket C | 8 | 5 |
| Supermarket D | 4 | 1 |
| Supermarket E | 1 | 4 |
| Supermarket F | 7 | 6 |
| Supermarket G | 2 | 3 |
| Supermarket H | 6 | 8 |

**(a)** Show that the value of Spearman's rank correlation coefficient between their rankings is 0.55 correct to two dp.

**(b)** Interpret in context the value of the correlation coefficient given in part **(a)**.

**(c)** Ben also ranks the quality of the white bread.
The value of Spearman's rank correlation coefficient between his rankings and **Paul's** rankings is −1.
Write down the ranking that he gives to the bread sold in Supermarket A.

© AQA 2017

**4.** The table shows the distance travelled (miles) and the cost (£) of nine taxi journeys.

| Distance (miles) | 1.5 | 2 | 3 | 3.5 | 5 | 6 | 6.5 | 8 | 9.5 |
|---|---|---|---|---|---|---|---|---|---|
| Cost (£) | 4.00 | 5.50 | 4.50 | 7.50 | 7.50 | 11.00 | 8.50 | 10.00 | 13.50 |

The data are shown on the scatter diagram.

**(a)** Circle the most likely value of Spearman's rank correlation coefficient for the data.

   −0.87    0.08    0.93    8.45

**(b)** The mean distance travelled for these nine journeys is 5 miles and the mean cost is £8.

Use these mean values to draw a line of best fit on a copy of the scatter diagram.

**(c)** Use your line of best fit to estimate the cost of a 7 mile taxi journey.

**(d)** Jack paid £15 for his taxi journey.

Use your line of best fit to estimate the distance he travelled.

**(e)** Which of the answers, (c) or (d), do you think is more reliable? Give a reason for your answer.

© AQA 2015

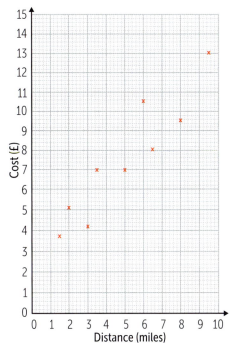

**5.** Eight dancers take part in a competition.
Each dancer performs a dance which is marked by two judges.
The table shows the scores (out of 10) the judges gave to each dancer.

|          | ALEX | NINA | TANYA | RACHEL | SAM | CRUZ | JESS | MIRA |
|----------|------|------|-------|--------|-----|------|------|------|
| Judge A  | 6    | 5    | 10    | 3      | 9   | 3    | 7    | 7    |
| Judge B  | 7    | 7    | 9     | 5      | 7   | 6    | 7    | 6    |

Calculate Spearman's rank correlation coefficient for the values.

You **must** show your working.

© AQA 2015

**HIGHER TIER**

**6.** A sports coach analyses the goal scoring record of a large sample of Premier League Football players over a season.

Part of his analysis involves calculating values for the product moment correlation coefficient ($r$).

**(a)** $r = +0.65$ between number of shots on goal and goals scored. This is probably correct. Explain why.

**(b)** $r = −0.83$ between boot size and goals scored. This is probably incorrect. Explain why.

**(c)** $r = −1.14$ between age and goals scored. This is definitely incorrect. Explain why.

© AQA 2013

# 12 | Standard Deviation, Skew and the Normal Distribution (HIGHER TIER)

## In this chapter you will learn to:

HIGHER TIER **Interpret and calculate standard deviation**

HIGHER TIER **Interpret and calculate skew**

HIGHER TIER **Recognise skewed and symmetrical distributions**

HIGHER TIER **Recognise the main properties of the Normal distribution**

HIGHER TIER **Compare distributions using standardised scores**

### New Vocabulary

**Standard deviation**

**Pearson's measure of skew**

**Positive and negative skew**

**Distribution**

**Normal distribution**

**Standardised score**

Everything in this chapter is tested on the Higher tier only.

We already have several options of how to measure the spread of a data set. We can use:

- the range (which uses both end points of the data set)

- the interquartile range (which uses the central 50% of the data and so eliminates the effect that any outlier may have)

- the interdecile or interpercentile ranges (which can use a greater percentage of the original data than the interquartile range)

None of the above measures of spread actually use every single data value. **Standard deviation** is an alternative way to measure the spread of a data set by using every single data point. This is a similar situation to comparing the use of the mean (which uses all of the data) and the median (which only uses the order of the data).

A data set with a smaller standard deviation is more consistent and therefore less varied or spread out than a data set with a larger standard deviation.

You will need one of these formulae to calculate a standard deviation.

Standard deviation = $\sqrt{\frac{\sum x^2}{n} - (\frac{\sum x}{n})^2}$ whhere $\sum x^2$ means the sum of each data point squared, $\bar{x}^2$ is the mean squared. and $n$ is the number of data points.

The standard deviation is also equal to = $\sqrt{\sum \frac{(x - \bar{x})^2}{n}}$ where $\sum(x - \bar{x})^2$ means the sum of the squares of each data point from the mean.

The second formula shows you a little more about what standard deviation is actually measuring, that is, the average difference between a data value and the mean.

**advice**

*You may see this symbol $\sigma$ used to represent standard deviation. This is a lower case-Greek letter, sigma. We use the upper case sigma, $\Sigma$, to mean "sum of".*

### EXAMPLE

Artemis grows tomatoes. He has counted the number of tomatoes from each plant. This is his record.

| 6 | 3 | 12 | 8 | 5 | 14 | 7 | 5 | 10 |
|---|---|----|---|---|----|---|---|----|

8    12

Find the standard deviation of these values.

### SOLUTION

By counting, we see that there are 11 data points, so here $n = 11$.

We need to find the mean of the data set, $\bar{x}$:

$\frac{[6 + 3 + 12 + 8 + 5 + 14 + 7 + 5 + 10 + 8 + 12]}{11} = 8.18...$

It is easier to use the first formula here:

$\sum x^2$ will be found by $6^2 + 3^2 + 12^2 + 8^2 + 5^2 + 14^2 + 7^2 + 5^2 + 10^2 + 8^2 + 12^2 = 856$.

So the standard deviation is $\sqrt{\frac{856}{11} - 8.18...^2} = 3.3$ (to 1dp).

This can also be done on the statistical functions of all scientific or graphical calculators. However, the models vary too much for us to show how here. It may be worthwhile for you to find out how to do this on your calculator, so that you can easily check your calculations.

**advice**

*It's best to keep using the full calculator display value for the mean to avoid rounding errors in the standard deviation.*

## EXERCISE 1

1. Calculate the standard deviation of these data sets.

   **a.** 32  48  12  6  10  55  41

   **b.** 1  9  11  5  7  3  4  8

   **c.** 12.3  11.7  6.4  5.9  7.7  10.9

   **d.** 101  10  103  104  105  106

   **e.** 1  2  3  4  5  6

   **f.** 51  52  53  54  55  56

   **g.** Compare the standard deviations for parts (d), (e), and (f). What conclusions can you make?

2. **a.** Use the Internet to find out the maximum temperatures yesterday in 10 UK cities.

   **b.** Use the Internet to find out the maximum temperatures yesterday in 10 capital cities.

   **c.** Calculate the standard deviation of each list.

   **d.** Compare, in context, the standard deviations of each list.

3. Dave and Keeley deliver parcels. The table shows the mean and standard deviation of the mass of last week's parcels in kg for each of them.

   | | MEAN | STANDARD DEVIATION |
   |---|---|---|
   | Dave | 12 | 1.8 |
   | Keeley | 14 | 2.2 |

   Make two comparisons between the mass of Dave's and Keeley's parcels.

4. Data set A has a mean of 5 and a standard deviation of 2.3.

   Data set B has a mean of 5 and a standard deviation of 3.2.

   What comparison can you make about the two data sets?

5. The table shows the numbers of goals scored in some football matches.

   Work out the standard deviation of the number of goals scored.

   | NUMBER OF GOALS | FREQUENCY |
   |---|---|
   | 0 | 11 |
   | 1 | 2 |
   | 2 | 6 |
   | 3 | 6 |
   | 4 | 2 |
   | 5 | 3 |

**advice**

*Here, you will need to use "0" eleven times and "1" twice etc. Don't just use them once each; you have a total of 30 data points here. There will be shortcuts available on your calculator for this. It's worth spending a little time finding out how to use them.*

6. Theo and Cleo work in a restaurant. The table shows the mean and standard deviation of last week's tips for each of them, in £.

|  | MEAN | STANDARD DEVIATION |
|---|---|---|
| Theo | 125 | 12 |
| Cleo | 104 | 5 |

Compare statistically, Theo's and Cleo's tips.

7. Write out two data sets that have the same standard deviation but where the mean of the first one is double the mean of the second one.

8. Using the formula standard deviation $= \sqrt{\sum \frac{(x - \bar{x})^2}{n}}$ and the values $\sum(x - \bar{x})^2 = 16$ for a data set containing 12 values, calculate the standard deviation for the data set.

9. A data set of 20 values has a mean of 1.8 and $\sum x^2 = 341$.

Calculate the standard deviation of the data set using the formula standard deviation $= \sqrt{\frac{\sum x^2}{n} - \bar{x}^2}$ .

10. Sal has calculated the standard deviation of a data set using the formula standard deviation $= \sqrt{\sum \frac{(x - \bar{x})^2}{n}}$. He has found the standard deviation of the data set is 0.69.

From his notes, Sal can see that $\sum(x - \bar{x})^2 = 19.9962$. How many values were in the data set?

# Calculating skew

As well as assessing the skew of a data set by eye from a box plot, histogram, or cumulative frequency diagram, there are several ways to calculate a value for the skew. Once calculated, the skew values, like averages and measures of spread, can be used to compare different data sets.

A commonly used calculation for skew is **Pearson's measure of skew**. This is found by using the formula:

$$\text{Skew} = \frac{3(\text{mean - median})}{\text{standard deviation}}$$

If your calculation produces a positive value, then the data has a **positive skew**. Conversely, a negative value means **negative skew**. A value of 0 indicates that the distribution of the data is symmetrical (see the next section for more about this).

The size of the number indicates a greater or lesser amount of skew. For example, a skew of +1.9 shows a much greater skew than that of +0.35.

**advice**

*A little like correlation coefficients, any positive values often include the + sign for emphasis.*

Other formulae for skew exist (see Q5 in the next Exercise), so the emphasis here is being able to:

- evaluate the measures from a data set or diagram if necessary
- substitute the measures into a given formula
- interpret the outcome, possibly comparing two or more values of skew as above

### EXAMPLE

Calculate Pearson's measure of skew for this data set.

| 4 | 5 | 12 | 21 | 7 | 14 | 20 | 10 | 9 |

### SOLUTION

The mean of the data is: 11.3333...

The median of the data set is: 10

Standard deviation of the data set is: 5.7348835...

Pearson's measure of skew is found by using $\frac{3(\text{mean} - \text{median})}{\text{standard deviation}}$, giving: $\frac{3(11.33333..... - 10)}{5.7348835....} = +0.6975$

Continuous data (skewed or symmetrical) can be illustrated by a sketch of the possible **distribution** (in a similar way to sketching out a possible box plot of the data).

The diagrams below show the possible shapes of how the data is distributed:

**advice**

*Notice how the shape of the distribution changes as the mean, median, and mode alter their relative positions within the data set.*

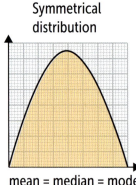

Symmetrical distribution

mean = median = mode

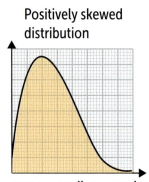

Positively skewed distribution

mean > median > mode

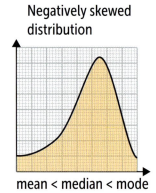

Negatively skewed distribution

mean < median < mode

## EXERCISE 2

**1.** Calculate Pearson's measure of skew for this data set.

   6    3    7    12    10    9    14    19    21

**2.** Calculate Pearson's measure of skew for this data set.

   104   112   195   154   162   107   183   199   131
   155   167

**3.** Compare the skewness of these two data sets.

   **A:** 123   132   145   154   163   136   150

   **B:** 121   144   156   167   199   208   210   222   223

**4.** Calculate the skewness for each of these data sets.

| | MEAN | MEDIAN | STANDARD DEVIATION |
|---|---|---|---|
| Set 1 | 30 | 35 | 15 |
| Set 2 | 50 | 50 | 10 |
| Set 3 | 60 | 55 | 30 |

**5.** An alternative measure of skew uses the formula:

$$\text{Skew} = \frac{\text{mean - mode}}{\text{standard deviation}}$$

Use this measure of skew to calculate the skewness of the data set.

   6    3    7    12    10    19    14    19    21

**6.** The table shows the prices (in £) of some houses for sale.

| 210000 | 540000 | 205000 | 304000 |
|---|---|---|---|
| 335000 | 415000 | 219000 | 295500 |
| 296500 | 366000 | 222500 | 465000 |
| 237000 | 489000 | 269500 | 409500 |

   **a.** Find the mean house price.

   **b.** Find the standard deviation of the house prices.

   **c.** Comment on the skewness of the house prices.

   **d.** Give a possible reason why house prices are skewed this way.

**7.** Wendy has calculated Pearson's measure of skew to be −0.5886 for her data set.

Here are some of her correct workings:

mean = 4.5263                    median = 5

Work out the standard deviation of the data set.

8. Draw an approximate distribution curve for continuous data with a skew of:

   **a.** 0      **b.** −1.5      **c.** +0.6

9. Draw a possible box plot for data with a skew of

   **b.** 0      **b.** +0.9      **c.** −2

10. A continuous distribution has a mean of 10, a median of 12, and a mode of 14. Circle the shape of this distribution.

    negative skew      symmetrical      positive skew

11. A positively skewed distribution has a mode of 50 and a mean of 60.

    Circle a possible value for the median of this distribution.

    45      50      55      60      65

# The Normal distribution

Wc have seen that a distribution with a skew of zero is symmetrical.

One of the most important types of continuous, symmetrical distributions is the **Normal distribution**.

It is characterised by what is known as a "bell-shaped" curve and looks like this.

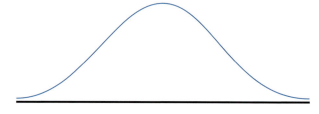

The mean, mode, and median are all equal in a Normal distribution, but the exact height and width of the curve varies according to the standard deviation.

You need to be aware of how different curves (for different distributions) will appear relative to each other based on their means and their standard deviations. These important results are true for all Normal distributions.

- almost all data are within three standard deviations of the mean (it is actually 99.8%)

- 95% of all data are within two standard deviations of the mean

- about two-thirds of all data are within one standard deviation of the mean

**advice**

*It is well worth learning these three facts as you will need to know them.*

In the real world, we would see lots of examples of data that are very close to following a Normal distribution. For example, heights of people, scores in a fair exam, times taken to finish a race, and so on.

## EXAMPLE

When it is raining, Bruno has walks which follow a Normal distribution with a mean of 48 minutes and a standard deviation of 10 minutes.

When it is not raining, Bruno has walks which follow a Normal distribution with a mean of 65 minutes and a standard deviation of 5 minutes.

**a.** Show both distributions on the same axes.

**b.** What is the probability that when it is raining, Bruno's walk will be between 28 and 68 minutes?

**c.** What is the probability that when it is not raining, Bruno's walk will be less than an hour?

## SOLUTION

**a.** Firstly, we need to know the limits of each distribution. Since we know 99.8% of all data in a Normal distribution lies within 3 standard deviations of the mean, we can use these as the upper/lower limits.

When it is raining, we have $48 \pm 3 \times 10 = 48 \pm 30$, so limits are 18 and 78.

When it is not raining, we have $65 \pm 3 \times 5 = 65 \pm 15$, so limits are 50 and 80.

These are the limits that we should try to draw the curve to each time.

advice

*Make sure your sketches are also symmetrical and labelled appropriately.*

The "raining" data has a higher standard deviation so will be a shorter, more spread-out curve.

Both curves are centred around their means.

All this information leads us to sketch the curves as follows.

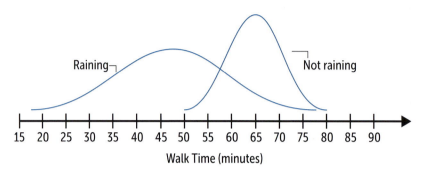

**b.** Between 28 and 68 minutes is within two standard deviations of the mean. We know that 95% of all data in a Normal distribution lies within two standard deviations of the mean, so we can say that the probability is 0.95.

**c.** One hour (60 minutes) is one standard deviation below the mean for the data when it is not raining. Look at the sketch of this situation.

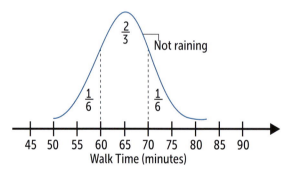

advice

*A sketch can be very helpful in these situations to help you see what's going on.*

We know that $\frac{2}{3}$ of the data is within one standard deviation of the mean, so here this is between 60 and 70 minutes.

By using symmetry, this leaves $\frac{1 - \frac{2}{3}}{2} = \frac{1}{6}$ in each section outside 60 and 70.

Therefore, the probability of Bruno's walk being below an hour is $\frac{1}{6}$.

## EXERCISE 3

**1.** On a labelled axis, sketch the shape and position of the distribution for a Normal distribution with a mean of 20 and a standard deviation of 4.

**2.** Three students pack boxes for a charity in their spare time.

Jack packs with a mean of 25 minutes and a standard deviation of 3.

Foo packs with a mean of 30 minutes and a standard deviation of 4.

Leona packs with a mean of 32 minutes and a standard deviation of 2.

**a.** On the same axes, draw sketches to show the shapes and relative positions of the distributions of the three students' times for packing boxes.

**b.** What assumption have you had to make to answer part (a)?

**c.** Laura says that it is highly unlikely that any of these students will take 40 minutes to pack a box.

Investigate Laura's claim using your sketches or appropriate calculations.

**3.** The mass of jam in jars is Normally distributed with a mean of 401 grams and a standard deviation of 0.5 grams.

**a.** Copy and complete these statements:

It is almost certain that the mass of jam is between __ g and __ g.

There is a 95% chance that the mass of jam is between __ g and __ g.

There is a two-thirds chance that the mass of jam is between __ g and __ g.

**b.** The jar is labelled as containing 400 g of jam.

Work out the probability that the jar contains less jam than the label claims.

**4.** There is a 95% chance that Amy runs a 10 km race in between 55 and 65 minutes.

Assuming her times are Normally distributed, what is the mean and standard deviation of this distribution?

# Standardised scores

We can assume that two (or more) distributions are a Normal distribution and then use this to compare the data sets by calculating **standardised scores**. To do this we need to know their mean and standard deviation.

The formula we use is:

Standardised score is $\dfrac{\text{actual score} - \text{mean}}{\text{standard deviation}}$.

This shows that a standardised score works out the number of standard deviations you are actually away from the mean.

So, if you are given an actual value, say a score in a test,

- a standardised score of 0 indicates the actual value is the same as the mean

- a negative standardised score shows the actual value is below the mean

- a positive standardised score shows the actual value is above the mean

- the larger (in size, ignoring sign) the standardised score is, the **less likely** that the actual value is to have occurred

This is particularly effective when comparing performances in two different exams, for example, where it might not be obvious where the better performance lies.

### EXAMPLE

For her plumbing qualification, Pippa has taken a practical test and a theory test.

The table shows her marks, together with the mean and standard deviation of the tests, over a long period of time.

|  | PIPPA'S MARK | MEAN | STANDARD DEVIATION |
|---|---|---|---|
| Practical | 65 | 60 | 10 |
| Theory | 56 | 44 | 16 |

Assuming the scores are a Normal distribution, in which test did Pippa perform better? Give evidence for your decision.

## SOLUTION

We know that the better performance will be the one with the higher standardised score.

Standardised score is $\frac{\text{(actual score−mean)}}{\text{(standard deviation)}}$, so:

For the practical, her standardised score $= \frac{65 − 60}{10} = +0.5$.

For the theory, her standardised score $= \frac{56 − 44}{16} = +0.75$.

This shows us that Pippa did better in the theory test (even though she had a lower score) because her standardised score was higher.

## EXAMPLE

Think back to the Bruno dog-walking question.

When it is raining, Bruno has walks which follow a Normal distribution with a mean of 48 minutes and a standard deviation of 10 minutes.

When it is not raining, Bruno has walks which follow a Normal distribution with a mean of 65 minutes and a standard deviation of 5 minutes.

If his walk on Friday walk lasted 58 minutes, is it more likely to have been raining or not raining?

## SOLUTION

If we calculate the standardised score for the actual value of 58 using both the raining and not raining distributions, the score that is closer to 0 gives the more likely situation.

Standardised score if it was raining $= \frac{58 − 48}{10} = +1$.

Standardised score if it was not raining $= \frac{58 − 65}{5} = −1.4$.

Therefore a 58-minute walk is more likely when it is raining as 1 is closer to 0 than −1.4.

**advice**

*Whether the score is positive or negative makes no difference here.*

## EXERCISE 4

Throughout this exercise, you may assume that the distributions in each question are Normal.

1. A quiz has a mean score of 50% and a standard deviation of 15%. Calculate the standardised scores for a quiz result of

   **a.** 50%    **b.** 65%    **c.** 42.5%    **d.** 95%

   **e.** Put the scores in parts a) to d) in order, from most likely to least likely.

2. Here are Sophie's overall scores in all her end of Year 10 exams together with the mean and standard deviation for each exam.

| EXAM | SOPHIE'S SCORE (%) | EXAM MEAN (%) | EXAM STANDARD DEVIATION (%) |
|---|---|---|---|
| Maths | 68 | 44 | 12 |
| English Language | 54 | 51 | 4 |
| English Literature | 80 | 64 | 8 |
| Chemistry | 61 | 60 | 10 |
| Biology | 34 | 62 | 14 |
| Physics | 75 | 48 | 9 |
| Statistics | 55 | 60 | 5 |
| History | 78 | 62 | 5 |
| Art | 95 | 70 | 8 |
| German | 40 | 32 | 12 |

   a. Calculate the standardised score for each subject.

   b. Put her performance in order, from best to worst.

   c. Comment on the validity of the assumption that has to be made about the scores.

3. Sadiq goes shopping each week.

   The amount he spends has a mean of £120 and a standard deviation of £20.

   The time it takes him has a mean of 65 minutes and a standard deviation of 10 minutes.

   a. Work out standardised scores for:

      i. Shopping costing £160      ii. Shopping taking 50 minutes

   b. Which is more likely, shopping costing £130 or a shop taking 59 minutes?

   c. One day both shopping cost and time had the same standardised score.

      Give two possible pairs of values for shopping cost and the shop time.

**4.** Two pizza firms deliver to Pepe's house.

TopCrust have a delivery time with a mean of 40 minutes and a standard deviation of 12 minutes.

GetStuffed have a delivery time with a mean of 30 minutes and a standard deviation of 8 minutes.

   **a.** One day, Pepe orders at 7.25 p.m.

   Which firm is more likely to deliver by 8 p.m.? Show evidence for your decision.

   **b.** On another day, Pepe orders a pizza from TopCrust.

   He says, "I am 95% certain that the pizza will arrive in under an hour".

   Is Pepe correct? You must show your working.

**5.** Eleanor grows sunflowers and measures exactly how tall each plant reaches.

She notices that:

• 50% of plants grow to 80 inches or more

• 95% of plants are between 68 and 92 inches

Work out the mean and standard deviation of the heights of Eleanor's sunflowers.

**6.** Clough obtained a standardised score of +1.2 in a college entrance exam with a score of 60%.

Work out a possible value for the mean and standard deviation.

# You should now be able to:

HIGHER TIER **Interpret and calculate standard deviation**

HIGHER TIER **Interpret and calculate skew**

HIGHER TIER **Recognise skewed and symmetrical distributions**

HIGHER TIER **Recognise the main properties of the Normal distribution**

HIGHER TIER **Compare distributions using standardised scores**

# Exam Practice Questions

**1.** Sarah works as a receptionist at a doctor's surgery.

Each day she records the number of missed appointments.

The table shows the number of missed appointments for a 90-day period.

| NUMBER OF MISSED APPOINTMENTS ($x$) | 0 | 1 | 2 | 3 | 4 | 5 | 6 | 7 | 8 |
|---|---|---|---|---|---|---|---|---|---|
| NUMBER OF DAYS ($f$) | 5 | 7 | 21 | 18 | 15 | 7 | 6 | 7 | 4 |

**(a)** Write down:

**(i)** the mode

**(ii)** the range of the number of missed appointments

**(b)** You are given that:

$$\sum fx = 315 \qquad \sum fx^2 = 1483$$

**(i)** Calculate the mean number of missed appointments.

**(ii)** Calculate the standard deviation of the number of missed appointments.

© AQA 2013

**2.** Jakob is a warden at a nature reserve.

The diagram shows the distribution of the masses of adult male lions in the park. The masses follow a Normal distribution.

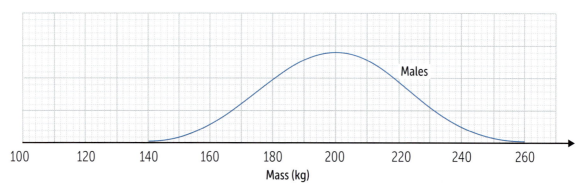

**(i)** Write the best estimate for the standard deviation of the masses of the adult male lions.

20 kg          60 kg          120 kg          200 kg

**(ii)** The masses of adult female lions in the park have a Normal distribution with

mean mass = 150 kg
standard deviation = 10 kg

Draw a sketch of the distribution of the masses of adult female lions.

**(iii)** Compare the masses of male and female lions in the park.
Write your comparisons in context.

© AQA 2018

**3.** Three types of bluebell plant grow in a garden: English, Spanish, and Hybrid.

Alex measures the widths of the leaves of random samples of each type of bluebell. She finds that the widths follow **Normal distributions** with different means and standard deviations.

| | ENGLISH BLUEBELL | SPANISH BLUEBELL | HYBRID BLUEBELL |
|---|---|---|---|
| Mean (mm) | 11.9 | 26.1 | 19.6 |
| Standard deviation (mm) | 1.7 | 3.6 | 4.5 |

**(a)** Alex concludes:

"Nearly all leaves on English bluebell plants in the garden have widths that are less than 17 mm".

Use your knowledge of the Normal distribution to show that Alex is correct.

**(b)** One of the bluebells has a width of 23.5 mm.

Use standardised scores to work out if the bluebell is more likely to be a Spanish bluebell or a Hybrid bluebell.

© AQA 2016

**4.** The daily intake of **magnesium** for females aged 11–18 years has a Normal distribution with mean, 183 milligrams, and standard deviation, 51 milligrams.

95% of these females have a daily intake of magnesium that is between $a$ milligrams and $b$ milligrams.

Calculate the values of $a$ and $b$.

© AQA 2017

**5.** A team of biologists are investigating a type of frog that lives on a small island. They capture at random a sample of 800 frogs, 440 females and 360 males.

Some information about the masses, in grams, of the captured frogs is shown.

| Female frogs | Male frogs |
|---|---|
| Sample size = 440 | Sample size = 360 |
| Mean mass = 45.3 g | $\sum x = 13860$ |
| Standard deviation = 18.6 g | $\sum x^2 = 573300$ |

**(a)** Work out the mean mass of the male frogs.

**(b)** Work out the standard deviation of the masses of the male frogs.

**(c)** Compare the masses of the male frogs with the masses of the female frogs.

© AQA 2016

6. A manufacturing firm regularly uses a mail distribution company, 'Expo', to send documents from its factory to its Head Office.

Management at the manufacturing firm decide to check the journey times (in minutes) of a sample of 36 deliveries made by 'Expo' drivers.

(a) A summary of the times is:

$$\sum x = 3636 \qquad \sum x^2 = 367677$$

(i) Show that the mean time is 101 minutes.

(ii) Show that the standard deviation of the times is 3.5 minutes.

(b) Assume that the delivery times are Normally distributed.

(i) One of the delivery times was recorded as 115 minutes.

Use the values of the mean and standard deviation to calculate the standardised score for this delivery time.

(ii) It is later claimed that the time of 115 minutes had been incorrectly recorded.

Based on your answer to part (b)(i), explain why this claim is likely to be correct.

(c) A rival delivery firm, 'Rapid', claim they can make the deliveries in a shorter time than 'Expo'.

As a check on this claim 'Rapid' were given a number of trial deliveries to make.

Give a reason why the results of the trial deliveries by 'Rapid' may **not** be a suitable basis to use in comparison with the delivery times for 'Expo'.

(d) A random sample of 28 of the delivery times recorded by 'Rapid' showed that 21 deliveries were made in under 102 minutes.

(i) Estimate the percentage of **all** 'Rapid' delivery times that would be completed in under 102 minutes.

(ii) To improve the accuracy of this estimate, it is suggested that the variability should be reduced by one half.

What size sample would be needed to achieve this level of improvement?

© AQA 2014

**7.** The birth weights of new born babies are Normally distributed with mean 3.4 kg, and standard deviation 0.6 kg.

**(a)** Between which weights is it almost certain babies will be born.

**(b)** An expectant mother is worried that her baby will be born weighing less than 2.8 kg. What is the probability of this happening?

# 13 | The Statistical Enquiry Cycle

**In this chapter, you will see how everything you have learnt can come together through the Statistical Enquiry Cycle to carry out a statistical investigation.**

Right at the beginning of the book, we talked about the Statistical Enquiry Cycle (SEC) and how this is the framework for statistical study.

We didn't say too much about it then as we hadn't covered all the statistics you needed to be able to make sensible choices about how to sample, collect, represent, and analyse data.

Hopefully, you now know a great deal more about statistics, so in this chapter we shall discuss how to carry out a statistical investigation to bring it all together.

Firstly, here is a reminder about stages of the SEC.

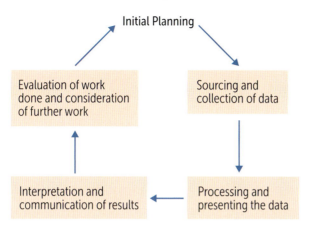

Let's look at the SEC again now and carry out an investigation. Most investigations come from a desire to check, find out, or disprove certain information that is suggested as fact.

Holly and her mum were disagreeing about the length of time modern music hits last compared to those about 30 years ago. Holly said it would be a good topic on which to complete a statistical investigation, so they agreed to investigate.

*"Songs that are Number 1 in the charts now are longer (in minutes) than they were 30 years ago".*

Let's look at each part of the SEC labelled (a) in each section and how it relates to this investigation labelled (b) in each section.

## 1. Initial planning

### a. Constraints involved in designing an investigation

Without careful initial planning, many investigations will fall flat before they even get going.

What exactly are you trying to find out?

Will you be answering a <u>research question</u> such as "Do people drink more coffee than tea?" or will you be testing a <u>hypothesis</u> such as "People drink more coffee than tea."?

Who will you ask? Where will you find these people in order to keep bias out of your investigation? How will you phrase what you ask them? Will you interview them, give them an online survey, a paper one, deliver to their door, telephone them, and/or email them?

How will you record your data as it is collected? How will you process, present, and interrogate your data? Some of this might be easier once you have your data, but you should always think ahead and plan.

In an ideal world, you would always be able to carry out an investigation exactly as you wanted. There would be no limits to your time, your budget to pay for things, and the number of people just desperate to fill in your questionnaire for you! However, we don't live in an ideal world, so these are just some of the constraints that you may face when you want to investigate something:

**advice**

*"Interrogate" here means thoroughly look at in detail, finding out everything your data could tell you.*

| | CONSTRAINT | POSSIBLE SOLUTION |
|---|---|---|
| **Time** | Often, the real world will put a time limit on your investigation. A large company will want to see results as quickly as possible. | Design methods that are efficient and collect quality data as quickly as possible. |
| **Cost** | People collecting the data need to be paid and this can be very costly. | Can you obtain a sample efficiently or change the method of collection to something cheaper? Or perhaps get some of the work generated by using a computer or a simulation? |

| | | |
|---|---|---|
| **Confidentiality** | Often, people won't want to answer sensitive questions if they are not confident that their answers will remain confidential. Dishonest answers would affect the results of your investigation. | Provide firm assurances that individual answers will not be associated with the individual where possible. If this is not possible, you need to explain how you will keep the answers confidential and for the purposes of the investigation only. |
| **Availability** | Can you find enough people to answer your questions/perform the test? If you are looking into a specialised area (maybe for a new medicine), there may only be a few people who are qualified to answer. | Offer incentives to encourage as many participants as possible. |
| **Ethical issues** | You may want to test a new medicine, but is it safe? Will participants be worried about side effects? | It is still possible to test on animals, but there are now very strict rules that must be followed. You could offer financial rewards for human volunteers, but you will need to monitor them very closely for side effects and be honest about potential risks. |

Can you think of any more issues that might stop you from carrying out a statistical investigation?

**b.** For this investigation

As we saw, Holly and her mum decided on the hypothesis: *"Songs that are Number 1 in the charts now are longer (in minutes) than they were 30 years ago".* It is perfectly possible to use a research question such as *"Which lasts longer, current Number 1 songs or those from 30 years ago?".*

Holly chats with her mum about the planning stage of the investigation.

**Mum:** *Should we design a questionnaire to ask how long people think the tracks were then?*

**Holly:** *No, the length of time a track lasts is a fact, so we need real data from somewhere.*

**Mum:** *That will be a lot of data! It'll take ages to collect.*

**Holly:** *If we need to, we'll do a sample instead; that would reduce the amount we need to collect.*

**Mum:** *What will we do with the data once we have it?*

**advice**

*Notice the difference between a hypothesis and a research question. The hypothesis is a statement which is supported (or not) by the statistics later on.*

**advice**

*It is essential that when you use other people's data, you acknowledge the source.*

*There's so much choice!*

**Holly:** *Time is continuous data, so it would be good to use averages and measures of spread such as mean, median, interquartile range, and standard deviation.*

**Mum:** *Will there be any diagrams? Reports like this look great with some diagrams in them.*

**Holly:** *We could use box plots, cumulative frequency diagrams, or histograms.*

**2.** Sourcing and collecting your data

**a.** We previously talked about the different ways of obtaining data from people, but your investigation might not need information from people. Instead, you may just need to scour the Internet for data that has already been collected by others (as long as you trust the source!).

If you are working with people, this part of the SEC is about designing the questionnaire or survey. You should also consider if the questions you plan to ask are sensitive in any way, as this might affect how freely and honestly people will answer.

When designing questions there are several other things to consider.

- Is the wording of your question unbiased?

It is known as a leading question if your wording implies support for one way or another in a situation.

For example, "Do you agree that eating meat is terrible?" is a leading question, whereas "What are your views on eating meat?" is not a leading question because there's no opinion forming part of the question.

- Will your questions be open or closed?

Open questions allow any response which might make the data be more difficult to analyse. Closed questions give specific options to choose from which might be preferred when, for example, someone is asked to give their age.

- In closed questions, how will you write your responses?

Numerical option boxes must cover all possibilities without overlap.

For example, if asking someone their age, these options have both overlaps (at 20 and 30) and gaps (over 60s):

less than 10, 10–20 , 20–30, 31–45, 46–60

You should also be considering how to obtain a sample from your population or whether it might be feasible to obtain data from the whole population.

Before we consider Holly's investigation, let's just look at difficulties that might arise in the sourcing and collection of data.

As a researcher carrying out a statistical investigation, you are reliant upon those who volunteer to be respondents (the people who will answer the questions for you) being available and doing things correctly for you.

Here are some of the things that can go wrong – can you plan for these issues?

| | PROBLEM | POSSIBLE SOLUTION |
|---|---|---|
| **Missing data** | Participants simply miss out or don't answer some of your crucial questions. | Perhaps source more respondents than you need, to allow for a certain percentage not answering every question. |
| **Incorrect formats** | You want someone to answer about their mass (weight) in kg and they give you it in stones and pounds! | Be prepared and look out for unusual answers that might simply be in unexpected units or written in a different way to how you expected. You may need to make a decision about whether to include such values when you do your analysis. |
| **Missing participants** | You have carefully selected your sample and then you find you cannot access some of them. | Have spare people chosen in advance so you can go to them instead. |
| **Unexpected results** | You find you are getting really unexpected results. | Do you need to stop and re-consider your plan? This is a good reason to trial a small scale version of your study to check that everything is going well before you proceed fully. |

| | | |
|---|---|---|
| **Extraneous variables getting involved** | This is where something else other than what you are investigating is affecting the outcomes of your investigation. For example, if you want to test a weight loss diet to see if it is effective, you will need to ensure that the amount of exercise is controlled between a group who have the diet and the group who don't. | Use a control group to compare effects between groups that perform the test and groups that do not. |

Another issue that you must consider is what level of control you need to have on the experiment or data collection. If you interfere too much (high level of control), you may well affect the outcomes as behaviour may not be normal amongst the participants (those taking part). If you exert little or no control, then the investigation may be badly affected by extraneous variables.

**b.** Holly's investigation will have secondary data available on the Internet. If she is lucky she might find a website which lists the length of each Number 1 track as part of the data kept about Number 1 songs. The worst case scenario would be to have to find which tracks have been Number 1 this year and Number 1 30 years ago and then go to a music streaming / download website to obtain the lengths of these songs.

There could be a primary data element to the data collection here, and Holly could measure the lengths of the tracks herself, but this would take a lot of time and is unnecessary when there is secondary data available. Importantly, there seems no obvious reason why the secondary data and the sources would not be reliable.

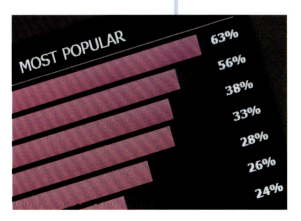

Finally, and somewhat unusually, with the ease of data collection here, it would seem appropriate to take a census of ALL Number 1s from the two years as that would entail, at most, 52 values for each data set, though in practice, many songs spend longer than one week at Number 1.

Whilst Holly was collecting the data, she came across a problem that she hadn't thought of. All the results are in minutes and seconds which might be difficult to process. (All would need changing to decimals if any calculations were to be carried out on the raw data.) So she decided to group the data to hide these complications as grouping was necessary for much of the representation she wanted to do.

**3.** Processing and presenting your data

**a.** This is all about how you will work with the data once it is collected.

What calculations will you want to carry out? What types of diagram should you be using? Who is going to be reading your work is important – if they have specialist knowledge you might use completely different methods to those you would choose for a non-specialist to understand. To investigate statistically requires measures of average and measures of spread to be evaluated and compared.

You should also consider how you can maximise the use of technology in calculations and diagrams (sometimes referred to as visualisations) - it's a lot easier than drawing them yourself.

**b.** As discussed above, the length of tracks is continuous data, so the first job after collecting the data is to group them into a reasonable number of class intervals. Histograms and cumulative frequency graphs (to get comparative box plots) are appropriate for grouped data.

Here are the grouped frequency distributions for the lengths of the Number 1s in the two years. Holly decided to use different class intervals for each year as she noticed fewer longer tracks in the data for 30 years ago.

**This year** (39 different Number 1s)

| LENGTH OF TRACK , $t$ (MINS) | FREQUENCY |
|---|---|
| $2 \leq t < 2.5$ | 1 |
| $2.5 \leq t < 3$ | 2 |
| $3 \leq t < 3.5$ | 6 |
| $3.5 \leq t < 4$ | 12 |
| $4 \leq t < 5$ | 14 |
| $5 \leq t < 7$ | 4 |

**advice**

*It is possible for all the elements of a box plot to be read exactly from the ordered data, but with about 40 readings in each year, this would be a lengthy task without technology to help.*

**advice**

*If you are working at Foundation Tier, your histogram does not need frequency density - simply draw the bars without gaps to the heights of the frequencies.*

**Thirty years ago** (41 different Number 1s)

| LENGTH OF TRACK (MINS) | FREQUENCY |
|---|---|
| $2 \leq t < 2.5$ | 2 |
| $2.5 \leq t < 3$ | 5 |
| $3 \leq t < 3.5$ | 9 |
| $3.5 \leq t < 4$ | 18 |
| $4 \leq t < 4.5$ | 5 |
| $4.5 \leq t < 6$ | 2 |

To get an initial visual comparison of the distributions, Holly decided to construct histograms.

Here's the working for the "this year" data:

| LENGTH OF TRACK ($t$, MINS) | FREQUENCY | CLASS WIDTH | FREQUENCY DENSITY |
|---|---|---|---|
| $2 \leq t < 2.5$ | 1 | 0.5 | 2 |
| $2.5 \leq t < 3$ | 2 | 0.5 | 4 |
| $3 \leq t < 3.5$ | 6 | 0.5 | 12 |
| $3.5 \leq t < 4$ | 12 | 0.5 | 24 |
| $4 \leq t < 5$ | 14 | 1 | 14 |
| $5 \leq t < 7$ | 4 | 2 | 2 |

Holly now used a software package to produce these histograms.

**advice**

*In an investigation, try to only include relevant and valuable work; here there is no gain in seeing the cumulative frequency diagrams as they are merely a way of estimating the measures for the box plot.*

**advice**

*Remember if you are doing Higher Tier to check for outliers.*

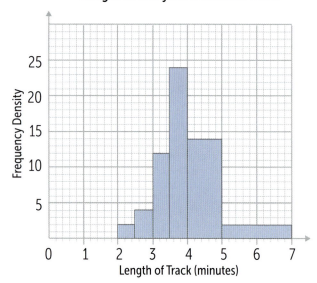

**Length of this year's Number 1 hits**

Even though Holly had used different class intervals for the two sets of data, she decided to use the same scales on the histograms for easier comparison.

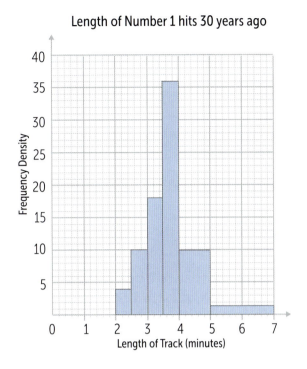

Length of Number 1 hits 30 years ago

Though we shall interpret these fully in part 4 of the SEC, it is immediately worth Holly noting that the histograms do appear to show that the 30 years ago data is lower on average and a little less spread out. There also didn't appear to be any outliers, so her options to use mean and standard deviation remain good ones.

However, next Holly decided to look more closely at a comparative diagram. She decided to obtain the minimum, lower quartile, median, upper quartile, and maximum values to complete two box plots from cumulative frequency graphs (not shown).

Here are the box plots.

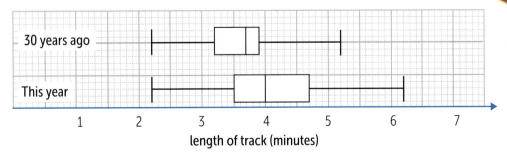

**advice**

*It is usually unwise to talk about a hypothesis being "proved". As all data from the two years was taken, it would be reasonable to say that.*

**advice**

*If you are working at Foundation Tier, use the interquartile range as your measure of spread. It is 0.7 for 30 years ago, and 1.2 for this year, so you get the same conclusions.*

By now, Holly was gaining confidence that the hypothesis was being supported by the evidence, but she decided to calculate the mean and standard deviation as a final check.

Her results from the raw data were:

|  | MEAN | STANDARD DEVIATION |
|---|---|---|
| 30 years ago | 3.78 | 0.87 |
| This year | 4.02 | 1.03 |

Holly felt that she now had enough information to interpret her results fully and draw some conclusions.

**4.** Interpretation and communication of results

**a.** The statistician should be spending as much of their time as possible interpreting and comparing their data set(s) rather than doing calculations and creating diagrams.

This is where the real skill lies, in reaching conclusions about the research question or hypothesis and in making inferences and predictions based on data in the context of

the investigation. It is also important to understand how reliable the findings of an investigation are likely to be.

All this has to be clearly communicated again, considering the target audience where appropriate.

**b.** Holly interpreted the diagrams and calculations as follows.

The histograms show that the tracks 30 years ago and the tracks this year have the same modal group, but the final group is longer for this year than 30 years ago, possibly showing that this year's tracks are longer. The histogram for this year seems to show a little positive skew whereas the box plot and histogram for 30 years ago are inconclusive about skew.

The box plots show much more clearly that the tracks are longer on average this year (when comparing the medians), and also more widely spread (when comparing the ranges or interquartile ranges).

There are no outliers, and so the mean and standard deviation can safely be used, which will give a stronger comparison of average and spread, as they use every piece of data. The means show that the Number 1 tracks this year are, on average, 0.24 minutes longer (this is just over 14 seconds and about 6% longer than those of 30 years ago). The tracks for this year are also more varied in their length as shown by the larger standard deviation.

Holly came to the following conclusion:

*"Number 1 tracks this year are generally longer than Number 1 tracks thirty years ago, and my hypothesis is supported".*

**5.** Evaluating your work

**a.** Once you think you have finished collecting, processing, and presenting your data, you should consider the approaches used to look for any weaknesses. Ask yourself the classic question, "If I were to do this again, would I do anything differently?" – this will prepare you for future work.

It is also the time at this point to consider whether you now need further investigation, perhaps with a slightly refined hypothesis. This is why the C in SEC stands for Cycle – you may be doing the whole process more than once.

**b.** One of the strengths of Holly's work was that she was able to take all the data for the two years without this being particularly time consuming, due to the good availability of trustworthy websites holding the data she needed.

Holly could have obtained exact values for the medians and quartiles by ordering all the data for each year, instead of obtaining estimates from the cumulative frequency graphs. Apart from that, all the work was accurate and relevant.

The hypothesis was certainly addressed in full, but one consideration would be how narrow it was, considering only Number 1 songs. If the real conversation was about tracks in general from the two years, the data was narrow and the investigation could certainly be extended with the current variables by considering all tracks, not just Number 1s.

Additional variables which could be considered could include the music genre and album tracks compared to singles.

## EXERCISE 1

Carry out one or more of these investigations (as described by these research questions or hypotheses) by following the Statistical Enquiry Cycle process:

1. Do boys have better memories than girls?

2. Do younger people have better reaction times than older people?

3. It rains more when it is windier.

4. Are shops busier at 5 p.m. on a weekday or 5 p.m. on a weekend?

5. Hair is longer in winter than in summer.

6. Diesel costs more than petrol.

7. Are apples bigger than oranges?

8. Is downloading slower in the evenings or at weekends?

9. Do students travel to school in the same ways as they did 40 years ago?

10. There are more charities in the UK now than there used to be.

11. In 2016, voters in the UK voted on whether to leave the European Union (EU).

The table shows the results for **some** of the regions of the UK and the total number of votes of people who voted to remain in the EU.

The final column shows the % of those who could vote who did vote.

| REGION | VOTES TO REMAIN IN THE EU | VOTES TO LEAVE THE EU | % WHO VOTED |
|---|---|---|---|
| East | 1 448 616 | 1 880 367 | 75.7 |
| London | 2 263 519 | 1 513 232 | 69.7 |
| Scotland | 1 661 191 | 1 018 322 | 67.2 |
| North-West | 1 699 020 | 1 966 925 | 70.0 |
| Wales | 772 347 | 854 572 | 71.7 |
| **Full UK result** | **16 141 241** | | **72.2** |

Source : www.electoralcommission.org.uk

a. Which of the five given regions voted that the UK should leave the EU?

b. There were 46 500 001 people who could have voted in the UK.
72.2% of these people did vote.
Calculate the number of people who voted to leave the EU (the empty cell in the table).

c. Why is your answer to **(b)** unlikely to be exactly right?

d. Sadiq said, "People were more likely to vote to leave the EU in regions where the percentage voting was higher". Using the data from the table only, comment on Sadiq's statement.

e. Sadiq finds a graph in a newspaper showing the percentage who voted in each region. Give **two** criticisms of the graph.

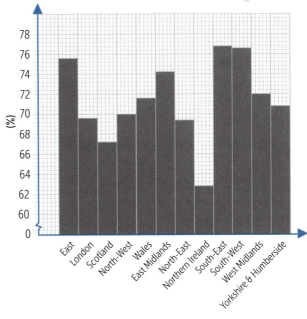

303

**f.** He finds the full list of which regions voted for the UK to remain in the EU or leave the EU.

| VOTED TO REMAIN | VOTED TO LEAVE |
|---|---|
| London | East |
| Scotland | North-West |
| Northern Ireland | Wales |
| | East Midlands |
| | North-East |
| | South-East |
| | South-West |
| | West Midlands |
| | Yorkshire & Humberside |

**(i)** Compare statistically the % who voted in regions who voted to remain with those who voted to leave.

**(ii)** Describe one issue with your results in part (f)(i) and how you might overcome this issue.

**THIS PAGE IS INTENTIONALLY LEFT BLANK**

# Glossary

**Action and Warning lines:** lines on a control chart marking the points at which action needs to be taken or extra attention paid to the accuracy of a machine's processes

**Arithmetic mean:** the full name for the numerical average usually referred to as the 'mean'

**Average:** the most common or typical value in a set of data

**Bar chart:** a diagram comparing discrete numerical or quantitative data using bars of different length or height but equal width

**Bar line chart:** a chart similar to a bar chart using vertical or horizontal lines rather than bars

**Bias:** a tendency to favour one person or thing over another

**Bimodal:** having two modes

**Binomial distribution:** the results of a trial where there are only two possible outcomes

**Bivariate:** data involving two variables

**Box plot:** a box showing the position of the lower quartile, median, and upper quartile with lines extending to the minimum and maximum values

**Capture-recapture:** a method of estimating animal populations; some animals are trapped, marked, and released, then some time later more are captured and examined, and a formula used to find the approximate population size

**Categorical:** data that has been classified in some way

**Causality:** exists when the effect of one variable increasing or decreasing causes the other variable to change accordingly

**Census:** where everyone or every item in the population is sampled

**Certain:** an event that is guaranteed to happen

**Chance:** how likely it is that an occurrence will happen

**Choropleth map:** a map showing the density of a distribution in each section as colours or through shading

**Class interval:** another name for a group of numerical data such as 10 - 19

**Composite bar chart:** a bar chart comparing multiple sets of data for each category stacked on top of each other

**Conditional probability:** a probability when the outcome of one event affects the outcome of another

**Continuous:** data that can take any value (within a range)

**Control chart:** a graph used in quality control to monitor the levels of key variables in the manufacturing of a product

**Control group:** a group that is not treated in an experiment but experiences the same conditions as those who are; used as a benchmark

**Convenience sampling:** sampling from those who are most easily available

**Correlation (association):** a connection between two variables for a set of data

**Cumulative frequency:** the running total of how many values have occurred so far

**Cumulative frequency curve:** (for continuous data) points on the diagram are joined by a smooth curve

**Cumulative frequency diagram:** a graph showing cumulative frequency

**Cumulative frequency polygon:** (for continuous data) points on the diagram are joined by straight lines

**Cumulative frequency step polygon:** (for discrete data) points on the diagram are joined in 'steps'

**Decile:** each of ten equal groups into which data can be divided

**Discrete:** data that is 'stepped'; it can only take on certain values

**Double mean point:** the mean of each set of data plotted

**Dual bar chart:** a bar chart comparing two sets of data for each category side by side

**Even chance:** an event which is equally likely to happen or not happen

**Event:** something that occurs

**Expectation:** likely number of outcomes in a situation

**Experimental data:** data collected through an experiment

**Experimental probability (relative frequency):** the proportion of times an outcome occurs in an experiment

**Explanatory (independent) variable:** the variable being investigated in an experiment

**Extraneous variable:** an unwanted variable that might affect experimental data

**Extrapolation:** an estimate of missing data values outside the data range

**Frequency density:** the height of the bar in a histogram with unequal class widths (frequency divided by width)

**Frequency distribution table:** a table showing the number of occurrences of each data point

**Frequency polygon:** a line graph showing the frequencies of different groups of data

**Geometric mean:** the value found by finding the $n^{th}$ root of the product of $n$ values

**Grouped frequency distribution:** a table showing the frequency of values in groups

**Histogram:** a diagram representing groups of continuous data in the form of bars; the area of each bar is proportional to the frequency of the class

**Impossible:** an event that cannot happen

**Independent events:** an outcome that does not affect the possibility of a different outcome from occurring

**Interdecile range:** the difference between any two deciles

**Interpercentile range:** the difference between any two percentiles

**Interpolation:** an estimate of missing data values within the data range

**Interquartile range:** the range of values in the central 50% of a data set; the difference between the upper quartile and the lower quartile

**Judgement sampling:** choosing the sample based on the researcher's judgement

**Likelihood:** a qualitative measure of how probable it is that an occurrence will happen

**Likely:** an event that has a good possibility of happening

**Line of best fit:** a line drawn through a scatter diagram that best expresses the relationship between the points longer than the other

**Lower quartile:** the value $\frac{1}{4}$ along a data set

**Mean:** the value derived by dividing the sum of a set of values by the number of terms in the set

**Mean seasonal variation:** the means of seasonal effects taken at the same point in successive years

**Median:** the middle term in a series of values arranged in order of size

**Modal:** relating to the most commonly occurring term in a set of data

**Mode:** the most commonly occurring value in a set of data

**Moving average:** a succession of averages found from successive sets of a series of values

**Multiple bar chart:** a bar chart comparing multiple sets of data for each category side by side

**Multivariate:** data involving multiple variables

**Mutually exclusive:** two outcomes that cannot happen at the same time

**National census:** a nationwide survey of every household in the country, conducted every ten years

**Negative correlation:** as one variable increases, the other decreases

**No correlation:** no apparent connection between the two variables

**Normal distribution:** a 'bell-shaped' symmetrical distribution where mean, mode, and median are all equal

**Observation:** recording what is observed without interaction

**Ordinal:** data where the order of each data point is clear, but not the degree of difference between each point

**Outcome:** the result(s) of a specific event

**Outlier:** a data point that lies well beyond most others in a set of data

**Pearson's measure of skew:** a measure of skewness

**Pearson's product moment correlation coefficient:** a more refined method of finding the strength of correlation in bivariate data than Spearman's rank correlation coefficient

**Percentage bar chart:** a composite bar chart where the total height or length of each column is the same (100%) and the composite values in each column represent percentages of the whole

**Percentile:** each of 100 equal groups into which data can be divided

**Pictogram:** a pictorial representation of data on a graph or chart

**Pie chart:** a diagram in the form of a circle divided into sectors, with each sector representing a portion of the whole

**Population:** everything or everyone being considered

**Population pyramid:** a type of back-to-back histogram giving a visual profile of the age distribution of a population, split by gender

**Positive correlation:** as one variable increases, so does the other

**Positive and negative skew:** the degree to which the tail of one side of a distribution is is different. (Right hand tail longer = positive skew; left hand tail longer = negative skew.)

**Primary data:** collected by the person carrying out the analysis of the data

**Probability:** a quantitative measure of the likeliness of an event

**Probability tree:** a tree diagram that helps display all possible outcomes of combined events and the chance of each event occurring

**Proportional pie chart:** two or more pie charts drawn for comparison in which each sector represents the frequency and the radii of the charts represent the total frequency , and the radii of the charts are adjusted so that the area represents the total frequency

**Qualitative:** data that is based on the quality of a variable (eg colour)

**Quality control:** a process of regular checking to ensure that a product is being made exactly as it should be without error

**Quantitative:** data that is number-based

**Questionnaire:** a document designed to obtain relevant data through a series of questions

**Quota sampling:** choosing a sample from specific groups within a population

**Random sampling:** every member of a population has an equal chance of being sampled

**Raw data:** data before it has been processed or organised

**Relative risk:** comparing the risk between two groups

**Reliable:** a property of an experiment that shows it gives consistent results

**Response (dependent) variable:** the outcome measured in an experiment

**Risk:** the chance of something happening

**Sample:** a small part or quantity of something designed to show what the whole is like

**Sample frame:** the members of the population who are available for sampling

**Sample size:** how many people or pieces of evidence are in a sample

**Sample space diagram:** a table that displays all possible outcomes of an event

**Sampling:** using a selection from a statistical population to represent the whole

**Scatter diagram:** a graph plotting two variables along two axes

**Seasonal effect:** the difference between a trend line and a specific data point

**Secondary data:** collected by someone other than the person carrying out the data analysis

**Simulation:** an imitation of a situation or process, often by means of a computer program

**Skewness:** the degree of distortion of a set of data from the symmetrical distribution

**Spearman's rank correlation coefficient:** a calculation tool to indicate whether a positive or negative correlation is present in bivariate data and how strong it is

**Standard deviation:** a measure of spread of a data set using every data value

**Standardised score:** a way of comparing different Normal distributions

**Stem and leaf:** a table where each data value is split into a 'stem' (usually the first digit) and a 'leaf' (usually the last digit)

**Strata and stratified:** strata are the different groups within a population; a sample is stratified if it includes evidence from every strata of the population

**Strong correlation:** a very clear connection, with the data points forming a nearly straight line

**Symmetrical distribution:** a distribution with a skew of 0, where the left side mirrors the right side

**Systematic sampling:** choosing items from a sample frame at regular intervals

**Theoretical probability:** a probability derived from theory

**Trend:** a general direction in which something is changing or developing

**Trend line:** a line indicating the general tendency or course of something

**Trial:** a single instance of an experiment

**Two-way table:** a frequency table with two variables

**Unlikely:** an event that has little possibility of happening

**Upper quartile:** the value $\frac{3}{4}$ along a data set

**Valid:** a property of an experiment that shows it tests what it is supposed to test

**Variable:** a number or property of something that will vary in a data set

**Venn diagram:** data sets represented as two or more circles, which may overlap

**Weak correlation:** a less clear connection, but with a general trend in the data points

**Weighted mean:** a mean where some data points are given greater emphasis or 'weight' than others